# Click and Play Agility
Clicker Training for Successful Dog Agility

by Angelica Steinker, M.Ed., C.D.B.C., CAP 2, NADOI
endorsed

Courteous Canine, Inc. Publishing
3414 Melissa Country Drive
Lutz, FL 33559
www.CourteousCanine.com

First Edition: 2006
Photographs by Joe Canova
Andrea Davis
Allison Marsh
Carol Murphy
Pet Action Shots
Suzanne Rider
Tony Rider
Spot Shots
Angelica Steinker
Saby Rochon /Sport Photography
Tien Tran
Todd Van Buren

Editors: Diana Bird, Mary Ann Campbell,
Andrea Davis, Brenna Fender
Layout: Andrea Davis
Cover design: Watermark Design

Library of Congress Cataloging-in-Publishing Data

Steinker, Angelica.
        Click and play agility : clicker training for successful dog agility
/ Angelica Steinker. – 1$^{st}$ ed.

ISBN 978-0-9679202-2-1
        1.    Dog training. 2. Dog. 3. Agility. I. Title.

Printed in the United States of America

This book is available in quantity discounts for multiple copy purchases.

Thank you to my husband, mom and dad and friends – I love you! A special thank you to Diana Bird, Mary Ann Campbell, Andrea Davis, Jean Donaldson, Dr. Rachel Kelly, Kay Laurence, Karen Pryor, Dr. Pam Reid and Dee Zurburg for their help with learning theory, thoughts, editing and support. You guys rock! Also thank you to Chris Bach and Chuck Tompkins who have both profoundly influenced my learning and this book. Many people have contributed to this book, indirectly or directly, thank you to Sue Ailsby, Robert Bailey, Rob Bitler, Guy Blancke, Brenda Buja, Elicia Calhoun, Rhonda Carter, Jan Casey, Diane Conroy, Ray & Lorna Coppinger, Dede Crough, Julie Daniels, Barb DeMascio, Greg Derrett, Beth Diehl, Dr. Jean Dodds, Beth Duman, Darlene Durham, Rachel Page Eliot, Kathleen Fahle, Ann Farmer, Helix Fairweather, Brenna Fender, Steve Frick, Dee Ganley, Susan Garrett, Bud Houston, Maren Jensen, Anne-Claire Jolivot, Deb Jones, Kathy Keats, Silvia Kent, Joyce D. Kresling, Kevin Krueger, Lisa Laney, Thad Lasinack, Terri Latronica, Sharon Loftly, Pati and Stuart Mah, Allison Marsh, Theresa McKeon, Adina McRae, Linda Mecklenburg, Joan Miller, September Morn, Jacque Munera, Leslie Nelson, James O'Heare, Brandy Oliver, Nancy Ouellette, Joan Orr, Chris Parker, Emma Parsons, Chris Peach and Bernie of Bordering on Insanity, Stacy Peardot-Goudy, Monica Percival, Jen Pinder, Val Ruthledge, Susan Salo, Rachel Sanders, Jane Stash, Ken Ramirez, Jesús Rosales-Ruiz, Suzanne Rider, Jo Sermon, Lynn Sickinger, Attila Skukalek, Sue Sternberg, Sally Treat, Ted Turner, Shannon West, Julie Weir, Steve White, Katie Wiles, Kim Wilson, Gayle York, Chris Zink and my favorite teachers, the dogs!

About the Author
Angelica Steinker, M.Ed. is the author of "Agility Success" and articles on clicker training, canine behavior and human sport psychology. Her writing has been published in the clicker magazine *Teaching Dogs*, the APDT (Association of Pet Dog Trainers) Newsletter, *Dog and Handler*, *Animal Trainer*, *Dog Fancy Clicker Training* special issue and *Clean Run*. Angelica Steinker is endorsed by the National Association for Dog Obedience Instructors (NADOI), is a Certified Dog Behavior Consultant (CDBC) through the organization International Applied Animal Behavior Consultants. She is also on the advisory committee of the Cynology College, an accredited online dog trainer education school committed to ethical force-free dog training and behavior modification. Angelica has special interests in clicker training, TAGTeaching, human and canine cognition, neuropsychology, psychology and aggression. She has testified as an expert witness in dog bite cases.

Angelica started competing in agility in 1992 with her Jack Russell Terriers Moose and Junior, and she currently competes in AKC, NADAC and USDAA. Angelica owns and operates Courteous Canine, Inc., a clicker training school in the Tampa Bay area. Angelica has presented at Camp Gone to the Dogs, Karen Pryor's Clicker Expo, The BARK camp and has given seminars nationally. She shares her life with a Miniature Pinscher, and three Border Collies. She is happily married to the world's most supportive husband, Ted.

Dedication
To Moose and Junior, my best teachers!

# Table of Contents

# Chapter 1  Click!  Let's Get Started

If I had the opportunity to live my life as a dog, I'd be a Border Collie.  Working and learning are addictive to me.  I thrive on gaining understanding and passing that understanding on to others.  This book is the result from my passion for learning, my desire to understand how people communicate with their dogs and my wish to share what I've learned about how to clicker train agility.

Agility is a sport that requires both precision and speed from the dog.  Clicker training enables a trainer to communicate precisely which behaviors are wanted and how they are to be performed.  Agility and clicker training is a match made in heaven!  When I began training my dogs to do agility, my Jack Russell Terrier Moose enjoyed the sport, but mostly he loved playing to the crowd.  Getting a reaction from a group of people was highly reinforcing (rewarding and fun) to Moose.  At one trial, Moose was running beautifully, completely clean, and I was already half celebrating our imminent qualifying run.  (Qualifying means a passing score that earns the dog one "leg" toward a title that requires three passing scores.)  A few obstacles before the finish, right in front of a small group of people, Moose kicked up his rear leg as if slipping on a banana peel and dramatically threw himself on his back, tongue dangling out of his mouth.  The crowd burst into laughter and Moose's "exhausted dog act" had just been trained.  In behavior terms, this is called one-trial learning.  It took only one instance for Moose to learn this "act" was going to get him tons of attention.  The next thing I knew, simple walks around the neighborhood had turned into one-dog-comedy-shows.

This was the beginning of my journey into the science of how animals, including humans, learn.  Traditional training methods did not work on my Jack Russells, so I concluded there had to be a better way.  There was.  I read Karen

Pryor's classic, *Don't Shoot the Dog!* This was the beginning of my love for clicker training.

## How to Use This Book
With each flip of the page, you will find fun training ideas, which I hope will become a useful and exciting part of your dog's agility journey.

This is a clicker training book.  If you are not familiar with the basics of clicker training, run, don't walk, to get a copy of Karen Pryor's *Don't Shoot the Dog!* Other useful books on clicker training for beginners include:  Kay Laurence's *Foundation, Novice* and *Intermediate* clicker training books.

## Terminology
As you read this book, you will periodically see a scientific term.  Don't panic; breathe deeply, all scientific terms are defined in the glossary at the end of this book.  If you are new to agility, relax, common agility terms are also defined in the glossary.  The first time a scientific or agility term appears, it will be defined in the text.  Think of scientific terms as a form of secret code.  While the code may be unfamiliar, your reinforcement will come from learning and understanding the code.  Understanding scientific terms will empower you to think critically and logically. Empowering you to analyze training suggestions.

Throughout the book when the term reinforcement is used, positive reinforcement is meant.  Reinforcement is anything that increases behavior.  Positive reinforcement refers to adding something to the dog's environment that increases the frequency of the behavior the dog was just engaging in.  Food, attention and toys are all positive reinforcers.

## Agility Photos
We tried to show a variety of breeds.  Agility is for all dogs. However, some pictures took many attempts so the dogs

that were most consistently available were the most photographed.

My own dogs are mentioned and pictured throughout, so I will introduce them here.

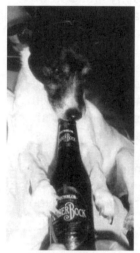

Photo by Angelica Steinker

Moose, my first agility dog, was a male neutered Jack Russell Terrier. Moose had numerous physical problems, such as microcellular shunting of the liver, causing him to have seizures, because of the toxins building up in his body. He had luxating patellas and as he matured he developed canine cognitive dysfunction. Despite all of these health problems and his addiction to beer, he was my best teacher. (Of course I am joking about the beer. Alcohol is dangerous to dogs.)

Junior, also a Jack Russell, was haunted by fears his entire life. Every change in environment frightened or stressed him. He had very poor bounce back; unable to recover from events that scared him.

Photo by Tien Tran

One time a screen door accidentally closed on him and he spent the rest of his life afraid of screen doors. His fears were resistant to counter conditioning and desensitization, the behavior modification techniques used to help dogs adjust. Doing agility with him was a struggle. He was plagued by teeter fears and never consistently performed.

3

We joked that Junior was always concerned about the men in black trench coats and the helicopters following him.  He achieved his AX title in AKC before I retired him.  I am grateful for everything I learned from him.  Despite the struggles, I miss him.

Nicki is my first Border Collie and first girl.  What an adjustment it was, and again she has been a fabulous teacher.  Today Nicki is 6 years and the biggest joy to work with.  Nicki is extremely soft and has taught me the best ways to encourage learning for sensitive dogs.  She had to retire from agility because of injuries she received in a

Photo by Angelica Steinker

roll over car accident.  I had her in a soft crate and my luggage fell on her.  Her left hind calf muscle was completely torn off the back of her knee.  There is currently no surgery to repair this type of damage in dogs.  Make sure your dogs ride in hard crates, and try to avoid being rear ended by drunk drivers while on a highway in an SUV, apparently this causes you to become a motorized projectile and roll three times.  Nicki competes in Rally Obedience, and is planning to enter competition obedience.

Photo by Suzanne Rider

4

Stevie is another Border Collie, male and a total blast. Stevie is four years old and competes in AKC, NADAC and USDAA.  Of all my dogs Stevie has been the easiest to train and I don't think it is was just my skills that where improving.  Stevie does everything quickly, saving months of training.  In a sport where speed is desirable he gave me from the start what you have to train other dogs to do. He also competes in Rally.

Turbo our Miniature Pinscher is also four years old and another boy.  For two weeks my husband and I fought about keeping this foster dog.  Turbo

Photo by Suzanne Rider

growls and bites if the wind blows or you do anything that is not precisely to his liking.  Turbo is agility trained but blind in one eye interfering with his depth perception.  He sporadically runs in agility but has not developed the same passion for the sport that my other dogs have.  Breed differences do matter!

Zoomie is another Border Collie, another male, do I sense a pattern? Zoomie is an absolute joy.  He is my most affectionate dog, always willing to work or cuddle.  Zoomie will begin competing in agility some time after he turns two.

Photo by Angelica Steinker

He is also preparing for Rally Obedience and Musical Freestyle competition and competes in Disc Dog.

## Agility Diagrams

Use the key below to familiarize yourself with what each of the symbols means. In general, the obstacle numbers are placed on the side of the obstacle that the dog will be approaching from.

*One square in the diagram at left represents 10-feet by 10-feet.*

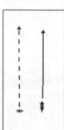

*In the diagrams, the handler's path is represented by a dashed line and the dog's path is represented by a solid line.*

*A dog, okay probably a border collie, but I didn't write the software program.*

*A person representing the handler, with his right arm forward signaling the dog's path.*

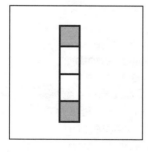

*A-frame - the tallest contact obstacle.*

*Teeter - arrow indicates direction the dog travels. It is the only obstacle that moves and one of three contact obstacles.*

*Table - dogs perform a sit or down and hold position for 5 seconds.*

*Dog walk - the longest of all the contact obstacles.*

*Chute – This obstacle is a solid barrel with a fabric tube attached.*

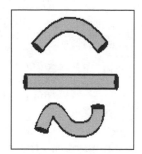

*Tire – The tire is a suspended hoop that the dog is required to jump through.*

*Tunnel - This diagram depicts three tunnels to show that they can be of a variety of shapes - curved, straight or even S shaped.*

*Panel jump – This jump is made of solid panels that obstruct the dog's vision.*

*Broad jump - The arrow indicates the direction the dog will take when going over this horizontal jump.*

*One bar jump – This obstacle only has one bar making it a little*

*Single bar jump – This jump has two bars. One is set at*

*more challenging for the dog to see.*

*the dog's jump height and one is at ground level attaching the two uprights, making it easier to see.*

*Two triple bar jumps – The dog will need to jump high and long.  The arrow indicates the direction the dog will travel. The top triple is wingless and bottom triple is winged.*

*Double jump – The double jump has two bars requiring the dog jump both high and long.  The double in this diagram also has wings, which are attachments of wood or PVC connected to the uprights, making the obstacle more visible to the dog.*

## Why Click?

Clicker training offers the agility enthusiast a fun and effective method of teaching behaviors.  Dogs that enjoy their training sessions can learn more and perform better.  Oh no, the horror, you and your dog will have fun!

How does clicker training work?  If the dog does what you want, you click at the moment the behavior occurs and immediately reinforce the dog with a treat or something else such as a toy or game of tug.  Examples of wanted behaviors are sitting, lying-down, being quiet or performing an agility behavior.  If the dog doesn't do what you want, you don't click and don't reinforce.  The click functions as a clear signal to your dog of the behavior that you want.  A critical part of the learning process for the dog is that one behavior gets the dog a click and reinforcement and other behaviors don't.  This is why force and correction have no place in clicker training.  Clicker training is "safe" -- it's playing a game with your dog.

When clicker training, there are three ways for you to get behaviors:  shaping, prompting or capturing.

Shaping refers to gradually building the behavior one tiny piece at a time, like a sculptor creating a work of art.

Prompting means you use a piece of food, a target or other prop to help the dog perform the behavior that you want.

Capturing is the easiest of the three methods, since all it requires is clicking and reinforcing the dog for a behavior that she naturally offers.  It is easy to capture a sit or a down since they are behaviors that all dogs naturally perform.

All three methods of encouraging behaviors will be explained in detail throughout this book enabling you to successfully communicate with your dog.

Trainers can get into verbal fisticuffs over which method is the best.  The bottom line is it depends on the behavior you are trying to teach, the dog and the creativity and skill of the trainer.

Clicker trainers don't view intimidation, or the use of physical punishment as a useful method for altering a dog's behavior.  This means that clicker trainers don't rely on coercive tools, such as choke chains, prong collars, shake cans, or spray bottles.  Clicker training is based on training a dog to *volunteer* behaviors.  The dog is not pushed, pulled or otherwise coerced into performing the wanted behavior.  Clicker training is not compatible with force.  Another reason to avoid punishment is that our dogs are emotionally connected to us in part by our reinforcement history with them.  Reinforcement history is roughly comparable to your bond with your dog.  Every time you do something your dog likes, that 'something' is associated with you, via classical conditioning.  Every belly rub, every game, every piece of food is a deposit into the bonding bank account.  When using training methods that are coercive, we damage that reinforcement history.  A damaged reinforcement history can dampen your dog's motivation, desire to play with you or may even cause aggression or other behavior problems.  Part of what prevents dogs from biting people is reinforcement history — how much a dog likes you based on how reinforcing you have been.

**Click and Play**
Most trainers use clickers in combination with food.  Click and then treat.  You can also click and play.  Any game

that your dog finds fun can be used as reinforcement.  Ask the best agility trainers in the world if they play with their dogs and you will hear a list of their favorite games.  It seems there is a strong connection between play and success in agility.  At its core, agility is a game and to be successful you have to *play* it.

**The Proofing Game**

Proofing is a dog trainer term for generalization training. Generalization has happened when a cued behavior becomes more probable in the presence of one stimulus or situation as a result of having been reinforced in the presence of another stimulus or situation (Pamela Reid, PhD).  This means proofing helps your dog learn to perform cues in different situations and contexts.  An agility trial is a very different context compared to an agility group class or your back yard, so proofing all of your agility behaviors is of critical importance.

Think of proofing as a way of asking your dog questions. Can you perform a sit and hold that sit position while I drop food on the floor next to you?  If the dog says "no", you made the question too hard.  Pick up the food and try again, but make it much easier by moving the food further away.  Proofing is a game and you always try to play it at a level that sets the dog up for success.  If the dog answers your proofing question with "yes, I can do that," you click and reinforce the dog.  The more challenging the question you ask the dog, the more "money" you pay your dog for getting it right.  Money to a dog is anything that the dog finds reinforcing.

Proofing is at least 50% of the training.  Once you have a behavior on cue, it is only half trained until you have proofed.  Only when you have proofed and proofed and proofed some more, can you actually say that the behavior is learned.

## Stress

Stress is at odds with learning and certainly it is at odds with fun.  A stressed animal is going to have memory and perception problems.  This is why using what is scientifically called positive punishment (yelling, hitting, spraying or throwing things at the dog) and negative reinforcement (yanking on a dog's leash until the dog does what you want) usually slows or even stops learning.  Skilled clicker training makes use of a high rate of reinforcement with lots of cookies/play in a short period of time.  If you are training a brand new behavior and you are not clicking and reinforcing every few seconds, your rate of reinforcement is probably too low.

Clicker training, when done properly, minimizes stress. "Yes, but… ," I hear you say you have seen dogs being clicker trained that were barking and clearly frustrated. Some mild frustration is part of learning, learning is like solving a puzzle and frustration is a part of that process. However, a dog barking out of frustration while you are training is usually a sign that something is wrong.  The art of training is reading the dog and knowing how to minimize learning frustration.  The Kay Laurence videos that accompany her clicker training books, demonstrate lovely clicker training sessions that show dogs learning happily. Wouldn't it be cool if all dogs had fun while learning?

## Stages of Learning

Learning occurs in two stages.  1. Acquisition – the dog is learning a new behavior.  2. Maintenance – the behavior has been learned, been put on cue and you are playing proofing games.

The challenge is that you don't always know when the dog is in acquisition or maintenance.  If you have trained your dog to turn left and right on verbal cues and you don't practice the left and rights for three months, your dog may not remember the cues and revert to acquisition.  Seems a little frustrating, but training your dog to do agility is not like

11

riding a bike. The dog will eventually forget the behaviors if you don't practice and reinforce. Behaviors that are self-reinforcing will be more resistant to falling back into acquisition. Behaviors that are less self-reinforcing will require periodic reinforcement in order to be maintained. Murphy's Law says that usually the self-reinforcing behaviors are those we don't want.

## Overshadowing

Imagine this. The phone rings while your friend is dictating a phone number to you. You answer the phone and now have no idea what phone number your friend was giving you. The ringing phone "overshadowed" the hearing of the phone number. When two stimuli happen at the same time, one will dominate the other even though both would be effective if presented one at a time. A stimulus is anything a dog can perceive (Pamela Reid). Dogs don't multi-task well, and neither do most humans.

While your dog is learning, she needs quiet to focus and to become aware of your cues. If you are constantly talking to your dog while attempting to teach a new behavior, your talking may overshadow your cues or what you are trying to teach her. To prevent overshadowing quietly observe your dog while she is learning, then after clicking and while reinforcing, cheer and chatter all you want.

## Blah, Blah, Blah

"My dog is blowing me off." The trainer calls and calls "come, come, come, Fido, come now," and the dog standing by a tree conducts a precise investigation of a crumpled leaf. The trainer's calls reach a feverish pitch yet the dog blissfully ignorant of her trainer's wishes, continues her leaf information gathering. To this dog the cue, "come" means nothing. Come doesn't predict anything important and the dog can't discriminate between the repeated words and cues. "Come" becomes white noise. The dog has been trained to ignore the cue. Training is what the dog does, not what we want the dog to do. Give all cues

— verbal or body — only *once* and only when you are certain the dog will respond.

Cues are precious information.  Avoid using cue words or physical cues as part of your praise.  Praising your dog with "good sit," is weakening the link between cue and behavior.  A cue is a signal for your dog to take action; if a dog is already sitting, she can't sit again.

### Does a Hammer Work?
Some trainers will comment that they tried the clicker but it did not "work."  It is possible that these trainers inadvertently taught the dog that a click means nothing, an example of learned irrelevance.  A clicker is like a hammer: it can work, but how well it works depends on who is using it.  If the noise of the clicker is not consistently paired with a reinforcer, or if the reinforcement is not something the dog really wants, then the click loses its meaning or never gains meaning in the first place.

There is a lag time while the dog learns that the click marks the behavior.  They learn the click = reinforcement link quickly, but working out that they can *make* the click happen may take longer.  The clicker may seem not to be working, because the dog has not yet understood that she can control the click.  Repeat what I click and I will click again.  The clicker still works, but the training may need to be modified.

### Fluent Responses
The process of training fast and accurate responses to cues is called fluency training.  Just like a person can be "fluent" in a language, you want fluency in your dog's response to cues.  If a dog reliably and promptly responds to a cue, then that behavior is fluent.  Successful agility requires fast and accurate responses to cues.  To see some great fluent agility training, watch world-class agility competitor Greg Derrett's "Foundation Training" video.

Somebody please clone this man, so that my home state of Florida can have its own Greg Derrett.

*First Fluent Then Fast*
Karen Pryor says, "fluency is precision teaching so that cues are consistently well-executed, quickly and easily performed in various environments without hesitation." Fluency and speed training however are not the same thing, but you can't get speed if you don't have fluency.  It is possible for a dog to fluently respond to a weave cue, but then to weave very slowly.  A quick response to the cue does not equal a quick execution of the entire behavior.  First, the dog must be able to fluently respond to a cue, and then you can begin to only click and reinforce the dog for performing the actual behavior quickly.  This is why it is important to change a cue when retraining a behavior.  In order to do the best agility your dog is capable of performing, you want her to respond to your cue and perform that behavior quickly.  Only then add your verbal or physical cue.

Fluent = dog responds quickly to cue.  The actual behavior may be performed slowly.
Speed = dog performs the behavior quickly.

You achieve fluency by clicking and reinforcing your dog for fast responses to cues (starting to do the cued behavior is clicked and reinforced).

You train speed after you have a fluent response to the cue, by reinforcing only fast behaviors.  Some dogs naturally do everything fast.  If you have a dog like this, count your blessings, you just saved months of training.

*Energy*
Be sure to bring energy to the training session when working on fluency.  If you are behaving casually and moving slowly, so will your dog.  Over time, dogs usually match our body language.  A super fast dog with a very

14

slow moving trainer may eventually match that trainer and slow down or the trainer may have no ankles left from the dog's frustration biting.  If you want fast, crisp responses, then your training and attitude need to be fast and crisp.  Get on the balls of your feet and let's see some peppy movement.  Otherwise, don't expect it from your dog.

There are some exceptions.  Some shy dogs may become stressed if you bring a great deal of energy to your training.  Part of the art of training is reading the dog and evaluating what that dog needs.  If your dog is shy or overly reactive, bringing a lot of energy to your training should be done gradually so the dog can adjust to it.  Don't just do something because you read about it — listen to your dog.

*Relax*
If you are training a dog naturally wired to do everything fast, you may want to stay relaxed and calm during training.  You won't have any difficulty getting fast behaviors, but it may be a challenge to get the dog to focus enough to pay attention to your cues.  The trainer staying calm and relaxed will help a dog like this.  Also teaching a dog like this to relax by very lightly and slowly massaging her will be helpful.  You can put the relaxing on cue by saying "relax" before you begin a gentle and slow massage.  The word "relax" predicts the massage prompting a relaxed state.

Assuming your dog is neither extremely excitable nor shy, you will be setting her up for success by playing with her and getting her excited before asking her to do a behavior quickly.  Play tug with your dog, pretend to grab her feet to get her going.  Then with an excited voice, suddenly cue her to down.  If she does so quickly and enthusiastically, click and release the dog from the down and start playing again.  You can have your cake and eat it too by getting a fluent response and a fast execution of the behavior.  If the dog does not respond to a cue, just wait a few seconds

15

and try again.  Fluency training is for cues in acquisition. Speed training is for cues in maintenance.

You get speed by clicking and reinforcing the dog for fast behaviors and not clicking and reinforcing slower ones. The cool thing is that if you teach your dog to perform all her cues quickly, reinforcing only speedy behaviors, then speed will begin to permeate all of your dog's training. Speed is contagious -- isn't it wonderful?  Soon you won't be able to get your dog to do anything slowly, but don't send me email complaining about it.

When working on fluency or speed, less is more.  The fewer repetitions you do, the more success you will have. If you ask your dog for a fast down and she slams down quicker than you have ever seen, click, release and reinforce her with tug and make a big fuss over her.  Have a party and then don't ask her to do it again! If you do, she may think that you did not want "fast" after all, and perform a slow down.  I am still missing some hair, from pulling it out, after I made that mistake.  Nicki and I would be playing table games and I would get an amazing fast down.  I would click and reinforce and then the obsessive part of me would start whispering, "get her to do it 50 more times." So I would ask her to perform the down again and the moment the cue left my mouth, I knew it was a horrid mistake.  In Nicki's eyes, I saw the Border Collie brain wheels turning and sure enough, I got a slow down.  ARG! I would want to slap myself, why didn't I just leave it alone? So if you want your 50 fast downs on the table, reason with yourself that you can't have them all at once.  Play short intense games and move on to the next behavior.  You can always come back to the table.  Know your dog; if she is the thinking type, like Nicki, don't use a lot of repetition. Even if she is not the thinking type, repetition is boring. Mix your training up to keep it more fun and interesting.

*Fluency Assessment*
Take the fluency assessment to see how your dog is doing in terms of fast and reliable sit and down cue responses.

1.  Can your dog sit immediately on the first cue while another dog walks around her?
2.  Can your dog down immediately on the first cue while another dog and handler run around her?
3.  Can your dog sit while squirrels play in a tree near by?
4.  Can your dog down if you just released her from playing tug?
5.  Can your dog down while recalling toward you?
6.  Can your dog down while you do jumping jacks?

Scoring
6 "yes" responses – your dog has passed the sit and down fluency test with flying colors.
4 – 5 "yes" responses – your dog is doing well; keep working on it until you score a 6!
3 – 0 "yes" responses – keep working on what your dog can do and build on success from there!

*Fluency and Patterning*
One way to attain fluency and speed is to use patterning. Asking the dog to repeat the same behavior repeatedly can help some dogs gain confidence and speed in the behavior and in their response to cues. Although physical wear and tear can occur. Doing many repetitions, when it comes to a physically demanding sport such as agility, is less than ideal. In addition, patterning is boring, causing loss of attitude and motivation in some dogs. Dogs that are still building drive for agility, soft dogs like Nicki, who think more than they need to, probably will not reach their best potential with patterning. While pattern training works for some dogs, clicking and reinforcing only excellent responses works for *all* dogs.

If you want your dog to notice your cues and respond immediately, be aware of your every word and body cue in the presence of your dog.  Every interaction with your dog is training.  If you are aware, you train effectively.

*Clean Behavior Cues Game*
After your dog responds fluently to all of her cues, the next step is to stack the cues one after another and still get that same fluent response.  The process of doing this is the game of clean behavior cues.

When you first begin stacking cues start with the cues your dog knows the best.  Kay Laurence labels these cues "A." Cues that your dog is performing reliably, but are newer are labeled "B" and "C."  Laurence then recommends a simple formula for chaining cues together:  ABACAB.

A – very familiar cue (sit)
B – newer cue (down)
A – very familiar cue (sit)
C – another new cue (stand)
A – very familiar cue (sit)
B – newer cue (down)

By following this simple formula you are creating a list of stacked cues that ping pongs the dog between the easy very familiar cue and the newer, less generalized cues. This sets the dog up for success.  Once you have practiced the ABACAB game for a while, you can begin playing the clean behavior cues game.

A list of behavior cues is clean when every cue you give is responded to fluently and the cues are only given once. All the cues you give the dog and all the responses flow because the dog cleanly goes from one behavior to another.  This flow may even be reinforcing to some dogs. This means that the activity of performing the cues fluently one after the other is inherently fun.  Agility is a chain of alternating cues and behaviors.  If you strive to train to

18

keep your chain of cues clean and free of repetition or hesitations, you are creating flow. Flow is fun and reinforcing. The activity of doing agility with you is reinforcing -- every trainer's dream come true.

Rather than clean behavior cues, it is common to hear cues like this: Spike, Spike, Spike, Spike, sit, sit, SIT, stay, STAY, STAAAAAAY, okay, okay!, Spike, jump, no! jump, jump, Spike, come, come, COME!, COMMMMMME! Spike, tunnel, tunnel, tunnel. While the dog is performing a behavior chain, this handler is repeating cues and adding unnecessary words.

A behavior chain is the method used to teach a complex sequence of responses. If you are stacking cues, then you are creating a behavior chain. Alternatively, if you give one cue that triggers your dog to respond with a series of behaviors, that is also a behavior chain. If the stacked cues you are giving are repeated like in the example with Spike above, flow can't be achieved.

A list of clean cues would be: "sit," "okay," "jump," "jump," "come." All unnecessary words have been removed. Now this team can flow around the agility course! A list of clean behavior cues is much easier on both the dog and the handler. The dog running agility with clean behavior cues will be faster than the dog that has to go on a treasure hunt to find the next cue.

In order to successfully run a Master's level agility course, your dog will need to perform a minimum of 25 stacked cues fluently. In order to over-prepare be able to perform more than you anticipate in the competition ring, your dog may need to play the game of clean behavior cues with up to 50 cues. These cues include verbal and body cues.

Beth Diehl's Jack Russell Terrier, Hustle is given clear verbal cues so she consistently runs speedy agility courses.

Photo by Tien Tran

## A Good Behavior Chain Gone Bad

Agility is a series of behaviors cued by the handler.  If your dog gets up from her sit at the start line and begins running the course, you have trained a behavior chain that includes not holding the sit until released.  Allowing inconsistencies in behavior chains is guaranteed to undermine your training.  One step forward, two steps back.  Don't let a good behavior chain go bad, if your dog gets up at the start, reposition her and try again.

Coming up next!  Chapter 2 presents and discusses methods of clicker training that will help guide you and your dog to agility success.

# Chapter   2 Click! And Play Pyramid

### The Click and Play Pyramid
Imagine that you are building a pyramid that is constructed by layers stacked on top of each other.  In order for your pyramid to be stable, it requires five layers to support the final structure.  Without all five layers, the structure will be incomplete.  This five-layer pyramid is your "**click and play**-training foundation."

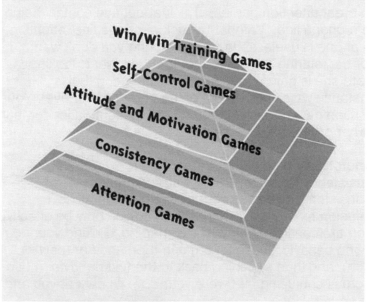

1. Attention Games
2. Consistency Games
3. Attitude and Motivation Games
4. Self-Control Games
5. Win/Win Training Games

### Attention Games
The first and most important layer of your pyramid is attention. Attention is the foundation of everything to come.  Without attention, you are unable to communicate with your dog.  And if you aren't giving her attention, your dog can't communicate with you either.  Attention ideally

precedes all training.  Your daily training sessions should include attention games to help you maintain your attention foundation.  You cannot get your dog to sit on the start line if she is not paying attention to you.  Without attention, it is impossible to have a flowing and flawless run.

Attention games are any game you play with your dog that involves the dog giving you eye contact.  Your dog looking at you while you drop a piece of food on the floor, or your dog maintaining eye contact while you bounce a ball are two great attention games.  Think about eye contact being like a phone line.  Without the actual phone line, attention, the phone is useless.  In the agility ring you don't want your dog staring at you, you need a dog that is looking where she is going.  But, you do want a dog that is constantly watching you out of the corner of her eye.  Your attention games will help you create the foundation for that "corner of the eye" attention.

**Consistency Games**
Consistency is the key to the learning process.  Inconsistency weakens your pyramid and leads to confusion for the dog.  Clicker training can only be effective if you are consistent.  If you are shaping, clicking your dog for one behavior (nose touch) and then another (paw touch), and then switching back to the first behavior (nose touch) is confusing.  If I were your dog, I'd bark at you and bite your ankle!

So, be consistent in your training, and with your verbal and body cues, making sure that both you and your dog are on the same page.  Your goals are to create a cue system that is clear and allows your dog to play with you at her optimum level and to test that system for its effectiveness.

*Consistently Meeting the Dog's Needs*
Your dog needs you to be consistent before you click so she can learn, but your dog also needs you to consistently meet her needs.  Daily exercise, mental stimulation,

security, socialization, companionship, chewing, health care, quality food and fresh water are some of your dog's needs. Without having her needs met, your dog will not be easy or fun to live with. Are your dog's needs being met?

*Consistent Exercise*
Daily exercise, such as retrieving games are critical to your dog's health and mental well-being. By exercising your dog, you avoid behavior problems and keep your dog fit to perform. Hiking and swimming are excellent forms of exercise.

How many hours does your dog spend crated? Crates are used for housetraining and safety. They are not something a dog should live in, especially active dogs. Putting your dog's mental and physical well-being first, means working to minimize the time your dog spends in a crate. Crates don't allow dogs to walk and many don't allow room for the dog to stretch. It is not natural for a dog to be confined to a box. In physiological studies, researchers use crates to de-condition dogs to compare them to other dogs that are conditioned. According to animal welfare studies on kenneling, socially isolated dogs have higher levels of stress (cortisol) especially if they are female. Keeping your dog in a crate most of the day is not going to help your dog maintain fitness.

*Consistent Mental Stimulation*
Dogs need to use their brains just as we do! Using your clicker to teach your dog new behaviors is a great way to keep your dog mentally stimulated. This book will provide you with many ideas and fun games to play with your dog that will help you meet her need for mental stimulation.

*Consistent Security*
Just like us, dogs need to feel safe to perform their best. Some dogs require more from their handlers to feel safe. Most of us either have a dog that has anxiety issues or know someone who does. Your dog's safety concerns are

part of agility training. While modifying aggression or fear responses is beyond the scope of this book, you will find a list of resources in the appendix.

Everyone can help his or her dog feel safer. Don't allow groups of people, especially children to rush up to your dog. While most kids enjoy petting dogs, many dogs are fearful of kids. Keep both kids and dogs safe by assertively monitoring happy interactions. Enforce a one person at a time rule.

Don't allow dogs to rush up and greet your dog. This can start a dog fight. Speak to the handler, observe the dog's response to the environment, to other dogs and your dog and then decide if saying "hi" is a good idea. You are responsible to help your dog feel safe.

*Consistent Socialization*
In order to be safe and comfortable around other dogs and with people, your dog needs to be socialized both as a puppy and as an adult. Socialization is most critical for dogs from four weeks to four months. Socialization is accomplished by gradually allowing your dog to investigate, at her own pace, different looking people, children, environments, objects and dogs. It is critical that the dog is exposed to novel stimuli (new things) on a *voluntary* basis, and not forced to interact with beings or objects that frighten her. When socializing your dog, if your dog shows fear responses, she may bite. If the dog wants to back away, allow her to. Forcing approach will only increase the chance that the dog will become aggressive. Fear and stress are the basis of almost all aggression. James O'Heare author of *The Canine Aggression Workbook* and *Aggressive Behavior in Dogs* says, "Unpleasant experiences can create an unpleasant or aversive association with the stimuli involved (in this case people). So rather than developing a positive emotional reaction to these things the emotional reaction can be negative. The dog will likely learn avoidance or

escape behavior (these are usually aggressive behaviors) in these cases. The key to socialization is to provide as much as is possible while being careful not to overwhelm the dog. Socialization must remain a pleasant experience at all times. This is a key principle in socialization procedures."

An under-socialized dog is more likely to become stressed and/or bite in unfamiliar environments and situations; this may make competing a challenge or even impossible. Stress causes the dog brain to be bathed in neurochemicals that interfere with learning. Stress and fear block the brain from processing most other information.

Socialization is only part of what forms a dog's personality or temperament. Brain chemistry and genetics are also a huge part. Because of this, in spite of ideal socialization, some dogs remain unable to accept the presence of strangers or unfamiliar dogs. It is inappropriate and unkind to blame the trainer of the dog for this. Training controls only so much. Genetics and biochemistry control possibly as much as two-thirds of behavior.

Ray and Lorna Coppinger, in their book *Dogs – A Startling New Understanding of Canine Origin, Behavior & Evolution,* discuss how 80% of a dog's brain is fully formed by four months of age, from four months to a year the remaining 20% of the brain develops. Once the brain's growth stops, it becomes far more challenging to "change the wiring." If you are planning on getting a puppy for agility, carefully research the socialization program of the breeder and once you get the puppy take the pup to a different environment to meet different people and dogs every day.

*Consistent Companionship*
Dogs are social creatures. Most dogs enjoy the company of people and of other dogs. To deprive a dog of this

social contact by keeping a dog crated, outside or home alone for most of her life can be a recipe for disaster. Unsupervised outside, the dog is bored and lonely. Barking and digging are sure to become her companions. A dog left home alone excessively may become destructive and/or develop canine separation anxiety. Avoid problems by providing your dog with the social contact that she needs to be happy.

*Consistent Chewing*
Dogs need to chew every day.  Provide your dog with chew toys on a constant basis.  This will help prevent unwanted chewing of your belongings.  Nylabones, bully sticks and large basted bones are great for most dogs. Raw hide can cause choking and is best avoided.

*Consistent Health*
To be the best agility dog she can be your dog needs proper health care, including daily massage and possible chiropractic care, human grade quality food and fresh, pure water.  Dogs can't meet these needs on their own. Meeting your dog's health needs will make her an easier pet to live with and enable her to shine as an agility dog.

**Attitude and Motivation Games**
Before training your dog to do a behavior, your dog needs to be motivated to learn.  Enter training for attitude! If your dog isn't smiling then there is no point in clicking and reinforcing the behavior.  Ask the dog to do several familiar behaviors, click and reinforce each.  Get her playing and then give the behavior that triggered loss of attitude another shot.  Attitude is everything.

Sea World's Vice President of Animal Training Chuck Tompkins says one of the ways to motivate animals is to bridge (click), not only for the behavior, but for the high energy attitude.  Chuck also emphasizes that in all stages of training, if the animal isn't having fun, training should not proceed.  Fun is first.  Putting fun first is easy.  Examine how you train.  Is your dog smiling?

Turbo my Miniature Pinscher smiling!

Photo by Tien Tran

*Resisting Fun*
For some people the idea of having fun isn't fun.  Having fun may be associated with bad prior experiences or with a lack of control.  If you experience resisting fun, just give it a try.  Allow yourself to explore what being playful is all about.  You owe it to your dog to give it a try.  Make it a goal to have each training session be a play session.  That is how you get and maintain attitude and motivation, and you'll have fun along the way.

If your dog has not learned to play with toys, you can make food delivery a game.  You can praise while you give the food treat, have the dog jump up high to get the food treat from your hand, or give the food treat in small pieces, one piece after the other.  If the dog does something fabulous, click and give her an entire handful: that's a jackpot!

An advantage to playing with toys in agility is that you may get more speed.  This is because playing with toys and doing agility are closely associated with play behavior systems, running and chasing, which are genetically programmed into the dog.  Play behavior systems are closer to what we want in agility training than the food behavior systems sniffing, chewing and eating.

In order to increase motivation, learn to be silly and play games with your dog.  If your dog has a motivational problem, you have a great excuse to become a kid again and spend lots of time playing with your dog.

*If You Can't Get Your Dog to Play*
Dogs read our body language; if you don't feel like being playful; your dog will know it.  To succeed, your desire to play with your dog must be sincere.  What types of activities encourage you to loosen up and laugh?  Whatever it is, do it before playing with your dog.  If you are not in a happy mood, consider skipping training that day.  Whatever attitude you bring to your training session is the attitude you may get from your dog.

*Context*
Dogs learn context very well.  If you only use food in your training, then the food may become part of doing agility.  Food is present = dog does agility.  Food not present = dog doesn't do agility.  Now you have a dog only motivated to do agility when food is present, and you can't take food into the agility ring.  Using games, toys, praise, petting and a variety of reinforcers gives the dog many contexts for agility.  Moreover, all those things will be at an agility trial and praising is allowed in the competition ring.  If you are trying to build your dog's "play motivation," set aside some time to have short fun play sessions every day.  This book will give you ideas for games you can use to **click and play**!

**Self-Control Games**
To reach your team's maximum potential, you need accuracy and speed.  Many dogs enjoy playing the game of agility and seeing agility equipment will trigger a high arousal state.  Agility dogs are ideally prepared for competition when they have learned to handle those high arousal states, by playing self-control games.

Suzanne proofs Rev's down with three food bowls and a treat in her hand. Rev ignores the distractions and gives Suzanne attention.

Photo by Angelica Steinker

Self-control games include exercises that require the dog to hold a position despite intense distractions and a high arousal level. A food-motivated dog that is asked to sit and hold that position while treats are dropped all around her is demonstrating excellent self-control. A dog that is easily aroused by motion but can hold an A-frame contact despite other dogs running past her is also showing excellent self-control.

Think of motivation and self-control as dependent on each other. The more motivated your dog becomes to play agility with you, the more self-control you will need to teach. The art of agility training is to balance motivation games with self-control games. If you play too many motivation games and hardly any self-control games the dog may become out of control. If you play too many self-control games but not enough motivation games, the dog will be accurate but not run at her full speed.

*Arousal and Generalization Training*
Pretend we could measure our dog's level of arousal: sleeping would be zero, and bouncing off the walls excitedly would be ten. Understanding arousal is important for agility because a dog in group class may only be at a level four arousal but at an actual competition the arousal may become an eight. This means that whatever the dog learned in group class might not be "remembered" in this

new higher arousal state.  "This link between [arousal] state and [memory] recall is called state dependent learning.  This state dependent learning was initially observed in experimental animals that were given certain drugs, and then taught to perform certain tasks.  Researchers repeatedly found that the animals' subsequent test performances were best in the same drug states (Arkhipov, 1999; Pusakulich and Nielson, 1976; Overton, 1966, 1964).  Research with human subjects later showed that state dependent learning can be associated with mood states as well: Material learned during a happy mood is recalled best when the subject is again happy and sad-state learning is recalled best during sad states (Eich, 1980; Bower, 1981)." (Comer, Ronald. 2001. Abnormal Psychology fourth edition.  Worth Publishers)

The mental state of the dog is linked to what the dog learns.  If the dog only learns to sit when she is calm, the dog is less likely to understand what the cue "sit" means when aroused.  Because of state dependent learning, it is important to train agility behaviors in a state of high arousal, since most dogs are in a high state of arousal when competing.

During play, gradually increase the arousal level of your dog so she can generalize cues to different arousal states.  Your dog is learning self-control.  By increasing arousal you are playing the self control game!

*Dog Self-Control*
A well-trained dog is able to hold her sit position despite temptation such as a hamburger or toy next to her.  Take note of the training games you play that create the most excitement and which ones create less.  When training self-control, start by playing a game that creates a low level of arousal, then stop playing and give the dog a cue.  If the dog responds immediately, click and reinforce.  Once you are getting consistent success, move on to a game that creates a little more arousal.  Set your dog up to

succeed.  If you accidentally got the dog too aroused, take a few minutes to click and treat the dog for eye contact as this will help the dog lower her arousal.  When you see she has calmed, you can try again.

It is normal for some young, reactive dogs to nip, bite or bark at you while doing agility.  Note when these behaviors occur, so you can determine what is triggering them.  Find ways to set your dog up for success to avoid triggering the nipping, biting or barking.  Lower the dog's arousal, ask for fewer behaviors and increase your rate of reinforcement (more reinforcements for fewer behaviors).  This will help decrease any frustration that may be feeding the dog's high arousal state.  Build up slowly to higher arousal levels and more behaviors one at a time.

*Handler Self-Control*
Self-control is good for the agility handler too.  Agility training requires patience and the delaying of gratification, passing on something you want now in order to reach a better goal down the road.  Not only does the process of gradually teaching your dog the obstacles, handling cues and common sequences take time, but waiting to trial your dog until she is well prepared can also take considerable will power on your part.  You can do it!

In 1980, *Time Magazine* did a cover story on the Intelligence Quotient (IQ) versus Emotional Quotient (EQ).  The concept of IQ versus EQ is based on research that showed people with emotional skills did better in life than people with intelligence skills.  In other words, people who are able to strive toward long-term goals, delay gratification and demonstrate self-control do better in life than those who cannot.  They had less interpersonal conflict and generally were more satisfied in their careers.

The article begins by saying, "It turns out that a scientist can see the future by watching four-year-olds interact with a marshmallow.  The researcher invites the children, one by one, into a plain room and begins the gentle torment. You can have this marshmallow right now, he says. But if you wait while I run an errand, you can have two marshmallows when I get back. And then he leaves."

The fascinating results of this study are also comical. A video camera captured the children's responses to the delaying gratification dilemma. Some kids gobbled up the marshmallow the moment the door shut, while others tried to distract themselves from the marshmallow and finding the temptation too great, eventually swallowed the marshmallow whole. However, some kids were determined to wait. They covered their eyes or used other strategies to keep themselves occupied until the researcher returned. Of course, these kids were reinforced with the second marshmallow. Next, the researchers waited for these children to grow up. What they found was, "that those kids who delayed gratification grew up to be more successful in life." Those kids who did not resist the marshmallow temptation were more "lonely, easily frustrated, stubborn, buckled under stress and shied away from challenges."

So what do four-years-olds, marshmallows and delaying gratification have to do with agility? Delaying gratification and using self-control have everything to do with agility training. Agility training requires a high EQ. It takes emotional strength to strive towards long-term goals and to train at the pace the dog sets. It takes emotional strength to creatively think your way out of a frustrating training situation. Tap into your emotional intelligence and think long term. Give yourself and your dog, the time you need to gain the skills that you want. Even if you were one of the kids that grabbed the marshmallow, it's never too late to change your behavior. Just like you can teach an older dog agility, you can also teach an adult human to delay gratification.

**Win/Win Training Game**
Agility is a game that creates a partnership between trainer and dog. A partnership can only occur if the relationship is a win for both parties. All other possibilities, involving one or both parties losing, offer less.

There are four possibilities whenever you interact with your dog:

*Win/Lose*
You get what you want and the dog does not get what she wants. An example of this is any type of forceful training, when physical manipulation or correction of the dog is performed. A dog trained the win/lose way may be accurate, but is less likely to develop the speed and attitude desired for top agility performance. Win/lose training will ultimately end up lose/lose as it damages your reinforcement history and bond with your dog.

*Lose/Win*
You don't get what you want and the dog gets what she wants. Lose/win is when your dog engages in an unwanted behavior that is annoying to the trainer. Demand barking and pulling on her leash are examples of lose/win. If the dog is controlling the environment instead of the trainer, the trainer is in a lose situation. Lose/win scenarios don't build up the team that you and your dog create and can damage your reinforcement history and bond with your dog.

*Lose/Lose*
You don't get what you want, and the dog does not get what she wants. Sounds like fun, huh? Pardon the sarcasm. Using a physical correction may seem like a win/lose, but ultimately it is a lose/lose. The moment that the physical correction is given, it is reinforcing to the trainer. The trainer feels powerful and in control and momentarily the dog may comply. Physical corrections can ultimately create learned helplessness, a form of shut

down, which is definitely a lose/lose situation.  You can't do agility with a dog that is curled into a ball.  Most lose/lose trained dogs will have a tendency to work slowly because they are fearful and stressed attempting to avoid the next correction.  Training that results in lose/lose is usually a sure way to decrease your dog's motivation because it can cause stress and fear.  How much fun can a game be when one of the players is physically corrected for making a mistake?  Some dogs are so driven to work that they appear not to care about the physical corrections they are given.  But look into that dog's eyes, see the fear and stress, and ask yourself if that is the look you want in your dog's eyes.

*Some Causes for Lose Situations*
Using pack theory in your training is another way to psychologically create a power struggle and a win/lose situation.  According to pack theory, a misguided owner thinks he must win and the dog lose, because that is how you demonstrate that you are alpha over your dog.

James O'Heare, author of *Dominance Theory in Dogs* says, "If you examine the dominance concept, you will find that it may not be able to help us predict much dog behavior, because dominance is fluid, changing from context to context and over time."  It is probably helpful to eliminate pack theory and dominance from your dog training vocabulary, as they are only likely to distract you from focusing on the dog's behavior.

*Win/Win*
You and your dog both get what you want — the true partnership.  The win/win training game goal is to increase your bond with your dog in a mutually cooperative setting.  Both team members win.

The win/win: even though the performance wasn't perfect (bar down in far right) Suzanne and Rev leave the ring filled with joy.

Photo by Tony Rider

# Chapter 3 Click!  And Play

Let's discuss some of the training games you can play to begin your **click and play** pyramid journey!  These games link to the **click and play** pyramid, creating a solid foundation for all that you and your dog will learn.

### Attention Games
When interacting with your dog and before giving any cues, wait for her to offer attention or use her name to get it.  Let's say you want to ask your dog to sit at the door before letting her outside.  Wait for eye contact before cueing the sit.  When she sits, release her to go outside.  This will teach her that eye contact precedes all your cues, games and reinforcements.  In behavioral terms, eye contact becomes her default behavior — the behavior with the strongest reinforcement history.  For most dogs, sit is the default behavior.  Whatever you choose as your dog's default behavior, include eye contact.  Ultimately, in the agility ring your dog will not be staring at you, but rather at the obstacles she is performing.  But you will need her to watch you out of the corner of her eye for body cues and listen for verbal cues.  With a solid attention foundation, you will succeed.

One way to teach your dog to give eye contact is to shape the behavior by clicking and reinforcing when she looks near your face, then at your face and finally at your eyes.  For a very soft dog, clicking and reinforcing for looking at your chin may be less intimidating.  As you build a reinforcement history for eye contact with your chin, you can eventually raise criteria to actual eye contact.  When shaping eye contact be sure to build duration so that you train more than just a glance.  Clicking and reinforcing a glance can create darting eye contact rather than a consistent watch.

By teaching your dog to watch you, your dog will be able to notice the cues you give her.  You can use both food and toys to reinforce for eye contact. It is myth that precision can only be trained with food. Many great obedience dogs have been trained to the highest level of precision using only toy reinforcement.

*Lost Attention Game*
If you lose your dog's attention, immediately play an attention game before continuing the training session. A dog wandering off while you are training is your cue to run the opposite way as fast as you can and hide. If you have built up enough reinforcement history, your dog will frantically search for you. Good! That is what we want. When she finds you, click and play! Obedience trainers have played this attention game for decades and it is a great way to keep your dog watching you, lest the sneaky human runs off and disappears!

For those dogs that still need to build more reinforcement history, you can play other games and sporadically "test" to see if you have gotten enough "money" in the attention bank for the dog to want to search for you.

*Attention is Fun*
Who wants to watch you if it is not fun? Look for intensity, tail wagging and a happy attitude. Then click it! Be playful when playing attention games.

An environment with many distractions will challenge your training. If necessary, move your dog away from those distractions until she can succeed. Let's say you are training at a park and your dog is highly distracted by squirrels. Move away from the little critters, until you regain her attention. Once you have her attention, slowly move closer again. Build on success and be patient with this process. Turn the process into a game. You are **click and play** training!

In every training session, make it a habit to play some sort of attention game. Require eye contact for sits and downs.

Make it part of everything you do with your dog. This will help you maintain wonderful eye contact once you have created it.

*The Chris Bach Eye Contact Game*
Chris Bach developed a fun version of the eye contact game that results in the behavior itself becoming reinforcing to the dog. Bach accomplishes this by including proofing in both the acquisition and maintenance phase of learning. Any distraction in the environment becomes a cue to resume or continue giving eye contact.

You and your dog are playing the eye contact game. While watching each other, you bend over and softly drop a boring rock on the ground. Your dog keeps staring to you, click and reinforce. If the dog glances at the rock and then looks back at you, click and reinforce. If the dog stares at the rock, pick it up and try again. Consider this process asking the dog questions. "Can you keep watching me while I drop this rock on the ground?" The dog said "yes" if she kept looking at you: click and reinforce. You have shown the dog that the distraction is actually an *opportunity* to be reinforced. With more training, the distraction itself will become a cue to keep watching you. Looking at you creates the hope of earning reinforcement. Isn't it wonderful?

Smile at your dog while playing the eye contact game and invite her to want to look at you. Dogs read our expressions like you are reading this book, so smile when playing the eye contact game.

While it seems simple to teach your dog to look at you, maintaining attention in a highly distracting environment can be challenging. Agility trials are very distracting places, with cars, kids playing, dogs barking and spectators. Surprises and funny noises lurk everywhere.

Even though Suzanne holds out a piece of food with her right hand, Rev continues to hold eye contact with her.

Photo by Angelica Steinker

*Attention and the Startle Response*
Distractions can startle your dog and her physiological startle response can draw her eyes away from you. It is important to understand that no amount of training can prevent your dog from startling. Currently scientists theorize that the startle response is probably a reflex. This means that startling is not something that a dog has control over; it just happens. Assuming that your dog will startle, what needs to be trained is the recovery of eye contact after the startle. Click, and reinforce after the startled dog makes the decision to look at you again. This is invaluable in difficult circumstances when the dog may become stressed. Standing outside the agility ring playing the attention game, you hear a loud crack on the PA system. Your dog flinches, looks away, but then recovers and looks back at you — click and reinforce the recovery! This teaches the dog that no matter what happens, resuming eye contact with you is a great response.

So if the triple jump suddenly collapses, your dog may startle, but immediately recover and check in with you with minimal loss of time and confidence.  Then the two of you complete the course to celebrate at the finish line.

*Distraction Ideas*
A very simple distraction commonly used by Bach, is to hold a piece of food beside your face.  You are giving the dog a choice: you can look at me, or look at the food.  If the dog looks at you, click and reinforce.  If her eyes lock on to the food, remove it and hide it behind your back for a few seconds.  Then try again, but hold the food further away from your face to set up for success.  To get the dog started you can click and reinforce for just looking away from the food.  Then raise criteria and only click and reinforce if the dog looks at your face instead of the food.

Keep changing the type of attention proofing games you play.  "Can you look at me while I hold an entire hot dog out the full length of my arm?"  "Can you look at me while I drop food on the floor?"  "Can you look at me while another dog runs the agility course?"  Every time you play the game, ask the dog a different question.

Most agility dogs love to be mentally challenged, but it is still important to make it easy enough for them to succeed.  If you placed a child's noisy toy on the ground and your dog is now incapable of keeping eye contact, move her away from the toy until she can succeed again.  Generously click and reinforce attention when you are a distance from the toy, and then gradually raise criteria by moving closer.

In clicker training, a failure never indicates the need to correct a dog.  Rather it sends the dog a message that this behavior will not earn reinforcement.  Repeated failure sends the *trainer* a message that he needs to adjust the training plan, so his dog can succeed.

The goal of good attention training is a dog that checks in with you like Mickie is doing here.

Photo by Tony Rider

*Passive Attention Game*
The passive attention game is when your dog gives you attention even when you are not giving her any. You could be talking to a friend, taking a walk and looking where you are going or watching TV, and your dog still watches you, waiting for a cue or a click and reinforcer.

Passive attention is extremely important in agility, as we need our dogs to be ready for a cue at any moment. The following game trains passive attention and is a great way to train your own peripheral vision, which you will need during handling to monitor your dog's position on course.

While you are looking at another person click and reinforce your dog for watching you. Either use your peripheral vision to watch her (make sure not to look at her directly) or ask the person to click when you are being watched so you can feed.

Photo by Angelica Steinker

*Attention and Breed Differences*
Recently I saw two litters of young puppies. One litter had the default behavior of staring at whichever human happened to be nearby. It is no surprise, that the puppies

were Border Collies. Compare this with a litter of similarly aged Jack Russell Terrier pups. I observed every single terrier pup being busy with an activity that had nothing to do with any human in the room. For hundreds and thousands of years humans have been artificially selecting dogs for certain behavioral traits. Artificial selection works! There are exceptions, but usually herding breeds will be more likely to watch their owners. Conversely, terriers and hounds may be much more into creating their own fun. Of course all dogs that are mentally and physically capable can be trained to do a variety of things, but we don't see many bloodhounds in agility.

There is a reason for this. My personal experience has been that it is possible to attain the same results with both my Jack Russell terriers, my Miniature Pinscher and my Border Collies, however I will work anywhere from 10 to 100 times harder training the terriers. Consider breed differences when selecting your next agility dog. If you don't enjoy the challenge of working with terriers (who are in my opinion the best teachers in the world) select a dog that is more people-oriented in nature.

*The Power of Now*
In agility, attention is a two-way street. The dog stays focused on the trainer, and the trainer stays focused on the dog and the course. Pete Rose, the Hit King of Baseball, attributes his phenomenal success to his ability to keep his attention focused on the ball. In agility our "ball" is both the dog and the obstacle course. In order to succeed, we need to be committed to giving our full attention to our ball when training and competing.

To develop your own concentration and focus skills, consider non-agility tasks in your life that have required your complete attention. What skills assisted you in focusing? Determine what they were and implement them in your agility training and handling.

It is impossible to be in the moment if you are thinking about the past or the future. You can only be in the moment if you fully focus on what is happening now. This type of focus on the here and now takes practice.

Some skills that can help your focus are:

o   Setting small attainable goals. Ideally set goals that you can control. If you can't control something, it is likely to make you nervous. Nervousness decreases your focus. The best goals focus on process. Like doing a front cross between obstacle eight and nine or smiling the entire run. Setting small attainable training and competition goals is one way for the trainer to pay full attention to the current task.
o   Consistently ask yourself while interacting with your dog, "what am I training now?" Be aware.
o   Focusing on the here and now. Staying in the here and now is critical to both good training and handling. If you are worried about who is watching, or what others are thinking, you can't be attentive to your dog and the course. You can't help your dog learn if you are not fully present in the moment. The past is unalterable, the future is unknown, the only time we can alter anything is in the moment. So use your moment to focus on what you are doing with your dog.
o   Meditation. Meditation is a great way to focus your mind. It can open your mind to new solutions, a new perspective or a new idea. It can help de-clutter your mind so you can attend to what is happening right now in your dog's training. Only when you are fully present can you be aware. Only when you are fully aware can you control your own behavior, your movements, your timing or your attitude. Eckart Tolle has written a cool book called "*The Power of Now*" in it he describes how to meditate.

My personal favorite is the tremendous power that can be found when focusing on the now.  While Tolle's book may appear to have little or nothing to do with agility, it actually does.  Just think about what happens to us when we stress at a trial.  Our bodies create all kinds of unusual sensations because we are nervous.  We shake, we feel nauseous and we feel like we need to use the bathroom.  All these sensations interfere with our ability to focus and give our dog and the agility obstacles the attention that they need.  Where are these physiological responses coming from?  We create them!  We create them with our thoughts and feelings.  To top it all off these thoughts and feelings usually have nothing to do with what is happening in the moment, but rather are linked to our past experiences or our future goals.

So how do we rid ourselves of stress?  We rid ourselves of the thoughts and feelings.  Emotional intelligence = self-control and focus on the now.  In the moment of handling your dog, there is no reason to think or feel anything.  In the moment, you just do one thing.  In the next moment, you do the next thing.  It is only in the moment that you can alter the dog's path.

The attention games that you play with your dog, and with yourself, will become habits.  It will become a habit to click and reinforce your dog for eye contact.  It will become a habit for you to enter the now and be fully present when the situation calls for it.  In this sense, you will always be playing the attention game.  That is why attention is the bottom of the pyramid.  Everything is layered on the foundation of attention: the dog's attention, and ours.

**Consistency Games**
Is being consistent a challenge to you?  Well, if you have a dog, just sit back, watch and learn.  Most dogs are supremely consistent.  Just take a piece of food and tuck it barely out of the dog's reach under the couch.  Now see

how long the dog will attempt to get that food.  When adequately frustrated, watch the dog begin to train you to retrieve the food for her.  Most humans are very quickly trained in food recovery by their dog's frantic scratching at their $4,000 couch.  If you think your dog has never trained you, you just haven't noticed.

Dogs have a tireless dedication to consistency.  If you own a terrier-type dog, you know this dedication can drive you to the brink of insanity, and beyond.  I had my "beyond" experience when Moose started to lick the walls whenever I worked on a paper for graduate school.  Moose wanted my attention and wall licking pressed my buttons, so he always got what he wanted.  Insanity aside, consistency enables fast and efficient learning for both people and dogs.

*Consistency Check*
Take a moment to make a list of your verbal cues on a sheet of paper.  Examine your cues list for similar sounding cues.  Table, tire and tunnel all start with "T" and this could make them sound similar.  If your dog has a hard time verbally discriminating between these "T" cues, you may want to change at least one of them to a different sounding cue.

Be sure to include *all* the verbal cues you use.  List the ones you use in the house, in obedience, while on walks, etc.  The goal is for this list to be as complete as possible.  Look for junk cues, a cue that really means nothing.  Once I noticed that I kept telling my Border Collie Stevie, who used to love to aggravate my Jack Russell Junior, the following junk cue, "stop that — you know he hates it."  Border Collies are smart, but they definitely don't understand a reasoning sentence.  Having caught myself, I learned to cue Stevie to "lie down" when he went to tease Junior.  For some reason this worked much better!

In the handling chapter, you can make a list of your handling cues.  Once you have completed both lists you may want to review them for consistency with body language.  Each of your body language cues should be distinct and clear to your dog.

*One Cue*
A key element to successful agility is for your dog to respond immediately to the first cue given.  This is stimulus control.  It is "said to have occurred when a stimulus (also known as signal or cue) systematically affects the performance of a behavior (Pamela Reid)."  In other words, the dog does the behavior when you ask her to and doesn't do it if you don't ask her to.  To consistently do well in agility, you want your dog to respond to the first and only cue at least 90% of the time.

*The One Cue Game*
Make a commitment to saying your cues only one time!  To help you get in this habit, you can play the 'One Cue Game.'  You need two people to play so find a training partner.  One person is the trainer, the other the recorder.  Before playing, the trainer makes a list of all the dog's cues.  Hey, you just did that!  Draw a large capital "T" onto a sheet of paper.  On the left side of the T the recorder notes all the cues that the trainer said one time and one time only, these cues are under stimulus control.  On the right side, the recorder notes those cues that were repeated or that the dog did not respond to, the cues needing additional training.

Each cue given will be recorded as either being under stimulus control or needing training.  This game is a great way of gaining information about your dog's cues.  If you have stimulus control then you can throw a party.  If you have cues that need additional work, that is great to know and gives you something to focus on in your training sessions.

An advanced version of the one cue game is to play it in different contexts so that you can see if the dog is able to respond to one cue in distracting environments. Those cues that are responded to immediately, in different environments, are under stimulus control.

*Multitasking*
Multitasking is what agility is all about. An agility handler needs to be able to simultaneously engage in several tasks yet also be able to react to unexpected events. To successfully direct a dog over an agility course the handler must be able to:

1.  Memorize and recall the course.
2.  Have spatial awareness of the placement of all obstacles.
3.  Actively watch the dog.
4.  Be aware of his verbal and body signals, the timing of cues and when to make necessary adjustments.
5.  Be aware of his position on the course in relation to the obstacles and the dog.
6.  Clearly signal the next sequence.
7.  Know where the dog is in relation to the path being signaled.
8.  Know what behavior the dog is currently performing and whether it requires a release cue.

Is it any wonder why many agility competitors are obsessed with attending handling seminars? The best competitors manage to do it all and make it look effortless by gaining body awareness and expert familiarity with the tasks at hand.

Certain aspects of handling your dog need to be learned to the point where the activity no longer requires conscious thought. Practicing course memorization, verbal cues and handling on a daily basis (both with and without a dog) will help free up mental space for other activities.

*On/Off Switch Game*
Duration behaviors, like holding a sit are ideally taught with one cue that turns the behavior on and a second cue that turns the behavior off.  If you cue your dog to sit, you have flipped the sit "on" switch.  Train her to continue sitting until you flip the "off" switch, release cue with "okay."

Sit = on switch
Okay, or other cue = off switch

Down = on switch
Okay or other cue = off switch

Touch on contacts = on switch
Okay = off switch

Table (dog runs to table and automatically downs and holds position) = on switch
Okay = off switch

Every time you give your dog a cue (flip the on switch) continue to be aware of what your dog is doing.  If you tend to forget your off switch cue, have a friend play music or sing a song while your dog is switched on, to help remind yourself that you are still working your dog.

Another cue that is of utmost importance is your on duty and off duty cues.  On duty, means for the dog to be ready for the next cue and remain focused.  Off duty means, you can go and have free time.  For me any cue I give my dogs is the on duty switch.  The off duty switch is "no more."

*Success Rate Game*
When training, rehearse success, not failure.  Consistency is extremely important to the dog's training progress.  To establish your dog's success rate set up a video camera or have a friend help you.  Kay Laurence in her book "*Clicker Intermediate Training,*" describes how to calculate a success rate.  Count the number of behaviors the dog

offered, including sniffing, and any behaviors other than the one cued. Count out how many treats you will be using so you don't need to count the number of clicks. To calculate your success rate use the following formula:

Number of clicks ÷ Number of behaviors offered × 100 = success rate

Before starting, hold one piece of food between your thumb and forefinger ready to feed and keep the other pieces tucked in the palm of your hand ready to 'reload.'

This picture shows how to hold your treats for fast delivery. One treat is stored between the thumb and forefinger the other treats are tucked in the fist.
 After you use the first treat you can use your thumb to roll out the next treat.

Photo by Suzanne Rider

Hold your clicker in the opposite hand. Pick a simple behavior, such as sit that you think your dog knows well and cue it. While you focus on the timing of your click and reinforcement delivery for correct responses, your friend counts the times your dog performs a behavior, other than the sit cue for the total number of behaviors. These other behaviors are non-responses.

Total number of clicks: 20
Total number of behaviors: 25
20 ÷ 25 = 0.8 × 100 = 80% — This shows evidence of learning and is almost at the 90% you are shooting

for.  If the percentage is over 50% it is generally considered evidence of learning.

Total number of clicks: 20
Total number of behaviors: 48
$20 \div 48 = 0.41 \times 100 = 41\%$ — This dog may need a slightly less distracting environment to reach 50% or higher which would indicate learning.

When you reach 90% or better, you know the behavior is learned, *in that context*.  Use your success rate calculations to help you determine which behaviors are in maintenance and which ones need more work.

*Consistent Teaching Games*
There are three learning games you can play to get a behavior and to put it on cue.

1.  The Shaping Game.
2.  The Prompting Game.
3.  The Capturing Game.

I touched on these three games earlier but they are so important that I want to take the time to discuss them some more.

*The Shaping Game*
Shaping is the process of training your dog by reinforcing a very small part of the end behavior.  Gradually over time, you ask more of the dog until you have "shaped" the goal behavior.  Shaping truly is a game!  Let's say you want your dog to wave.  You start by clicking and reinforcing the dog for shifting her weight off her left paw.  Next, you click and reinforce the dog for lifting the left paw.  Next, you require that the dog lift the paw one inch, then two inches, and so on until you only click and reinforce if the dog has lifted her paw to eye level.  Once you get this behavior consistently, you add the cue "wave."  Ta da!  Another great behavior has been shaped.  Exciting isn't it!

51

*Cone Game*
If you are not familiar with shaping, here is a great game that can help you learn.  Grab a traffic-type cone and choose an easy behavior to shape, like the dog touching her nose to the tip of the cone.  Shape the dog to approach the cone, and then touch it.  If she touches it with her nose, lucky you, click and reinforce.  If she paws at it, don't panic, click and reinforce this one time and then wait.  It is very likely that she will become mildly frustrated and bump her nose on the cone, click, reinforce and celebrate!  You have shaped your first behavior!  The shaping game is ideal for training the nose touch for the contact obstacles, creating great attitude on the table and more.

Whenever you or someone else is shaping, observe how the timing of the click influences the behavior.  Shaping is cool!  Shaping exposes the trainer's abilities.  A skilled trainer will knock your socks off and make it all look so easy, like Laurence shaping a behavior on one of her videos.  Unskilled shaping can yield sloppy results and a frustrated, barking dog.

During shaping your timing is critical: your dog will repeat what you click, even if you intended to click another behavior.  Shaping requires a clicker savvy dog as well as a skilled trainer.  Beginners need to keep it very simple, in order to build their skills. Observe how your treat delivery influences the behavior.  If you deliver immediately next to the cone, how does that influence the behavior?  If you deliver away from the cone, does that influence the behavior?  Observe what happens if you click the same behavior twice, three times or more.  Clicking the same behavior may cause the dog to get 'stuck' at that point, because the shaping process may seem to be over.  You may have taught the dog that the current behavior is the end behavior.

Virtually any safe object can be used for a shaping session. A spoon, a wad of paper, a cardboard box, a ball — anything can mean fun for you and your dog. Laurence advises trainers to play shaping games with specific behaviors in mind.

*Creativity*
Some clicker trainers play a "be creative" game that encourages the dog to throw new behaviors, since only new behaviors are clicked and reinforced. While this game is mentally stimulating to the dog, Laurence warns that shaping is based on the dog repeating the behavior you just clicked and reinforced. If the dog instead keeps moving on to "new" behaviors you will have to work harder at playing the shaping game for other kinds of tasks.

For those trainers who enjoy reinforcing creativity, consider inserting the "be creative" game once between two shaping sessions. That way you are helping the dog understand that these two games are different. Laurence recommends using an environmental cue, such as a mat to play the 'be creative' game on. That way the dog associates the mat with that game and is less likely to offer 'creativity' when you may not want it.

*Shaping Tips*
Regardless of whether you are new to training or have been doing it for years, advice from Karen Pryor is always helpful. In "Don't Shoot the Dog!" she lists the laws of shaping. Pryor states the first four laws come straight from the psychology lab and have been experimentally demonstrated. The others have not yet been the subject of formal study, but can be recognized as inherently valid by anyone who has done a lot of shaping. The laws of shaping are:

1.    *Raise criteria in increments small enough so that the dog always has a realistic chance for reinforcement.* Imagine you are teaching a dog to

come when called, but you are doing it outside in a very distracting environment. You call the dog and the dog does not come, so you try again, and again, and again. But, each time the dog does not come. By choosing to try coming when called outside too soon and with too many distractions, training criteria were too high and the dog failed. Training failures are always a signal that the trainer needs to change something. Moving the session inside, the trainer asks the dog to "come" and when the dog does he clicks and reinforces. Ideal training sets the dog up for success!

2. *Train one thing at a time. Don't try to shape two criteria simultaneously.* Dogs are just like us in that they don't want to be bombarded with information. Training more than one thing at a time will likely create trainer frustration and/or confuse the dog. It is much easier and faster to avoid these problems than to fix them once they have been created.

3. *Always put the current level of response onto a variable schedule of reinforcement before adding or raising criteria.* While a dog is learning a criterion, she will be getting one click and treat for every behavior she performs. Once you have your ninety percent success rate, begin delaying reinforcement until after you get two or three responses in a row. Then raise criteria, because now you can be certain that the dog understands what you want.

4. *When introducing a new criterion, temporarily relax the old ones.* When adding a new aspect or a new behavior to a chain, you can temporarily relax the criteria on the previous behavior. It is good training to allow the dog to briefly work through some confusion.

5. *Stay ahead of your dog. Plan your shaping program completely so that if your dog makes sudden progress, you are aware of what to*

*reinforce next.* Doing and observing shaping will help you develop the ability to adjust your training plan for when your dog makes a sudden learning leap.

6. *Don't change trainers in mid-stream. You can have several trainers per dog but stick to one trainer per behavior.* Every trainer has an individual style. While a dog is learning, you don't want to switch trainers for that behavior. Switching can cause the dog to become confused and may either slow down or hobble the learning process.

7. *If one shaping procedure is not eliciting progress, find another. There are as many ways to get a behavior as there are trainers to think them up.* More than one path leads to the top of the mountain. Be flexible and open to different paths.

8. *Don't interrupt the training session gratuitously, that constitutes a punishment.* In agility, it is very common for handlers to forget to reinforce the dog after a sequence when they are eager to hear what the instructor thinks about what went wrong or right. Instead first reinforce your dog, and then ask the dog to lie down so you can focus your attention on your instructor. The dog comes first!! Be aware of how you end your sessions, since the end of a training session means the end of fun for your dog.

9. *If behavior deteriorates, "go back to kindergarten"; quickly review the whole shaping process with a series of easy reinforcements.* If your dog is having a bad day, go back to the most basic part of the behavior and quickly remind her of what you are working on. Find the dog's success point and go from there.

10. *End each session on a high note, if possible, but in any case quit while you are ahead.* Attitude is everything, maintain attitude by ending sessions with a jackpot— a handful of treats.

Keep these laws in mind when training and refer to them when you are stuck or frustrated by a training challenge. They can make the process of learning easier to understand and more enjoyable for both you and your dog.

*The Prompting Game*
Prompting is the process of training your dog by using some sort of physical prop or toy to get the goal behavior. Hand targeting, a target stick and toys are all forms of prompts. Although useful to 'get the behavior,' prompts must be faded (gradually removed) so that the behavior does not become dependent on the prompt.

*The Doorbell Game*
Ring your own doorbell! What happens? In most dog homes, the sound will elicit barking. Click and reinforce the dog for barking. Repeat three times. Now add the cue "speak," then ring the door bell. When the dog barks, click and reinforce the barking. Repeat five times. "Speak" should now predict the doorbell, which prompts barking. You are aiming for the dog to respond to "speak" without requiring the bell. Cue "speak" and don't ring the bell. If the dog barks, click and reinforce the barking. If not, just repeat the previous step a few more times. Ultimately, you will have the behavior of barking on the cue, "speak."

Now that you have taught your dog to bark, you can also cue her to be quiet. To prompt the dog to stop barking, cue the dog to speak and when she does, say "quiet". The new sound, "quiet" will likely interrupt the dog's barking. If so, immediately click and reinforce the silence. In this case quiet is initially both the prompt and the cue.

*The Capturing Game*
For the trainer, capturing is the easiest of the three methods. It only requires good observational skills and good timing. Capturing is clicking and reinforcing your dog for a behavior that she frequently engages in. To capture

a behavior you must be able to click and reinforce it several times a day ideally several times in a row.  It is difficult to capture behaviors that occur infrequently.  My mom and dad's Jack Russell Terrier Arnie, offered a head stand behavior but only sporadically.  It took six months to capture the behavior because it did not consistently occur.

This behavior was difficult to capture and put on cue, because it was offered infrequently.

Photo by Angelica Steinker

Observe your dog for unique behaviors.  Does your dog sneeze at predictable times?  Stretch after certain activities?  Any cute habits your dog engages in can potentially be captured.  To capture a behavior, it must consistently be offered by the dog.  Consistency is a central theme woven into many aspects of the science and art of training.

## Motivation Games
Motivation games help create a fun attitude.  Attitude in turn helps create speed.  If you enjoy something, you generally complete the task with intent and speed.  Training motivation in part leaves the realm of science and enters the realm of art.

*It Depends*
In motivation training everything depends on individual factors.  Having many factors come into play means that

the answer to most motivational training questions is it depends.

How fast can you train your dog to run agility?  It depends on:

- o   The dog's structure.
- o   The trainer's ability.
- o   How much time is devoted to the training process.
- o   The dog's level of fitness.
- o   The dog's genetic predisposition for agility.

Before becoming frustrated that your terrier isn't running like a Border Collie and your Bassett Hound isn't weaving like a Sheltie, evaluate what your dog is mentally, physically and genetically predisposed to do.  Dogs that are genetically programmed to do scent work, and have very laid-back personalities may not be ideal candidates for agility training.  This does not mean laid-back dogs can't succeed in agility, it means the goals should be realistic and training will require more effort.  Training a dog that is challenging to work with is one of the most wonderful ways to truly learn and grow as a trainer.

Motivational games exist to help your dog develop a love of play and agility, but they are also effective in gauging your dog's current motivational level.

*The Tug Gauge Game*
Before beginning a training session, wait for your dog to give you eye contact and then cue your dog to play a game of tug.  While you are tugging, notice how hard the dog is pulling.  Compare this to how hard she usually pulls. Use this "tug barometer" to read how motivated your dog is.  If she tugs intensely, she is probably keen to play agility.  If she is not tugging as hard as usual, you may want to continue playing until she becomes more excited and tugs with enthusiasm.  Then begin your training session.  Also, the dog may be experiencing stress and

you may want to establish the source of stress and remove the dog from it.

*The Food Gauge Game*
The intensity of a food motivated dog's interest in treats can be used to evaluate her motivational state.  Stress and food motivation are incompatible.  A stressed dog likely will not want to play or eat, or she may take treats very roughly.  If the dog doesn't want to eat, it is not an indication of lack of reinforcement history, nor is it a signal that the dog needs deprivation (the withholding of food to force increased hunger).  It is an indication to the trainer that he needs to make changes to the dog's environment to help the dog reduce her stress level.  Another indication of stress can be a failure to perform known behaviors.  Stress reduces a dog's ability to perform.

*Creating Motivation*
Playfully teasing your dog with a toy is a fun way to build motivation for toys and playing.  Be sure to move the toy slowly enough that the dog has a realistic chance of being able to grab it.  For puppies whose motor skills are still developing, slow means SSLLOOWWW.  While moving the toy, observe the dog and experiment with various speeds.  Which types of movements entice the dog into playing?  Many trainers quickly become discouraged if the dog doesn't show an interest in playing with a fast moving toy.  (Sometimes they don't notice the first attempts — eyes brightening, a quick lunge etc.  If those first attempts aren't reinforced and the dog may give up.)  Persistence, with a fun attitude, is likely to be reinforced by the dog eventually beginning to play.

If your dog doesn't grab the toy regardless of whether you move it slowly or quickly, you can shape the dog to learn how to play.  Begin with clicking and reinforcing the dog for watching the toy, then touching it with her nose.  Gradually raise criteria to opening her mouth, and eventually to mouthing.  From mouthing, you can move to picking up, tossing, carrying and so forth.  It may take some time, but it will be worth it every time your dog plays with you.

This shaping method can be used to get the dog tugging.  As soon as the dog starts tugging even lightly, click and reinforce.  Gradually build duration from there.  Playfully grab and tickle the dog while you tug to increase excitement over the game.  When the dog seems most into tugging, pull the toy away and put it out of her reach.  Playing this game of "keep away" will increase her desire for the toy.  Eventually, her "fun button" will be pressed, and a game of tug will become self-reinforcing.  This process may take months, but the effort will be reinforced by many years of play.

After the dog starts to play, you can incorporate play into your training.  Start asking her to play before receiving any food.  As the tugging becomes self-reinforcing to the dog, become unpredictable and intermittently follow playing tug with food until the food is completely faded.  Now you have two ways to reinforce your dog in agility training— with food and with a game of tug.

Photo by Angelica Steinker

My Min Pin Turbo, rescued at 1.5 years, had no desire to play tug.  Turbo did not play with toys or even respond to a rolled ball.  Today he will retrieve balls and tugs on his leash.  The process took months, but was well worth the effort as we have had a lot of fun.

### Clicking Smiles
Yes, dogs actually smile.  A dog smile is usually open mouthed, with the corners of the lips pulled back and up exposing some of the dog's molars.  The facial

muscles are relaxed and the eyes are wide-open, with a soft expression.

A dog smile, heaven on earth to a clicker trainer.

Photo by Suzanne Rider

Another body language signal called a "submissive smile" is pictured here. The submissive smile is not something all dogs engage in. It isn't the joyful expression that I am trying to draw your attention to.

Photo by Saby Rochon/Sport Photography

If you see a dog smile while you are training with your dog, click it! While the dog may not connect her emotional state with the click, her movements and behaviors will be of a certain "happy" quality. This is precisely what agility trainers are after. They want their dogs to have fun.

Another indicator of a dog's emotional state is the tail. A fast wag that includes the rear end is likely indicating a happy emotional state. A slow tail wag is usually not an indication of a happy state and can be a precursor to aggression. Dogs are also able to signal stress or arousal with a very fast tail wag (this fast wag is not happy). As a rule, if the rear end isn't wiggling then it is not a happy wag. Unfortunately, many people have misread a stress or arousal tail wag to signal "friendliness." Click and reinforce your dog for happy tail wags with butt wiggles.

Fergie demonstrating a very happy tail wag!

Photo by Carol Murphy

One way to know a dog is truly wagging her tail is to watch the dog's rump for movement. If the tail wag includes the rump it is a happy wag!

*Intensity*
A dog very much into her task has an intensity about her. My mom's Jack Russell closes his mouth and gets a serious look on his face when he is feeling intense. Other dogs even curl their toes when very excited. While we can't read a dog's mind, we can make a good guess at what the dog is feeling by evaluating her body language.

A dog that is displaying intensity has an alert facial expression. Intensity can be seen in a dog's eyes, the tensing of her muscles, and maybe even in the toes. This intensity, especially when displayed in connection to a sit or down duration behavior is a great thing to click and reinforce. It is a great attitude, as mentally the dog is focused, and by holding the sit or down position the dog is demonstrating significant self-control.

*Vocalizations*
Vocalizations, the sounds your dog makes, hold the final clue to your dog's emotional state. Happy growls, grunts, moans or whimpers can be signs of joy.

My dog Stevie grunts when he is happy. I use this feedback to gauge whether or not I am doing a good job praising him. If I do a good job, he will grunt and lift his right hind leg. The happy leg with sound effects!

Stevie grunts and lifts his hind leg when happy.

Photo by Suzanne Rider

My Jack Russell Terrier Moose used to whine and grab my arm with his mouth when he was happy. The more I praised him the louder he got and the more he just had to get my arm in his mouth. Observe and listen to your dog, so that you can learn what makes her happy. Agility is about making the dog happy, that is the joy of the sport.

*Grrrr!*
Dogs often growl in play and this playful signal is a great sound to click and reinforce. A dog's play growl is distinctly different in tone and volume from a dog's "real" growl. Usually the "real" growl is lower in tone and sounds much more menacing. Also by practicing reading your dog's body language, you can visually see the difference in the dog's muscles and movements. Soft and flexible movements usually accompany a play growl. A stiff body usually accompanies a threatening growl.

Attitude and motivation are about having fun. Investigate what your dog enjoys and use those toys, activities and games to create the attitude you want for your agility training. You can click that attitude and reinforce by playing again. Motivation is about fun for both you and the dog. Become a fun and happiness detective.

**Self-Control Games**
Your dog's ability to control herself is critical to your success in the agility ring. Only through self-control will your dog be able to maintain her sit at the start line, and hold her contacts and table until released. Any behavior that requires duration will help your dog learn self-control.

Even simple trick behaviors can be used to teach self-control. Teach your dog to wave and continue to hold the paw up until you say the release word. You can also teach hand targeting as a duration behavior. On your cue to hand target, your dog touches her nose to your hand and holds it there until you release her.

*The Food Dish Game*
Another fun game that teaches self-control is the food dish game. Most of us feed our dogs twice a day. This gives you two opportunities a day to play the food dish game.

As long as Blink remains sitting, the food dish continues to be lowered. The moment Blink moves, the dish is pulled away.

Photo by Suzanne Rider

To play the game, ask your dog to sit while you hold her food dish in your hand. While she remains sitting, lower the food dish toward the ground. If she gets up, lift the food dish up and away. Then start over again, by asking the dog to sit. Continue to play this game until you have the dog holding her sit and the food dish is on the ground. When she gives you eye contact, release her to the food dish. Sometimes expect three seconds of eye contact, sometimes 30 seconds. Mix it up to keep the game fun and interesting.

Seminar presenter Dee Ganley created an advanced version of the food dish game. Ask the dog to continue sitting while you reach into the bowl, pick up some food and then deliver it to the dog's mouth. That is some serious self-control!

Since dinner time is often the highlight of a dog's day, this one game will teach most food motivated dogs self-control. Turbo is hilarious when we play this game. He is tiny, almost as small as his food dish, and he learned the game very quickly (obviously, he is a genius). When released to eat, he lets out a HUGE growl and throws himself into his dish. It makes me laugh every day, twice a day. I love that little dude!

If your dog is not successful playing the game, break it down further. If she can only hold the sit for two seconds, release her earlier and build up from there. If she can't give you eye contact, then firmly establish the duration of the sit and then add the eye contact. Find your dog's success point and build on it, rather than focusing on what is wrong. A success point is the specific criterion that your dog is able to meet in a behavior or behavior chain.

**Achieving Win/Win**
What is win/win? The final layer of your click and play pyramid is the win/win game, which presents an entire philosophy of being 'with' your dog. The premise is simple: in all interactions and situations both the owner and the dog win. The trainer recognizes the dog as a being separate from the trainer with her own sets of behaviors,

goals, responses and emotions. All dogs deserve love, respect, attention and caring. Win/win training does not view a dog as a possession or object. There is no "should," "has to," or "must" in win/win training. Win/win training is free of the use of force. The emphasis is on the dog voluntarily offering desired behaviors, which are either reinforced or not. Win/win training assumes that the dog is always right and that the trainer is the one needing to make adjustments. As Chris Bach would say, "the dog is always perfect at being a dog."

*Building a Bond*
As part of the win/win philosophy, it is critical to establish and build a bond with your dog. This bond is more than just reinforcement history. It is a close, personal nurturing relationship that includes some binding agreements. If you are reading this book, your dog is more to you than a pet. Your dog is a family member. However, like all relationships, your bond with your dog is subject to change. Both your behavior and the behavior of your dog can alter the bond. Your behaviors can either strengthen or weaken the bond with your dog. Your behaviors that strengthen the bond are a win for you and the dog, whereas those that weaken it are a lose for both.

The following is a list of activities that will help strengthen your bond with your dog.

  o  Clicker training using shaping is force free and based on a *voluntary* offering of behaviors. It is a great way to establish and maintain trust.
  o  Play is the most powerful way to increase your bond with your dog. Although I don't have a study to cite, it is what I truly believe. Grab a piece of paper and jot down how you feel about your dog. Write anything that comes to mind. Lay the piece of paper aside and during the next 24 hours play with your dog at least 20 times for two minutes or more. That's a total of 40 minutes a day, not much

time.  At the end of the 24 hours jot down your feelings for your dog on another sheet of paper. Compare what you have written on the two sheets. This is a powerful exercise.  Many trainers find that while they had a great bond to begin with, the intensive focus on play deepened that bond even further.
If your dog is choosing to engage in self-reinforcing behaviors rather than playing with you (i.e. running off, sniffing) play 20 times for two minutes daily over a month.  This can make a big difference in how your dog responds to you and will intensify your bond.

o   Manage your dog as if she is a star.  Every agility dog is a wonderful gift to her handler.  Part of valuing that gift is to manage the dog effectively. Protect her from stressful situations.  Allow her time to rest and be comfortable when spending the day at a trial or provide exercise while traveling. Manage excessive barking, lunging at other dogs or people while crated or other self-reinforcing behaviors that will tire or stress your dog.  Find ways to help your dog feel safe and comfortable.  A sheet draped over the crate, keeping her crated near you or away from the noise and dog trial traffic can all help.

o   Keep her well-exercised.  A well-exercised dog is a well-mannered and happy dog.  Many annoying behaviors can be eliminated or reduced by keeping your dog well exercised and mentally stimulated. For active dogs, the act of full speed running meets a need that can't be met by anything else.  It is critical to offer terrier-types, herding breeds, sporting breeds and others the ability to run full speed on a daily basis.  Full speed running will calm the dog, decrease problem behaviors and deepen your bond.

o   Take your dog to different places.  Public parks, nature trails and different dog schools are all places for you and your dog to have adventures.  The more adventures you have the stronger your bond will become.

Of all the things listed above play is the most important. Playing with your dog on a daily basis is the closest thing we have to magic.

Both the dog and the owner determine what is fun.  If either party does not think the game is fun, make adjustments, or find another game.  There is no forcing a dog to play.  Playing is the ultimate win/win.

*Unable to Play*
Flirt is a gorgeous Border Collie that came from a highly reputable breeder.  When she first arrived, her owner noticed that this puppy was suffering from anxiety.  The puppy had been shipped and some veterinary behaviorists now theorize that even one brief traumatic experience in a crate can trigger canine separation anxiety, an anxiety disorder that is triggered when the dog is left alone.  Other issues soon confirmed a problem.  When her handler would try to play with Flirt, she would sometimes be gung ho and other times curl into a ball and "shut down."  After many months of frustration and several veterinary consultations, it was discovered that Flirt had panic disorder, canine separation anxiety and hypothyroidism.

If a dog is unable to play agility coaches should not only consider the trainer but also the dog's history, medical and mental state.  Just like humans dogs can suffer from physical, mental illness or neurological issues that may interfere with the dog's ability to play.

Flirt's trainer worked hard and eventually did debut the dog in agility.  When it became apparent that Flirt had no passion for the game and running her felt like pulling teeth she was retired.  Today Flirt lives a happy life as a pet. Not every dog is made to be a performance dog.

Chris Bach, Trainer of trainers, says that dogs have drives (the desire to do behaviors) and sensitivities (things, people, other beings that they fear). Bach theorizes that for each dog either the drives or the sensitivities are stronger. When the drives are stronger the dog can learn to cope with her fears. When the sensitivities are stronger and the drive can't be increased to overcome the sensitivities, you have a dog that will be happier being a pet than a performance dog.

*Life Reinforcers*
Life reinforcers are rewards that are part of the dog's daily life. You are going to let your dog out of the crate, a reinforcement, no matter what, so you ask for a sit with eye contact before releasing her. You are going to let her go outside, a reinforcement, so ask for a down with eye contact before releasing her. It is the ideal win/win training. The dog gets to go outside (win) and you get a behavior with eye contact (win).

Other examples of life reinforcers are verbal praise, belly rubs, going for a walk, going for a car ride or any reinforcing event that happens in your dog's life. These reinforcing events can be used as part of your training program. If your dog loves to say hello to people, then put it on cue and create a win/win.

*Timing and Win/Win Training*
Develop your timing and treat delivery skills to make every training session a win/win. Ideal timing of the click is important for your dog's learning. Once you have clicked, it is only fair to quickly deliver the reinforcement to the dog.

Photo by Suzanne Rider

*Clicker Timing*
Deb Jones taught me the following timing game. Hold a clicker in your left hand and a ball in your right hand. Now toss the ball in the air. When the ball drops back down and touches the palm of your hand, click! A well-timed click should sound exactly when you feel the ball hit your hand. To time your click well, you need to anticipate the ball hitting your hand. If you wait until it hits, you will click too late. Play the ball tossing game until you consistently get the timing right, then switch hands and do the same exercise. This is a challenging exercise, but with practice you can do it! Training your dog is a physical skill and it is important to practice coordination and create body awareness. This becomes particularly important when you work on your handling.

Variations of this game are to click the ball at its highest point instead of when it hits your palm or to click the ball when it hits the ground. Be creative and make up your own clicker timing games!

*Timing of the Reinforcer*
The next physical skill you need is the timing of the reinforcement delivery. When you are preparing to train,

70

always have at least one treat between your fingers and be ready to deliver that treat to your dog at lightning speed.  If you want the dog to do things fast, you also need to do them fast.

It is critical to be aware of the behaviors that follow a click.

Avoid this scenario:

1.  Click a behavior you want.
2.  Reach for the bait bag.
3.  Realize the zip lock is sealed and fiddle with it.
4.  Extract a treat wiggling it out of the plastic bag and the bait bag.
5.  Finally deliver the treat to the dog.

Behavior Analyst Jesús Rosales-Ruiz and his students did a study where the treat was delayed for 5 seconds after the click.  In their study the dog targeted an object with her nose, was clicked and five seconds later received the treat. In all cases, the dogs became frustrated and began barking, whining, biting or pawing at the target prior to the treat delivery.  Some dogs got so frustrated they stopped targeting altogether.  The conclusion of the study was that treat delivery delay caused superstitious behaviors. Superstitious behavior refers to the modification or maintenance of a behavior by accidentally or unintentionally reinforcing it (James O'Heare). According to the frustration displayed by the dogs in the treat delay study, it seems that it may also be a motivation killer.  Avoid these pitfalls by practicing fast treat or toy delivery.

*Location of Reinforcer Delivery*
The physical position of your dog when she is reinforced and the location of your treat delivery are critically important to building some of the behaviors you are trying to create.  When training the dog to perform a behavior away from you, it is important to toss the reinforcer to the

dog rather than have the dog rush back to you to get her reinforcement. If you click the behavior away from you, but reinforce with food from your hand or play tug, you will find the dog reluctant to move away from you. It is better to toss your reinforcement away from you when playing training games that involve distance.

When tossing a reinforcer for a dog not motivated by toys, use either a food-filled toy or a food tube. Avoid tossing food on the ground because it may prompt sniffing.

Junior playing with a tossed food tube. Any plastic container can be a food tube as long as there is an opening in it so the dog can be fed out of the container.

Photo by Suzanne Rider

When training duration behaviors like sit or down, deliver the reinforcer to your dog's mouth while she is on the table to encourage the dog to hold the sit or down position. Contacts and start line training are also examples of stationary duration behaviors.

Because of classical conditioning, dogs come to anticipate whether you are tossing a reinforcement or delivering it to their mouths. You want this anticipation to work for you rather than against you. So use the type of delivery that helps you create the behavior you want.

Dogs are individuals and while dog training is based on science, the art of dog training is tailoring the reinforcer delivery to the individual dog. A dog that is more toy than food motivated, may do well learning to hold her sit until released by tossing the toy behind her.  By delivering the reinforcer behind the dog, she learns that good things can be behind her, which is helpful if she is eager to bust forward out her sit.

*Reinforcer Delivery Game*
This game helps you develop the physical skill of delivering your dog's toy or food tube to a precise location.  Use a flat object to mark a spot on the ground.

Photo by Angelica Steinker

Now practice tossing your toy to the spot you have marked.  Evaluate how the shape and weight of the toy affect your ability to toss.  Are you better at tossing under hand or over hand?  Raise criteria by increasing your distance from the spot marker.  Build up to at least 20-foot tosses.

What happens *after* the click can matter just as much as what happened when you clicked.  How you toss your toy is part of the training process.

If you don't want your reinforcer delivery to carry any information, such as when you are playing the shaping game, you can toss your food treat on the ground.  Only do this if you are indoors on a smooth surface, tossing food treats on grass usually makes it hard for the dog to find the treat and may create the "by product" of sniffing.

Don't let potential training errors frustrate your dog. Practicing your timing with the clicker and reinforcer delivery is a win/win. Planning effective reinforcer placement and selecting an ideal reinforcer is another win/win.

This treat was delivered to Madison's mouth supporting her sit position. Delivering higher could cause her to leap or get up from the sit; delivering lower may prompt a down or stand.

Photo by Suzanne Rider

*Customize Proofing for Success*
Proofing games are a win/win. You get to help your dog generalize behaviors while playing a game. That is like losing weight while eating chocolate! Customize your proofing to give your particular dog an optimum chance for success. Use the information below to design a 'proofing plan for success' program for your dog. This is so exciting— proofing games are my favorites!

Every dog is different. To design the ideal proofing plan, it is critical to understand what "gets to" your dog. Below are examples of proofing plans for two different dogs.

The first dog, my Border Collie Nicki, is more toy motivated than food motivated. I have numbered her proofing categories from what is most challenging for her to what is easiest. When working with Nicki our training will begin with the easy proofing games. As Nicki becomes more successful with those challenges, the level of difficulty of the proofing games will increase. Movement, especially fast movement, easily distracts Nicki. This is, of course, not shocking since she is a Border Collie. So, movement proofing games will be emphasized.

The second dog, my Miniature Pinscher Turbo, is prone to sniffing. He is not as interested in toys as he is in food. Turbo is a "show me the money" kind of dog. He will happily work for me, but I have no illusions, he is just doing it for the money. My Border Collies beg me for work and would do it free, Turbo does it for the paycheck. For Turbo proofing games with food lying in the grass are the most challenging.

Proofing for Success Worksheet (example for a toy motivated dog)
Dog's Name: *Nicki*
For the following proofing areas place a one next to the most challenging proof, then a two for the second most challenging and so on.

   _5_  Food.
   _4_  Handler's body position/movement.
   _2_  Arousal/toys.
   _3_  Handler's facial expression.
   _1_  Other: *movement.*

Other important issues: *Nicki is very distracted by movement. It will be necessary to include lots of specific movement proofing of other dogs running near her and around her while she is performing cues.*

Use the information above to brainstorm the proofing ideas you plan to use with your dog. Begin with listing the more simple proofing ideas and build up to the more challenging ones:

5. *Food: Nicki is not tremendously food motivated and I think we will have good success with food proofs. I will start with food that she is least interested in (kibble) and ping pong rapidly up to food that she is most interested in (roast beef).*

4. *Handler's body position/movement: Nicki likes to work away from me so I will start my body position proofing games by moving away from her. I will finish proofing with me moving into her because that is something she will find more difficult. Running past her full speed and leaning over her will be the two most challenging handler body proofing games.*

3. *Arousal/toys: I will use Nicki's Frisbee to increase her arousal. The Frisbee is one of her favorite toys and it gets her arousal level up high. Tugging also gets her very aroused, so that will also be a helpful proofing game. Any ball, Frisbee, tug toy or item I can drag around will be a significant challenge to her. I will begin by rolling the Frisbee a few feet away and ping pong up to tossing it as hard as I can. If she can hold position while I throw a Frisbee, that will be a significant success.*

2. *Handler's facial expression: Nicki is very sensitive to facial expressions, so I will focus on proofing a serious facial expression and pair serious facial expressions with play.*

1. *Movement: Probably the most challenging proofs will be those involving movement. If Nicki can hold her contact while another dog runs past her, I am going to throw her a party!*

Proofing for Success Worksheet (example for a food motivated dog.)
Dog's Name: *Turbo, a.k.a. Mr. Show Me the Money*
For the following areas of proofing place a one next to the most challenging proof, then a two for the second most challenging and so on.

___4___ Handler's facial expression.

__3__  Arousal/toys.
__2__  Handler's body position/movement.
__1__  Food.
_____  Other: *none.*

Other important issues:  *Turbo is very prone to sniffing, so food will be his big issue. (Note that for Turbo, movement is not an issue so the other category is blank, leaving only four proofing categories.)*

Use the information above to brainstorm proofing ideas you plan to use with your dog.  Begin with listing the more simple proofing ideas and build up to the more challenging ones:

4.  *Handler's facial expression: Turbo does not appear sensitive to my facial expression.  He is blind in one eye, so these proofs of looking serious should be relatively easy.  Come to think of it, any proof off the right side of his body should be a piece of cake!  Because of Turbo's physical challenge, I will need to make sure that all proofing games are played within his range of vision.*
3.  *Arousal/toys: Turbo is a rescue and did not know how to play.  He is more toy driven now than he has ever been, but food is significantly more important to him.  If I can wave a toy in his face while he is holding position, he can probably be successful.  I will start by laying the toy on the ground and then gradually work up to waving it in his face.*
2.  *Handler's body position/movement: Turbo is not particularly sensitive to my position so these proofing games should be relatively easy.  Turbo is reactive to my movement so running past him full speed while he goes into position and holds position will be challenging to train.*
1.  *Food: Since Turbo usually behaves as if he were starving, all food proofs will be most challenging.  Because of Turbo's fondness for sniffing, I will need to*

*proof his contacts with food lying around. If Turbo can do his contact with food on the ground all around him, I will reinforce myself by going to an agility training camp!*

Use the sheet below to develop a proofing for success plan for your dog.
Proofing for Success Worksheet
Dog's Name:
For the following areas of proofing, place a one next to the most challenging proof, then a two for the second most challenging and so on.

\_\_\_  Food.
\_\_\_  Handler's body position/movement.
\_\_\_  Arousal/toys.
\_\_\_  Handler's facial expression.
\_\_\_  Other (if applicable):

Other important issues:

Use the information above to create the sequence of proofing you plan to use with your dog. Begin with listing the more simple proofing ideas and build up to the more challenging ones.

Different things are distracting to different dogs. When designing your dog's 'proofing for success' program make sure that while the overall proofing process is getting more challenging, you don't accidentally make every repetition harder than the previous one. This may cause the dog to quickly lose motivation since each criteria raise is getting harder and harder. This means you can't consistently move to more difficult proofs, because some dogs may quit wanting to play. If a proof is too hard, Turbo will dramatically spin around and take off sniffing. Ping pong proofing from challenging to easy all within an attainable range to the dog, or suffer the consequences of the Turbo 'snub and sniff!'

*Nightmare on Elm Street Proofing Game*
Take a moment to think about the hardest proofing games for your dog. Holding the sit position while you throw food or a Frisbee? Your terrier-type giving attention while squirrels dance a jig? Whatever the proofing game your mind conjures up, visualize it and see your dog succeeding at playing this particular proofing game. Don't allow yourself to think that it is impossible for you to succeed at your dog's most challenging proof or it will never be true. In order for you and your dog to succeed, you will need to know that you can meet this training challenge. If Turbo can do it, any dog can do it!

The hardest proofs you can think of will need the best pay offs for your dog. Reinforcers are to your dog what money is to people. The amount of money needs to match the proofing game you are playing. For an easy proof, you pay a dollar: kibble, or a short game. For a super challenging one you pay $100: roast beef or a rousing game of tug!

Use the info that you gained from completing the proofing worksheet for any of the behaviors you are training. Agility behaviors that are self-reinforcing to your dog will require less proofing games, whereas behaviors that are less self-reinforcing will require more proofing games.

If your dog loves to jump, the act of jumping is self-reinforcing. You won't need to spend hours playing jump proofing games. Jumping itself is fun, so your dog probably won't notice activities, sounds or other distractions. However, this same dog may not like maintaining a sit position, requiring you to spend time playing proofing games while the dog is sitting. How do you know what is fun to your dog? Just ask her! The answer will be written all over her face and body. Does your dog ever run through a tunnel without you cueing her? This shows that she enjoys doing a tunnel. Is there

79

an obstacle that you have to work harder at?  This is probably an obstacle that your dog enjoys less.  Listen to and watch your dog, she always holds the answer.

Proofing for success is a cornerstone of win/win training.  If both you and your dog are working the layers of the click and play pyramid, success is inevitable.  Hold the presses, because here comes another great agility team!

# Chapter 4 Click! Speed and Motivation

Motivation is at the heart of your training.  No matter how fast and motivated your dog is, consistency, confidence, attitude and ultimately, speed must be focused on in every training session.  When it comes to motivation, some things are known scientifically, but finding how to motivate each individual dog is an art.

By experimenting with various games, the secret of motivating each dog can be found.  If one game does not work, try another.  If that one fails, try yet another.  Systematically trying different games will ultimately lead to success.

Patience and persistence are necessary because each dog is different.  My min pin Turbo loves to play tug with hair scrunchies.  Had I not persistently tried different "toys," I would never have learned about this obsession!  My Jack Russell Terrier, Junior, used to go crazy for wind up cars.  Who would have guessed?  They are an easy toy to hide, and pull out of a pocket to play.

Observing your dog play with other dogs or with an object can also give you motivational ideas.  My Border Collie, Nicki, loves to grab a toy by its end and swing it in a circle around herself.  I have no idea how she does this without getting dizzy, but she loves it!  After discovering this I promptly put the toy spinning on cue and now use it as reinforcement.

Playing games builds motivation to be with you because through classical conditioning, the act of playing becomes associated with you.  Classical conditioning is the process by which one stimulus becomes linked with and predicts the arrival of another stimulus.  If you (stimulus one) play fun games (stimulus two) with your dog, then via classical conditioning being with you becomes fun.  Classical conditioning works the opposite way too.  If you yell at your dog, or do anything the dog dislikes, you become unfun. Motivation is playing with a dog that wants to spend time with you, and considers you safe and fun.

### What is Agility Motivation?

Motivation is the reason your dog takes action.  In agility, we want her to take fast and accurate action.  We want our dogs to act because of the strong history of reinforcement for the game of agility itself.  This means that running agility with you becomes more fun than food or any toy. Agility with you has become a game.

### What Affects Your Dog's Motivation?

According to animal behaviorist and agility competitor Pamela Reid, three things affect motivation:

- o  Emotionality.
- o  Need.
- o  Perceived value of the reinforcement.

*Emotionality*

Emotionality refers to a dog's level of reactivity or arousal. For agility, many competitors desire a more reactive, more easily aroused dog, commonly referred to as "high drive." The opposite of reactive is laid back and calm, less easily aroused.  More arousal usually means faster at doing agility behaviors, while less arousal usually means slower.

A dog that is in the acquisition stage of learning requires a lower arousal state in order to concentrate and absorb what is being taught.  Ultimately, the dog must be able to perform the agility behaviors even when highly aroused.  If the dog is not aroused enough, she will not be motivated to give you her best performance.  If she is too aroused, she will have trouble thinking and performing the cued behaviors fluently.

Arousal is a double-edged sword.  Too much of it, and a dog can lose her ability to focus or think.  The Yerkes–Dodson Law demonstrates that an animal needs to be in an ideal arousal state in order to learn.  This ideal arousal state is a happy medium between low arousal (dog may not be motivated to learn) and high arousal (dog may be too excited to learn).  The Yerkes-Dodson law states that the fastest learning is possible with a medium level of arousal.

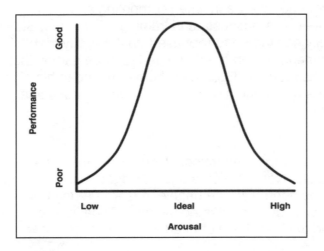

If your dog is very calm her arousal may be too low to learn.  If her arousal is too high her learning may be slowed or stopped.

Understand your dog's arousal baseline.  Do you need to decrease your dog's arousal or increase her arousal for optimum performance?  If your dog is easily aroused, how can you calm her so that she can go into the ring able to think?  If your dog has a tendency toward low arousal, what can you do to conserve her energy and pump her up right before you compete?

If your dog is very reactive and easily aroused, self-control exercises such as sit or down-stay may be helpful.  My Border Collie, Stevie, got so excited when I first began trialing him in agility that he would forget how to weave. I had failed to prepare him for the very high arousal state he would reach in the competition ring. Because of state dependent learning, he did not know how to weave when that aroused. When this would happen, I would calmly ask him to lie down, after one to two seconds release him and again cue him to weave. The brief lie down enabled him to settle enough so that he "remembered" how to weave. Part of the art of training is to try to anticipate the arousal state your dog will be in when competing and then duplicate that arousal state in training. Over time, Stevie gradually habituated to (got used to) the agility trial environment. When training, I added more games that raised his arousal. Eventually he habituated to his high level of arousal and his competition weaving became reliable.

*Need*
The need for food, exercise, elimination, etc. creates motivation. Need is also a double-edged sword. A dog that is too hungry will be unable to learn. A dog that is not hungry will not be motivated by food. Tune into your dog and find the ideal level of need.

A dog that is under-exercised because of excessive crating may also be unable to learn. This dog's need to run may be so high that nothing else will be processed by the dog's brain. While interviewing Attila Skukalek, a world-class musical freestyle (dog dancing) competitor, he explained that he has to run his Border Collie Fly for two miles before daily training sessions, otherwise Fly is unable to focus on her work. If Skukalek did not meet Fly's need for exercise prior to training, their training sessions would be more frustrating and less effective and they wouldn't be the great team that they are!

Understanding how your dog's needs work for you, or against you, is a critical part of solving the mystery of motivating your dog.

*Dopamine*
Another factor that is likely to influence your dog's
motivation is dopamine.  Dopamine is a neurotransmitter, a
biochemical signal that is associated with pleasure,
reinforcement and motivation.  In humans, low dopamine is
linked with depression and other mental illness.  In order
for dopamine to be processed humans need minerals and
vitamins, including B6, B12, C, Folic Acid, Magnesium,
Manganese, Iron, Copper and Zinc.  The canine brain
responds similarly to the human brain in terms of drugs
that target neurotransmitters, so theoretically it could be
that low motivation dogs may actually have a problem
processing dopamine.

*Hormones*
Hormones can affect behavior and motivation.  Dogs that
tend to stress may have higher than normal levels of the
hormone cortisol.  Cortisol is produced by the adrenal
glands.  In general, if one hormone is out of balance, it can
cause all the other hormones to become unbalanced.  The
result can be a dog that is resistant to learning via operant
and classical conditioning.

*Fast-Twitch Muscle Tissue*
Muscle tissue can be grouped into slow-twitch and fast-
twitch.  Slow-twitch is useful for physical activities that
require endurance, such as marathons.  Fast-twitch
muscle is ideal for sprinting and other fast-paced activities.
Ideally, we want the muscles of our agility dogs to be
primarily fast-twitch.

Olympic sprinters have been shown to have as much as
80% fast-twitch muscle tissue.  The question is, are these
individuals genetically blessed or did hard work create that
high percentage of fast-twitch muscles?  Researchers
have demonstrated fast-twitch to slow-twitch fiber
transformation in animal skeletal muscle.  The answer is
probably a mix of genetics and training.

Dogs that seem incapable of moving slowly may be genetically predisposed to more fast-twitch muscle tissue, thus creating an ideal agility dog, one that does everything very fast and asks questions later.

*Nutrition*
A large dog food company did a study on dog development and found that dogs supplied with certain nutrients that boost brain development ended up "smarter" than the control group of dogs.  This means that a dog starved or fed an improper diet as a puppy may have a different learning style and process information differently.  A brain that is not functioning at optimal levels is certainly going to impact a dog's motivation.

Some poorly trained dogs run very fast agility, simply because they default to doing everything fast.  Some well-trained dogs run slow agility for a variety of reasons — known and unknown — not all of which include the training or handling of the dog.  If you have a motivational issue, it is logical to evaluate your training and handling practices, but there are dogs that have motivational challenges despite good training and handling.

*Deprivation*
It's the double-edged sword thing again.  Deprivation is the withholding of food or other reinforcer to obtain an increase in the dog's motivation to perform behaviors (Pamela Reid).  However, extreme deprivation interferes with the dog's ability to think and learn.

The excessively food deprived dog becomes so desperate for food that she is unable to focus on anything else.  A very high drive dog that has been crated for hours may be unable to perform even simple cues because of her over-the-top needs for exercise and/or social contact.  Balance is key.  Some deprivation is okay, too much is not.  Extreme deprivation is force.  Skip extreme deprivation, **click and play** agility instead.

Thinking about deprivation with the dog's happiness in mind, using mild deprivation is ethically acceptable. Mild deprivation is not feeding a dog before you train her. Using a closed economy, where the dog works for every piece of food, is also a form of mild deprivation. To use a closed economy, put your dog's daily food ration in a container and use the food to play training games. Most dogs love the closed economy system, it is much more interesting then just eating out of a bowl. Briefly crating a dog for 30 minutes before you work her, if you usually spend time with your dog before training, may motivate your dog to be more interested in playing with you. If you have a lower energy dog, she may be refreshed from napping in her crate.

If you used mild deprivation and have not been successful, it is time to rethink your overall training program, rather than increase deprivation. Anything more than mild deprivation could end up being a losing situation for the dog, and for the trainer too. Go for win/win training!

*Cost and Benefits of Crating*
Some people in the United States use long hours of crating to control the dog's environment and build motivation. While this method may be successful for some dogs, it may not be necessary. In England and Europe, most dogs are never crated. Not even as puppies. They use laundry rooms or bathrooms to housetrain pups. Mary Ray, a world famous musical freestyle, obedience and agility trainer, says that some people in England use excessive crating in an attempt to increase motivation and drive for work. However, according to Ray these dogs don't win any more than the dogs that are loose in the house. Perhaps excessive crating is a superstitious behavior. Some people do it and they are very successful. People mistakenly attribute that success to the excessive crating and so the idea is perpetuated. Dogs that love to play

agility seem to want to play regardless of whether they are crated or not.

Photo by Andrea Davis

One potential problem with crating is that some dogs bite at the crate, damaging their teeth.  My Moose, in the early stages of doggie Alzheimers, pulverized all of his incisors by biting at his crate door.  Surgery was required to remove the roots of the teeth.  Dogs with separation anxiety also may bite the bars of crates.

Many dogs' lives have been saved by the proper use of crating, however before you crate your dog, ask yourself what your motivation is for doing so.

In the *"Handbook of Applied Dog Behavior and Training,"* Steven Lindsay cites several studies and explains that excessive crating is known to cause developmental problems because of social and sensory deprivation.  Excessive crating during critical periods of development can prevent a dog from developing the proper muscles and/or coordination.  Lindsay says that crating may cause neurotic behaviors, such as pacing and circling.  In addition, crating for more than 10-18 hours a day may result in crate dependency causing dogs to be unable to cope with life outside a crate because of cognitive and perceptual overload.  Lindsay particularly warns against excessive crating of active, young and curious dogs.

*Perceived Value of Reinforcement*
Perceived value of reinforcement is the second dynamic mentioned by Pam Reid in terms of motivation.  The value of reinforcement is determined by the dog.  What is fun to

your dog?  To clicker train your dog, you need to know what your dog enjoys.  The more games you have, the more fun training can be for your dog, because you can vary what fun things happen after the click.  So don't just stop after you have found five things your dog likes.  Keep going and adding to your list.

Begin exploring what your dog finds fun by using the categories of interactive games, sounds, taste and touch as a guide.  Become a fun detective.  The investigation begins now!  Spend the next few days playing with your dog, opening the fridge and testing out which foods your dog likes, and petting your dog in different ways as you watch her facial expression and body language.  Create a list of reinforcers that you can use to teach your dog.

Once you have listed all the things your dog likes, rate them on a scale of one to ten.  A level one positive reinforcer is something that your dog likes, but has very low potential for training.  A level ten positive reinforcer blows your dog's mind.  When training agility use reinforcers that are rated seven or higher.  These become sacred reinforcers and are saved for training with you only.

When Arnie really likes a treat, the whites in the corners of his eyes show while he reaches for it with his mouth.  We call these treats "eye-popping good."

Photo by Angelica Steinker

During training, be variable and sometimes give your dog a level 10 reinforcer and another time a level seven.  By mixing it up, you are turning the process of learning into a fun, unpredictable game.  Unpredictability of reinforcers helps make training exciting.  Consider the following categories of positive reinforcers to help you create a list of what your dog likes!

*Interactive Games*
"Interactive" refers to games such as tugging, which requires both you and your dog to play.

*Sounds*
What sounds does your dog like?  For many dogs the sound of praise is highly reinforcing, while others may go nuts over the squeak of a toy.  What did your fun detective work uncover regarding sounds?  This category will have some conditioned reinforcers in it.  The clank of the cookie jar, the jingle of car keys and, of course, the click are all sounds linked with reinforcement.  The sound predicts the activity, via classical conditioning.  However, if the sound is not consistently paired with the reinforcing activity, then the clank, jingle or even the click will lose its power.  The sound has power only because of what happens after the sound.

*Taste*
Taste is undoubtedly one of the most popular categories.  Most dogs thoroughly enjoy food and left to their own devices would eat until they burst.

List any foods your dog craves.  Experiment to find at least a handful of "taste" reinforcers that your dog finds eye-popping good.  Again, the idea is to have a long list of reinforcers so you can have fun surprising your dog with lots of different reinforcers.  If your dog does not like food, focus on the other categories and develop those.  Some dogs go through developmental stages where they don't like food, usually this passes by two or three years of age.  Develop other reinforcers during this time.

*Touch*
Observe your dog.  List the type of physical touch and the location of the touch that your dog likes.  Some dogs don't like to be touched.  You may be able to teach your dog to like touch by pairing touch with food or another reinforcer.  If you become a canine massage expert and observe what your dog likes she may eventually love to be touched.  Observe your dog's response to physical touch beginning with light feather type touching.  Watch your dog's face and body and look for visible signs of relaxation.  Deep sighs or moans can be a big hint that you are on the right track.

Observe how slow, soft strokes help your dog relax and how fast, quick rubdowns can energize your dog.  Let your dog tell you what she likes.  If the dog appears neutral, try giving the technique a few more times.  Some dogs take time making up their minds.

Canine massage is an excellent way to warm your dog up before exercising or a great way to help her cool down.  It is also a wonderful way to build your reinforcement history with your dog.  Once you know how your dog likes to be touched, you have two permanent reinforcers, your right and left hands.  They will be with you no matter where you go.

In agility, verbal and touch praise can be underused because it is so easy to use food.  It can be dangerous to rely on food as the only motivator.  The dog may become overly focused on food and using only one reinforcer is not helping your dog generalize her training to different contexts.  Praise and play can last for as long as you want and the dog never fills up.  Reinforcing for a longer time may cause your dog to be more motivated to play with you.

*Pairing*
Potential reinforcers, such as physical touch or praise, can be paired with food.  A dog that does not know how to enjoy physical touch can be clicked and reinforced with

91

food for allowing light petting and eventually for stroking. If you continue this process over several sessions, the dog may gradually begin to associate the touch with food and the touch may take on reinforcing properties. Some dogs dislike being touched and some of those dogs may never learn to enjoy petting, but they can learn to be *accepting* of physical touch. Like caviar can be an acquired taste, some dogs can learn to enjoy new forms of reinforcement, whereas others will never understand what the fuss is all about.

Hewy enjoying some long slow stroking from Suzanne.

Photo by Angelica Steinker

Regardless of which category your dog finds most reinforcing, never give up on getting a positive reinforcer to work until you have tried it extensively, this means months, not just a few times. Being as persistent as a terrier is what can pay off big. Frequently, dogs that did not seem interested in playing tug can develop a strong desire to play the game. Persist.

The most important category of reinforcers is interactive games. These are the most powerful. They are a great way to create a solid reinforcement history.

**Satiation**
If your dog has eaten prior to training, the value of food as a reinforcer may be reduced. Likewise, if your dog has just spent hours playing with other dogs, playing with you may not be very motivating. In both cases, the dogs are satiated. The dog's need for food or play have been met, so using them for motivation is likely to be unsuccessful.

## Misconceptions

"Not smart enough" or "too stubborn to learn" are labels. These labels and others lock the dog into being something unchangeable. While labels can't be avoided, they can rob the trainer of the mental framework and ability to make change. The dog has been pigeonholed. The truth is that a dog that appears to lack intelligence or appears stubborn may really lack motivation. Lacking motivation is a training issue that can usually be modified.

## Tips for Motivating

Solving the puzzle of how to motivate a dog is a fun challenge. When trying to increase your dog's motivation and speed, here are some tips to keep in mind.

Spend time every day playing with your dog. If you don't do anything else that day, play with your dog. Play will help you build a fantastic reinforcement history. Focus on your click and play pyramid.

Use a variety of reinforcers: Food, toys, praise, rubs. If your dog likes it, use it! Make it a rule to change something about how you reinforce your dog every day. Experiment so you can continue to find new games to play with your dog.

## Loving What Is

Whatever your dog's genetic predisposition, accept it and love it. It is part of who they are. Don't argue with reality, this will only cause you pain and needless suffering. Reality will never change. Acceptance and loving is so much easier and enables you to focus on what you can control and change. Chris Bach says every dog is "perfect," perfect at being who she is. Expecting your Bassett to behave like a Border Collie sets both you and the dog up to fail, instead love what is.

**Exploring Motivational Challenges**
Motivational training is the art of reading the dog's motivation and adjusting yourself accordingly. We are the trainers, we adjust. When we adjust, the dog will alter her behavior. By continuously adjusting we can tune into what it is the dog needs to give us her best.

Happiness creates speed. Consistent, enjoyable training with an interesting variety of reinforcers can help create a dog with a happy attitude who enjoys playing the game of agility with you. Motivational training is about creating such great attitude that your dog would rather play with you and respond to your cues than anything else in her environment. Much easier said than done! After all, you are competing with fascinating smells in the grass, darting squirrels in the trees and other dogs. It takes a lot of money in the reinforcement history bank account to be more fun than a squirrel! But it can be done.

Just as important as understanding what your dog enjoys is realizing what she does not enjoy. Below are some reasons dogs may lack motivation.

*Injury*
If a dog is hurting, agility is not a reinforcing experience and performance will become associated with pain. Many training challenges have been caused by undiagnosed soft tissue injuries, hip dysplasia, elbow, knee or spine problems. If your dog suddenly loses her desire to play agility, have her examined by a veterinarian who is experienced with performance dogs and their physical issues.

*Full-Out Running*
Someone once asked me, "How do you get your dogs to run so fast?" In addition to clicker training and game playing, the answer is full-out running. Every day my dogs spend some time running as fast as they physically can. This ritual began with my Jack Russells because it was

94

either that or I'd go insane.  High drive dogs benefit psychologically and physically from full-out running.

I recall my Jack Russells getting the zoomies (butt tucking bursts of speed) in the house while I stood outside talking on the phone.  The first few seconds I was entertained by their "Indi 500" imitation, but before I recognized the danger, it was too late.  Moose under-steered, swung wide and the burglar bar bounced off his leg and landed in the position that secured the house.  With a resounding 'clunk' I had been locked out.  Moose and Junior were just warming up.  Face pressed against the sliding glass door and in my pajamas, I watched as their laps expanded. Now the laps included the bed.  Pillows and covers were flying.  My objecting bangs against the glass door cheered them on.  (This was when I learned that some dogs are reinforced by attention including hysterical banging.)  It began to rain.  I gave up panicking and went to the neighbors.  When I got back into the house, I found two terriers asleep on my bed as if tossed there by hurricane force winds.  Surrounding them were the remnants of my pillows, blankets and sheets.  Apparently, the Indi 500 had morphed into outright vandalism.

I had hit rock bottom.  I needed help!  I began exercising my dogs on a daily basis focusing on full-out running.  It worked.  My dogs have never locked me out of my house or shredded my bed again.  It was "one trial learning" for me.  By keeping them exercised, most of my dogs' behavior problems decreased or disappeared.

*Fitness*
Exercising ensures that your dog's muscles are strong and flexible so she can work at her highest potential, and reduce risk of injury.  Agility is a physically demanding sport that requires running, biking or swimming with your dog to keep her fit.  Canine massage, acupuncture, chiropractic care and physical therapy are also helpful in maintaining fitness.  Certified canine massage therapist

Brandy Oliver, M.A. says, "Massage at any time, but particularly on a regular basis, can improve canine posture, flexibility, coat and even a dog's concentration. Concentration improves when pain or discomfort is reduced or eliminated by the release of endorphins." Being in touch with your dog's body and knowing how her muscles usually feel is important. My husband checks our dogs' backs for spasms every night. If he finds some, we massage the area until it's gone.

Fitness includes keeping your dog's weight at an ideal level. For a small agility dog, only one pound of extra weight can put a significant amount of strain on the joints. You must be able to feel the ribs and the tip of the pelvis bone on your dog's rump. An overweight dog is more at risk for injuries and is less likely to be motivated.

*Structure*
Structural flaws — straight angulation of the front shoulder assembly or rear hip, knee, hock joints, or others — hamper a dog's ability to jump and perform agility obstacles and can lead to injuries. Angulation refers to the degree of angle — viewing the dog from the side — of the front and rear legs. The shoulder assembly is from the tip of shoulder, to point of shoulder, to elbow. Generally, more of an angle is considered healthier then less of an angle. More of an angle allows for more shock absorption. Ideally, the front and rear leg angulation is balanced, meaning that both the front and the rear have similar degrees of angulation.

The ideal structure for an agility dog includes good length of neck so the dog can balance herself while jumping. The length of a dog's back should be slightly longer than the length of her leg, good shoulder lay back and a good rear. Ideally, front and rear angles are balanced.

Photo by Suzanne Rider

The dog pictured here has both good shoulder and rear angulation, which means he is balanced. Because of his good structure and fitness, this dog rarely has tight muscles or spasms.

According to Dr. Christine Zink, D.V.M., Ph.D., author of *Peak Performance: Coaching the Canine Athlete*, good structure is critical for the health of an agility dog. To evaluate structure you need to be familiar with canine anatomy. Determine rear angulation by locating the hip, knee and hock joints and visually assessing the angle that those three joints create.

This dog's front legs come straight down from his elbows to his toes.

Photo by Suzanne Rider

Zink prefers slightly east-west (toes turning slightly outward) for an agility dog. Zink says that slightly outward turned toes increase the dog's stability and the ability to turn quickly.

This dog's rear is straight from the hock to the toes. Dr. Chris Zink prefers a slightly cow hocked structure (hocks slightly turned in) for tighter turning in agility.

Photo by Suzanne Rider

Good structure is most apparent in the dog's movement. A well-structured dog at the trot will glide above the ground and appear to move effortlessly. The movement will be smooth with no jarring motions. A poorly structured dog moves in short choppy strides that compensate for the structural flaws. Rachel Page Elliot has written a great book on structure entitled *"Dog Steps."*

*Dog Training the Trainer*
Clicker trainer Steve White says, "Someone is always training, it is either you or the dog." My own education in "being trained" was conducted by one of my Jack Russell Terriers. My training sessions used to go something like this: Angelica asks Jack Russell to run a segment including the weave poles. Jack Russell performs everything flawlessly, but when he gets to the poles, he only hits the entrance and then pops out. Angelica thinks she is being a good clicker trainer, and goes back to work the weaves clicking for the third pole, since that is where the dog popped previously. Blissfully ignorant, I would assume that the problem was now "fixed." Next time I asked him to weave, he again popped out after the entrance. Our sessions would continue with these kinds of training issues for months, because my dog was smarter than I was! What my Jack Russell had learned was that my rate of reinforcement would drop when we went from acquisition to maintenance. He knew he had a better chance of getting more reinforcements if he messed up than if he performed flawlessly. I had accidentally trained him to make mistakes in order to prompt me to raise his rate of reinforcement. Is that dog smart? Or I am just trying to feel better about the whole incident? Don't allow yourself to be "Jack Russelled." Be unpredictable and keep the dog guessing when she might get the next click and reinforcement.

Some dogs love to be trained and other dogs love to train. Dogs that love to be trained may be easier to teach agility behaviors to than dogs that are motivated to train you.  But you do learn more working with the challenging ones.

*Lure Training*
Luring is the process of using a food or toy reinforcer to prompt the dog into performing a desired behavior.  While lure training can yield fast results, it can create a motivational problem.  Every dog is different, so some dogs may do extremely well with lure training.  Using badly executed lure training may cause some dogs to perform only if food is present.  Luring has created an assumption, rather than the hope of reinforcement.  If you have problems fading a food lure, avoid using it.  Use an object as a target to prompt, shape or capture instead.

Throw away your bait bag!  It is one giant cue that the bar is open for business.  It is also one giant cue that no food will be available if you are not wearing it.  If you own a dog with a motivational issue, your bait bag is a signal to your dog that the bar is open and you are available to be trained.

Take away the visual cue of having food available by hiding food treats.  (Use plastic containers to store food treats in various places around your home, training field, and training center.)  If the problem is a toy dependency – support groups are available – you can do the same thing hiding many toys in various locations.  Make it unpredictable to the dog where the toy may come from or at what point the click and the toy will come.

*Shaping Challenges*
Shaping is one of the best ways to create behaviors, yet it is probably the least understood of all training methods.  Training and motivation are linked.  Ideal training supports motivation, while less than ideal training can kill motivation.

If shaping is poorly done, it may cause the dog to lose motivation.  Using a low rate of reinforcement during acquisition or using confusing training methods can also cause a dog to lose motivation.

When training, evaluate what behavior you will be working on, what learning game would likely be most effective and consider what approximations you are going to use.

Kay Laurence explains in her *"Clicker Training Intermediate"* book that for some behaviors you can anticipate that free shaping without any guidance from the trainer will create a high level of frustration for the dog.  If you want to teach your dog to walk backwards around a cone, you can free shape this with no guidance and probably create a bunch of confusion for the dog, or you can use Laurence's guided shaping idea pictured below to help set the dog up for success.

To set the dog up for success backchain the entire exercise by beginning with only the last step of the backward circle around the cone, pictured at left.  Xtra is set up for success because I am blocking the exit with my chair.  It is easy for her to back up next to the cone.

Photos by Suzanne Rider

At left, Xtra is backing a quarter turn around the cone.  By using backchaining she is able to confidently move backwards around the cone.

Ultimately, the quarter turn is put on cue and the dog can be cued several times to accomplish a full turn.

As an experiment, I used one of the above methods on each of my dogs. Nicki was free shaped to go backwards around a cone with no barrier help. Zoomie was shaped using the guided "set up for success" method. Both dogs had been taught in a previous session that targeting the cone was not going to get clicks and reinforcements. Both dogs backed up on cue.

After one 3-minute session with each dog, Nicki was nose targeting the cone again, despite my not clicking it. And was *so* frustrated, she actually threw the cone at me. Nicki's rate of reinforcement was too low which caused her to frantically random sample, offering behaviors and dirty looks and lots of barking. The problem was that I was unable to get the criteria I was setting. I wanted her to back near the cone but since there were no barriers she backed into it instead. Once she felt the cone with her rear legs she became convinced that she needed to target the cone again and grabbed it with her mouth.

Meanwhile, during his 3-minute session, Zoomie, the dog set up for success with the ring gating, was confidently taking two steps backward around the cone. Using the barriers, I was able to shape Zoomie to walk around the cone forward into the barrier channel. By blocking the exit (see photo) he was prompted to lean back. I clicked and reinforced that, then got stepping back and finally several steps walking backwards around the cone. Lures, ring gating, targets and so on help dogs get it right and that is always good, but dependency issues must be understood and fading needs to be part of the training process.

Freeshaping is ideal for behaviors that you are certain you will be able to attain in seconds. Teaching a dog to nose or paw a target with freeshaping is likely to be successful.

The goal behavior and the dog that you are attempting to train, determine the method of training you choose.

Here are some potential challenges that you may face while shaping.

*Dog learns to wait for help.* The dog is offering very little behavior so the trainer starts helping (and helping and helping). This one is easy to fix, just stop helping and wait. Pretend you have all the time in the world, look for the tiniest movement or shift of movement in the right direction, click and reinforce.

*Being uncertain of criteria and missing opportunities to click and reinforce so that your rate of reinforcement drops too low.* Close your eyes and visualize your dog doing the end behavior you are training, visualize the dog doing only very tiny parts of the behavior. What does it look like? Use visualization to create a training plan that includes tiny approximations.

*Lowering criteria and getting stuck.* No big deal, just end the session and try again in a few minutes.

*Clicking a behavior more than once so that the dog thinks an approximation is actually an end behavior.* End the session, give the dog a handful of cookies for playing and try again later.

*Dog can't commit to a single behavior because she is trained to random sample.* This can be the result of failing to provide a framework for shaping. Kay Laurence recommends always sitting in a chair to signal your dog that a shaping session is about to begin. Continue sitting in the chair in different environments until the behavior is on cue and begin generalizing the cue to different body positions. Another cause for off cue random sampling can be the result of playing a lot of the "be creative game," you may have taught your dog to default to random sampling.

All of these training issues can affect your dog's motivation and your own motivation.  Have a clear plan for how you will teach your dog what you want her to learn.  If you don't have a plan, find a clicker instructor who will help you develop one.  Ideal training is motivating to the dog!

*Lumping*
Lumping refers to the training error of teaching the dog more than one criterion at a time or skipping training steps.  It may seem time saving, but in reality lumping damages the training process.  Lumping can cause a dog to misunderstand what you are training and/or may undermine the dog's confidence, causing decreased motivation.  Lumping can happen very easily, even with experienced trainers.  It can be difficult to see how a behavior can be broken down further.  As a result, the trainer unintentionally lumps.  For example, in one session a trainer attempts to teach the dog to jump on the table, one behavior; to lie down on it, a second behavior; hold that position for five seconds (a duration of the second behavior) and release on the "okay" cue, a third behavior. When the dog is slow to perform, the trainer gets frustrated.  This could have been avoided by teaching each of the behaviors separately.

1.  Lie down quickly on the ground, away from the table is one game.
2.  Jump up on the table.
3.  Teach the duration of down, with proofing games.
4.  Okay release game on flat.
5.  Okay release game off table.
6.  Train #1 on the table.
7.  Train #3 on table.
8.  Put all the behaviors on cue.
9.  Stack cues and ask dog to perform behavior chain.

This list may seem tedious, but what's *really* tedious is fixing a table problem.  It is much more fun and reinforcing to train properly to start with.

A great way to build your shaping skills is to play Kay Laurence's game Genabacab.  In this fun game, one person is the dog, and the other person is the trainer.  There is no talking while playing, so the game actually simulates the dog training process.  (See the appendix for information on how to get the Genabacab game.)

Another way to avoid lumping is to perform the behavior as if you were the dog.  This builds awareness of what you would need to do to get that behavior or behaviors.  Kay Laurence suggested this to me and soon I was doing some rather strange things out on the agility field.  While crawling across the A-frame I heard an ominous crack and briefly saw my life flash before my eyes.  But physically performing the obstacles at a crawl was an insightful exercise.  If you can physically do it, assume the position you are attempting to train with your dog.  If you can't physically do it, do as much as you can, so you can get some idea of what the dog will be experiencing.  Using visualization is helpful as an alternative to performing the physical behaviors.

Clicker trainer Bob Bailey teaches trainers how to split behaviors, the opposite of lumping, at his chicken clicker training camps.  The idea is to learn from clicker training a chicken and apply the information to dog training.  Chickens are challenging to train because they move very quickly so your timing has to be excellent.  It is also rather challenging to deliver food to a chicken so again physical skills and timing can be honed.  It was Bailey, along with Marion and Keller Breland, who developed the concept of splitting and lumping.  (It doesn't matter what you call this process of using small approximations —Kay Laurence calls it microshaping— but it does matter that you do it.)  The smaller the approximations the faster the learning will progress and the more confident and motivated your dog will be.

It is never too late.  If you lumped, you can go back and retrain with small approximations.  You may find your dog running with increased speed and motivation as a result.  Be sure to give the retrained behavior a new cue, as far as your dog is concerned, it will be a new behavior.

*Jealousy is a Wonderful Thing*
Describing a dog as being jealous is a humanization.  It is not scientifically known whether dogs experience the emotion of jealousy.  However, we can use frustration that looks like "jealousy" as a form of negative punishment.  If you are training your dog and she is demonstrating a lack of motivation and you have access to a second dog, you can put her into a crate for some "rest" and allow her to watch you work another dog.  After a few minutes, give her another chance to play with you.  Usually dogs will exit the crate with more enthusiasm for the training game.

If you don't have a second dog, you can still crate your dog and pretend to play with your "invisible dog."  Use high pitched tones and playfully work the imaginary teammate.  After a few minutes, give the real dog another chance.  Or borrow a neighbor's dog.  It doesn't matter if this dog doesn't know agility as long as he is willing to play with you or eat your treats.

*Save Special Toys for Playtime*
Be smart about your reinforcers.  Manage them effectively, making them available only for play with you at training time.  Then they will become precious to your dog and you can create more motivation for agility.  It is important for dogs to have access to chew toys and other toys at all times.  Access to toys keeps dogs mentally happy and balanced.  If dogs don't have their own toys, it sets them up for playing with yours.  Special toys, such as flying

discs, tug toys, etc., by contrast are put away and only available when playing training games.

*Not Reinforcing Often Enough*
The type and frequency of the reinforcement determine the success or failure of your training process.  If your dog isn't excited by a dry piece of kibble, then it isn't a suitable reinforcer.  The dog determines what is reinforcing, not the trainer.  Sometimes, in the excitement of training, a trainer asks too much too soon.  It becomes difficult for the dog to be right and the rate of reinforcement drops.  Before we know it, our dogs begin losing interest.

The term rate of reinforcement is used to describe the number of times a dog is reinforced per behavior performed.  A dog performing ten behaviors for one reinforcement is doing more work for less money (a lower rate of reinforcement).  A dog performing ten behaviors for five reinforcers (higher rate of reinforcement) is getting a better paycheck.  A dog learning a new behavior needs a high rate of reinforcement, every successful behavior should be clicked and reinforced.  A dog that is performing known behaviors can usually handle more sporadic reinforcement (a lower rate of reinforcement).  Learning is hard work and it should pay well so that your dog keeps playing the game with a happy attitude.

As trainers, we seem to think that once a behavior is learned it does not require reinforcement to be maintained. The truth is that most unreinforced behaviors will eventually disappear.

When your dog fails to perform a behavior and your rate of reinforcement is dropping too low, it is time to have your dog do a simple behavior like a hand touch, sit or down, and then reinforce.  Kay Laurence calls this a "reset" and it is tremendously helpful in preventing loss of motivation. Returning to you and making eye contact after failing is also a wonderful skill that can be clicked and reinforced, and used as a reset.  Very soft dogs have to learn resilience, the reset cookie teaches this.  Soft dogs can be so sensitive that missing a click and reinforcement is punishing to them, triggering loss of motivation.

*Learned Helplessness*
This occurs when a dog can't make sense of the physical corrections she is being given and she eventually "gives up."  The dog's eyes may glaze over and/or the dog may curl up and roll into a ball.  Some dogs in learned helplessness begin to show signs of stress if you do anything resembling "training."  Training has become a cue that the dog will be hurt, rather than playing a game.

To reverse learned helplessness, capture the dog doing a simple behavior like a sit or down and click and reinforce. If the dog will not take food, try meat flavored baby food, peanut butter or something else highly enticing.  If the dog refuses to eat from your hand, work on hand feeding when she is very hungry and slowly build up to longer periods of time of hand feeding.  Gradually the dog will regain the ability to learn.

Learned helplessness causes a dog to shut down, but a dog may also shut down because of inconsistent training. If the dog can't make sense of the training process she may opt to leave the training area or may begin sniffing. Sniffing, yawning, sneezing and shaking, can all be signs of stress and may be indicating confusion.  If a dog is consistently confused, that dog may develop avoidance behaviors that are similar to shutting down.

*Reinforcing Too Much*
Didn't I just spend the last few paragraphs repeatedly stating that lowering your rate of reinforcement can trash your dog's motivation?  Now this heading reads, "Reinforcing Too Much?"  No, it isn't a typo, it *is* possible to reinforce too much.  Here's how: if for weeks or months you consistently click and treat for every behavior (one

behavior gets one click and reinforcement), you may discover behaviors that are not reinforced at this extremely high rate of reinforcement, will degrade or even disappear. The reason is that the dog is used to the 1:1 reinforcement ratio so if you don't click and reinforce she may stop performing that behavior because it no longer 'works.'

During acquisition, the rate of reinforcement is 1:1. However, as soon as you have the behavior on cue, switch to differential reinforcement of excellent behavior (DRE). This means that only excellent responses to cues are clicked and reinforced.

*Fading the Click*
A common motivational problem occurs when a dog, used to a high rate of reinforcement in training, gets no clicks or reinforcements while in the agility ring. This dog can then develop a context specific problem. "When I am at the training place, I run fast and have good attitude and I get reinforced. In the competition ring, I run slow and have a poopie attitude." For this dog, the agility competition ring signals no hope for reinforcement.

To avoid this, play the counting cues game. You know that your dog will be asked to perform roughly 20 to 40 behaviors while in the agility ring, so while you are training, count the cues your dog is performing. When you've reached a certain number *and* your dog is performing desired behaviors, click and reinforce.

A training session might look like this:

| Number of cues | Number of clicks and reinforcements |
|---|---|
| 13 | 1 |
| 18 | 1 |
| 7 | 1 |
| 41 | 1 |
| 17 | 1 |
| 1 | 1 |
| 43 | 1 |

The average of the number of cues needed to run a Novice level course is about 20.  Notice that I did include a few low numbers and even a 1:1.  I did this because you want to keep things interesting and variable.  Being variable makes the training process more fun to your dog. The counting cues game is a great way to prepare your dog for competition.  It is a great game for terriers or hounds.  This game enables you to reinforce the dog when she leaves the ring and not lose attitude while she is still in the ring.

*No Hope*
Let's go back to the dog that has a sad attitude in the competition ring.  How do you fix that?  The answer is simple, yet complex.  The simple part is finding a way for that dog to have the hope that she will be reinforced in the competition ring.  The complex part is doing it when food and toys are not allowed in the competition ring.  Find fun matches.  If you can't find one, put on your own.  Transport agility equipment to a park and ask your family and friends to come for a BBQ so they can be the fake agility trial audience.  There you have it, your very own 'trial.'  Now reinforce your dog in the ring.

Another crafty way to create hope is to take allowable toys with you into the ring.  Teach your dog that your baseball cap, shoelaces or other clothing are toys, you will have those objects in the ring.

Finally, the counting cues game will also help instill hope since you can reinforce your dog *after* she leaves the ring. Duplicate the system in training, as you do in competition, to help your dog have hope in the competition ring.  Ask her to sometimes perform a segment, sometimes an entire course and then run out of the ring and reinforce her.  Just as you will in competition.

*Trainer Frustrations*
Becoming frustrated with your dog is usually a fast track to a demotivated dog.  Evaluate what causes you to become frustrated and prevent these triggers.  If you can't prevent them, give your dog a jackpot and end the training session as soon as your frustration begins.

Mild frustration is part of most trainers' learning process. Frustration isn't all bad.  A common source of frustration is failure.  If the dog fails to perform the desired behavior, the trainer takes it personally.  The dog's lack of, or incorrect, response is considered "deliberate" and this frustrates the trainer.

Depersonalizing canine, or human behavior, is a great emotional skill.  One way to do this is to understand that failure really doesn't exist.  When you are training, you only get outcomes.  The outcome is either one that you wanted or one that you didn't.  Either way, it is information and has nothing to do with you personally.  If your dog fails to perform a behavior, it is information to consider and use to make changes to your training program.

Trainers can have power over their emotions by changing their thoughts.  Emotions mostly follow thought, so by modifying your thoughts, you can control your emotions. Much easier said than done, but with practice it is a wonderful skill to have.  It will help you be a better trainer, and a better person.

*Learned Laziness*
Learned laziness is caused by non-contingent reinforcement.  It can occur if you give your dog access to reinforcement for doing nothing.  The dog learns to do nothing.  The dog is a victim of lack of mental stimulation and has not been given the opportunity to discover how to play learning games.

Reversing learned laziness requires you to analyze what is reinforcing to your dog and plan how she is going to gain access to those reinforcers.  Work to reduce the opportunity and need for self-reinforcing behaviors.  Place your dog on a closed economy.  For instance, have your dog work for all of her daily ration of food to help her learn that reinforcement is contingent on behavior.  This is also a great way to increase your reinforcement history with your dog.

*Training with Aversives*
Trainer Rob Bitler once described a seminar he had attended where the presenter described how the animals they were training became aggressive when even mild aversives were used.  In response, Rob jotted down in his notes, "How would the dogs that we train treat us in return if they had the power?"  How would your dog train you?  Let's strive to **click and play** train all dogs.  A happy dog is a motivated dog.

Training with physical corrections or other aversives, is ideologically at odds with building attitude, speed and playing with your dog.  Aversives include shouting at a dog, hitting, throwing things at your dog or squirting fluid at her.  No matter what your training goal, it is not necessary to use aversives.  World-class trainers have proven it is possible to succeed in agility and other canine sports without the use of aversives.  Every time your dog perceives you as using an aversive, you put a dent into your reinforcement history and damage your relationship.

Aversives can elicit fear and stress, which can be associated with the trainer, the agility obstacles or other aspects of training.  Fear and stress are incompatible with play.  If you are ever tempted to use an aversive, find another way.

Sea World Director of Training Chuck Tompkins often tells seminar participants about the lessons he learned regarding killer whale training and the use of aversives. When Sea World trainers first started working with killer whales, they used mild aversives to try to force the marine mammals into doing what they wanted.  Tompkins says that the first time he decided to take the chance and ride on the back of a killer whale, the animal threw him off his back, took him to the bottom of the tank and held him there.  The whale returned him to the surface, only to repeatedly dunk him under water.  Tompkins wondered if he would live through this ordeal.  In the end, the whale threw him out of the pool onto the stage.  While lying on the deck Tompkins thought, "We need to change what we are doing."  It was this experience in particular that led Sea World to make a commitment to exclusively train with the use of positive reinforcement, both for the sake of the animals in their care and for the safety of the humans.

Dogs don't have the physical strength of a killer whale.  A dog can't kill us in a split second with minimal effort.  Why did it take an animal that could, for marine mammal trainers (and ultimately animal trainers all over the world) to begin to change?

Nothing can dampen motivation more than worry.  Training aversives free is a fun way to avoid this problem and emphasize cooperation between dog and trainer.  It is easy to avoid the risk of damaging your reinforcement history and your bond with your dog, just **click and play**.

*Stress: The Ultimate Motivation Killer*
Dogs are non-verbal.  They growl and bark, but they don't use or understand words.  They live in a world of smells and body language.  It is possible to see a dog's stress level by reading her body language.  By watching for tiny changes in your dog's body language, you can learn what your dog is telling you.

Barking or nipping at the trainer can be signs of frustration. Frustration can occur because of inconsistent training, too much arousal or a too-low of a rate of reinforcement.

Your dog's facial expression, body posture and the position of the ears and tail are important.  Below is a list of some of the common signs of canine stress.  Use this list to help read your dog.

*Signs of Stress*
- o   Slow tail wagging — contrary to popular belief, a slow tail wag can be a sign of stress and may be a signal that a dog is about to become aggressive.
- o   Holding breath — observe the rib cage and body muscles for tension, or place a hand on your dog to feel.
- o   Panting — check the dog's facial expression for stress panting rather than regular "Gee, I'm hot!" panting; observe for tightening of muscles around the eyes, as if squinting; look for context if there is no reason for the dog to be panting temperature-wise, the motivation for the panting is more likely to be stress.

Notice that this dog's lips are not curled upward to reveal rear teeth.  The lack of lip curling shows that this pant is a stress pant.  The slight squinting of the eyes is also indicating stress.  In general, facial muscles appear tense.

113   Photo by Suzanne Rider

o Pacing — an inability to settle.
  Shedding and dandruff — commonly seen at the
  veterinarian's office.
o Excessive drooling.
o Gulping — swallowing hard and bracing for what is
  to come.
o Diarrhea.
o Urination — more common in male dogs than in
  females. In multiple dog households, one or
  several males may engage in stress induced urine
  marking.
o Licking of the lips — tongue flicking is a clear sign
  of nervousness.
o Coughing.
o Sneezing — if I give my Border Collie, Nicki, a cue
  she is not sure of, I get sneezing. Confusion is
  stressful to her.
o Turning away and avoiding eye contact — while
  this may be a training issue, it is important to take
  note and evaluate if this dog is experiencing stress.
  It can be a sign of worry when the handler leads out
  ahead of the dog at the start of a course especially
  if the dog is young or inexperienced.
o Trembling — usually extreme stress.
o Shaking (as if the dog were shaking off water) — if
  observed during training or at competition it may be
  a sign of stress.
o Yawning — no, you're not boring your dog, but she
  might be stressed.

Notice the extreme
tensing of the muscles
around the eyes, the
exaggerated large
yawn and pulling back
of the lips.

Photo by Suzanne Rider

- o Sweaty paws — a sign of severe nervous tension if the dog is not overheated.
- o Increased activity — a canine favorite is the zoomies, when a dog takes off and starts running around the agility ring full speed.
- o Decreased activity — some dogs will take a nap, flop on their side or curl up when feeling anxious. This is the denial nap, "this isn't really happening, when I wake up it will all be gone."
- o Scratching — if not caused by stress, be sure to check the dog's skin for rashes, allergies or parasites.
- o "Spacing out" — the dog mentally leaves the trainer after failure or confusion.
- o Refusing food — a sign of severe stress if the dog is normally food motivated.
- o Refusing to play — if your dog normally plays and can't play in a certain environment the dog is probably stressed.
- o Drooping ears — dogs that are stressed will pin their ears back or lower their ears.

Notice in addition to hiding behind some furniture, this dog's ears are being held back against his neck. He is also stress panting. Note the tense muscles around his right eye and the nervous curl of his lips backwards toward his neck. His eyes are also somewhat glazed.

Photo by Andrea Davis

115

If any of these behaviors appear while you are training, evaluate what in the environment is causing the stress. Is it your training? If so, back up a few steps in the training process, help her succeed, and then build up to the previous level of training. Increase your rate of reinforcement. Play a game, do something different. Experiment and learn what will help reduce your dog's tension. Is the source of tension a person, dog or object near by? You can determine this by carefully approaching the person, dog or object and monitoring your dog's body language. If the signs of nervousness increase, you know the person, dog or object is the source of the stress.

Gradually bringing your dog closer to what she is afraid of while playing and feeding her, will help her work through the fear. The speed of progress is dictated by the dog, not the trainer. When in doubt progress more slowly and resist the temptation to push your dog. Gradually desensitizing your dog to a fearful stimulus is a process and can take months or even years. Usually the more powerful the fear the longer the process will take.

The effects of tension are very powerful. A stressed dog may be more likely to act in an aggressive manner, so when you see signs of anxiety it is best to take steps to reduce your dog's stress level. If you can identify the stressor, move the dog away from it.

Tension is cumulative; if your dog is in the presence of several stressors, manage her even more carefully. A dog that is anxious in the presence of an unfamiliar dog will be very stressed at an agility trial. At the end of a long three-day agility trial, that same dog may not be able to handle that environment anymore. Tension has depleted the dog's coping resources. The dog now has fewer resources to call on and is at higher risk for aggressive behavior.

Help your dog deal with her anxieties by pairing stressors with play! If your dog stresses around loud noises, *gradually* expose your dog to loud noises while playing with the dog.  Ultimately, a loud noise will signal to your dog that it is time to play!

*Mental Illness*
While it has not been proven, growing evidence suggests that dogs suffer from a wide array of biochemical mental illnesses.  Just like humans, dogs are prescribed Prozac and other serotonin targeting drugs for a variety of symptoms that include aggression, anxiety and fear.  While medication may not offer a cure, it does offer a decrease in symptoms for some dogs.

If you think your dog is suffering from mental illness, no amount of training will modify the symptoms.  Causes for mental illness are not clearly understood.  This is not something that can usually be altered through behavior modification or motivational games.  Find a vet who is willing to work with you regarding medication, nutrition and exploring medical causes that may be causing the mental illness.

*Potential Solutions*
Motivational challenges present the trainer with puzzles that can usually be solved.  The more severe your dog's motivational issue, the more you can learn.  Trainers who have never worked with a difficult to motivate dog, have missed out on a fantastic learning experience.  If you have an opportunity to learn from your dog, make the best out of it!

Every dog is an individual.  What will motivate your dog depends on her personality and your persistence in finding what she likes.  The solutions to your dog's motivational challenges are only limited by your creativity and determination.

Be creative with your food and toy delivery.  Use different types of food in different quantities.  Have a variety of toys and use a different one every day.  Play a variety of games with the toys that you use.  Be fun and unpredictable. Don't allow toy or food dependency to creep into your games.

*Focus*
Sometimes a dog can appear to be lacking motivation, but in fact really lacks focus.  Here are some ideas and considerations for a dog that lacks focus.

Use clear signals to indicate when you are working and when you are not.  Consistently implement those signals. The signal that always means "work time" is a cue.  A special cue such as "all done," can signal that all training games have stopped and the dog is free to do as she pleases.  Only after you give the "all done" cue is your dog free to do as she pleases.  Avoid conversation with people while your dog is working; give her 100% of your focus.

Lots of short **click and play** sessions will help focus problems.  Play is the behavior most incompatible with stress and some dogs lack focus because they are easily stressed.  Carolyn Scott, musical freestyle and clicker trainer, showed me how to use a cheese stick as a toy. You grab the cheese stick by one end like a sword, tap it on the ground and swing it in front of the dog's face.  This teasing is really a fun game.  Scott emphasizes that the dog's movement, tugging and play, all act as de-stressing tools.  Scott also recommends pairing different games with different toys.  Creating a separate personality for each toy to help encourage us to be more fun and varied.

The counting cues game mentioned earlier in this chapter on page 108, is very helpful in building focus.  Dogs can suffer from focus fatigue.  Gradually build up the number of cues you give while playing the counting cues game.

The stimulus control game is a great one to add to your toolbox. Stimulus control means the behavior is performed consistently on the first cue, and the behavior only occurs when it is cued. It doesn't take a lot of thinking to realize that we all have many behaviors trained that require good stimulus control. Some behaviors like sit and down, will always occur off cue, but others can be trained to a level of optimum stimulus control. Every time your dog fails to respond to the first cue you give, is a signal to you that additional training is needed.

Fluency creates flow and flow is reinforcing. A break in flow will cause a lot of dogs to lose focus. Work to maintain flow and to teach your dog a default behavior for when flow is broken. If you get lost on a course, cue the dog to hand target or some other simple behavior to help her recover from the break in flow.

Non-response alert! Red flag all non-responses so that you are immediately aware that the behavior needs training. A missed cue not only interferes with your performance, it may also break flow and create stress or loss of focus.

Self-reinforcing behaviors can be a key to maintaining behavior chains. Which obstacles does your dog enjoy performing? Use those cues to reinforce other behaviors in the agility ring. Arnie, my mom's Jack Russell Terrier, hates to sit at the start line, but he loves to play patty cake (the trick during which the dog places alternating paws on the alternating feet of the trainer).

To exploit Arnie's love of the patty cake game, my mom sets him at the start, asks him to sit and then reinforces him with patty cake. She can take this game into the competition agility ring.

Photo by Angelica Steinker

119

**Maintaining Motivation and Speed**
Once you have your dog motivated and responding to cues consistently, increase your criteria. Click and reinforce only fast and accurate responses. Was the dog's response accurate? If the answer is yes, next ask yourself was the response fast? If the answer is yes, click and reinforce the dog. Go through this question and answer process quickly so the timing of your click is not affected.

If you lose accuracy, go back and work accuracy. Once you have accuracy you can use differential reinforcement of excellent behavior (DRE) to select for fast responses only. In agility training, once the dog is in maintenance, and the behavior has been proofed and generalized, the only clicks and reinforcers given will be for excellent performance. While you must fade the clicker, you will occasionally bring it back and unpredictably click and reinforce to avoid the degrading and resulting loss of motivation.

**Motivational Games**
Below are games that can be used specifically to build motivation.

The 'I'm-gonna-beat-you-game' was developed by Rhonda Carter. Playfully tell your dog "I'm gonna beat you!" and then gently slap and tap your dog's sides to get her revved up for a great game of tug. If "I'm gonna beat you" predicts play, then the phrase will take on reinforcing properties. You can then use this phrase to prompt a peppy and fun attitude.

The race game is a classic motivational game. Originally developed by obedience trainers, it is a great game to build confidence and to encourage the dog to work ahead of you. To play this game, ask your dog to sit-stay and toss a toy two-feet away from you. On your release "okay," race her to the toy. If she gets to the toy first, she brings it to you for a game of tug. (Only play this game if your dog knows how to play fetch.)  If you get to it first, you play with it by yourself to tease her.  With soft dogs, play this game many times allowing the dog to win.  Not letting a soft dog win may result in her not wanting to play.  For dogs that are not toy motivated, race them to a food-stuffed toy.  The winner eats the food.

Dogs that don't want to move ahead of their handlers greatly benefit from the race game.  Always start with a short distance and build up to longer distances.  As your dog speeds up, cheat by taking a head start.  This will encourage her to run as fast as she can.

The popping the clutch game.  If your dog has motivational issues when getting started with an agility course or segment, play this game a few times per week.  Popping the clutch is played by requiring a sit-duration (self-control) while you verbally wind the dog up.  Elicia Calhoun uses "ready, ready steady?"  When her dog hears this phrase, she becomes excited and tenses all of her muscles and is ready to play.  If the dog demonstrates the proper self-control, you can release her with an enthusiastic "okay" followed by a game of tug.  Self-control starts the game.  If she is unable to hold position, make it easier by whispering "ready, ready steady?"  This game is a great way to build motivation and to proof your start line sit!

*Flyball Games*
Dogs love the game of flyball.  The world of flyball has a lot of information regarding motivation and play training.  Flyball trainers love restrained recalls.  Grab the longest tug toy you can find, and have a person hold your dog by the chest, or in front of the hind legs as pictured below.

Angelica is restraining Rev while Suzanne is teasing him and running out ahead of him (not pictured).

Photo by Tony Rider

Tease your dog with the tug toy, then drag it on the ground behind you as you take off running.  On your release cue "come," your helper releases your dog, who dashes to you and the toy.  Once your dog gets the idea, vary the game by sometimes dragging the toy and sometimes hiding it and pulling it out when she catches up to you.  You don't want toy dependency.  Flyball people put a lot of energy into playing this game.  That energy makes it fun for both the dog and the human.

Be creative; invent your own motivational games.  Vary the games that your dog has already learned to keep things interesting and fun.  Read your dog's body language and let it guide you.

**Enhancing Speed**
Professional dolphin trainer Kevin Krueger explains that when he is training for speed, he often clicks and reinforces just for the initiation of the behavior.  He clicks for just starting to respond to a cue he has given and then reinforces.  To apply this to agility, click a dog for just approaching the table, weaves or whatever obstacle you are trying to build motivation for and then reinforce.

At every level of training be sure you are getting the attitude you want before raising criteria.  Don't ask your dog to do two jumps if you cannot get one jump with the right attitude.  Keep training one jump until you have your dog flying over that jump, then move on to two jumps.

All we can do is our best and all the dog can do is her best.  Motivation is part science and part art, and that is the challenge and the joy of it.  Training is a game, so play it for fun.  Dogs are truth detectors, they know whether you are truly having fun or not.  The single most powerful thing you can do to increase your dog's motivation is to have fun with her.

# Chapter 5 Click and Play! Training Games

If the five layers create a pyramid, then the games that you play with your dog are the mortar that holds the pyramid together.  Training games allow you and your dog to have fun, get great results and build a solid reinforcement history.  Let's get started and play some games!

**How Do You Get Your Dog to Play?**
Learn to read your dog's play signals by watching her play with other dogs.  Along with the obvious play signals such as play bows, observe her eyes and mouth.  Notice the speed of the tail wag and the specific movements of the tail.  When she plays with other dogs, what kinds of games does she enjoy?  Does she like to play fight?  To be chased?  Use your observations to develop a plan to invite your dog to play with you.

If you observed that your dog likes to play fight with other dogs, then use your hands to play with her the way the other dog used her mouth and allow your dog to mouth you.  Put the game on cue so the dog will only mouth you when you give the cue to play this special game.

If she likes to be chased, observe how she starts a chasing game.  What exactly does she do to initiate play?  Does she run up to her pal, nip her in the neck and then run away?  Does she run past another dog at high speed, carrying a stick?  Copy those movements and strategies when you invite your dog to play with you.

Research shows that dogs respond playfully to a human display of a play bow, so try this and see what happens.  How does your dog respond if you slap the ground?  What about if you hop up and down?  How about if you cover your hand with a towel and move it around?  Be silly and

123

creative and see what triggers playful responses in your dog.  Have fun!

**Assessing Your Dog's Play Drive**
Understanding your dog's natural desire to play (play drive) is helpful to the training process.  There are many reasons why your dog may act as if she does not want to play.  Some dogs are abused rescues, some dogs were deprived of early neurological stimulation and others may never have learned to play with a human.

The first four months of a dog's life are critical in terms of how the dog will relate to humans.  The first four months also likely affect the dog's play drive.  While it may be natural for puppies to play, directing play at humans is probably a learned behavior for adult dogs.  Dogs that were isolated or mostly around other dogs from birth to four months may be very reluctant to play with humans.

A dog with extreme fear issues may take a long time to develop the confidence to play with you.  Don't take it personally.  View this as a challenge.  Go slowly.  Attempt to play for a very short time, only a few seconds to start.  Monitor the dog for signs of stress (which signals you to change what you are doing) or for that doggie smile we all love to see (signaling that you are on the right track).

Take a moment to evaluate how playful your dog is.  Will your dog play with you if you:

1. Grab at her neck or collar? — only do this if your dog is NOT afraid of hands or collar grabbing.
2. Wiggle a toy on the ground in front of her? — experiment with different speeds and movements.
3. Reach for her feet? — avoid this if the dog has aggression or fear issues.
4. Give her a playful shove?  Poke?  Slap?
5. Turn and run the opposite way?  How about zig zagging and falling on the ground?

If you answered "no" to more than four of these questions, you might have a play emergency.  It may take longer for your dog to learn to play with you, but with patience and positive reinforcement, you'll get there.  If she is older, getting your dog to play will be more of a challenge than if she's a puppy that is naturally more playful.  Nevertheless, you can learn a tremendous amount about how to teach a dog to play by teaching an older dog the fun of play.  If you teach agility, knowing how to teach play skills is very important so you can pass it on to your students.  If you don't teach agility, the many hours of play will be its own reinforcement.  Playing with your dog is heaven on earth.

**Why Play with Your Dog?**
Nothing will build your reinforcement history with your dog more than play.  Think of reinforcement history as a giant bank account.  Playing with your dog deposits $100 into the account.  Food handed to the dog, may only deposit $1-50.  Food only lasts a split second and the dog can only eat so much.  Play can last as long as you want and the dog never fills up.  Play is the most powerful tool you have to create a strong reinforcement history.  Your mission in dog training, is for the games you play with your dog to be the most fun for your dog.

Suzanne tugging with Hewy, a rescue, who learned to play tug as an adult.

Photo by Angelica Steinker

**Building Reinforcement History with Your Dog**
As just discussed, if reinforcing your dog is a deposit into your bank account, then punishing your dog is a withdrawal. "Punishment is a consequence which decreases the probability of the target behavior reoccurring. The consequence is either the presentation of an aversive stimulus, a loud noise, a squirt of water or the removal of a pleasant or desirable stimulus, i.e. taking away something the dog wants, contingent on the animal displaying the target behavior (Pamela Reid)." Depending on the dog and the form of punishment, the withdrawal may be a large amount of money or even the entire balance. Your reinforcement history bank account is under your control so it is your job to both protect it and increase the balance.

*Play with Other Dogs*
There is no scientific evidence that letting your dog play with other dogs will decrease your dog's motivation to play with you. However, if your dog mostly plays with other dogs rather than with you, your dog may build a large reinforcement history with other dogs. This dog would then prefer the company of other dogs to your company. To prevent this, whenever your dog is playing with other dogs, call her out of play every few minutes. Reinforce her with a fun game between the two of you, and send her back out for more play with the other dogs. This is a win/win. Your dog gets to play with both you and other dogs.

*Self-Reinforcing Behaviors*
Be sure your dog does not open a bank account that makes deposits to accounts that are not yours. Playing with other dogs, sniffing, bug chasing and lizard hunting are all potential bank accounts. While your dog may have come genetically preprogrammed with some of these accounts, it does not mean you have let her make regular deposits to them.

Use self-reinforcing behaviors to measure your current balance. If your dog loves to sniff, ask your dog to give you attention while on a "sniffy" field. Be sure to pay your dog lots of "money" for giving you attention instead of sniffing. Gauge your account balance by observing your dog while she is on a potty break. The moment she becomes highly engrossed in the activity of sniffing call her to you. If she comes to you, your bank account balance is very high. If not, play some training games to increase your reinforcement history in the context where your dog often sniffs.

Self-reinforcing behaviors such as fence fighting, cat chasing and barking have nothing to do with agility. Letting your dog engage in self-reinforcing activities can come to haunt you. A dog that has had the opportunity to fence fight may develop dog aggression or may enjoy the game so much that she is unable focus on you when near a dog behind a fence.

To find out if you have a problem with your dog's self-reinforcing behaviors, experiment if you can call the dog out of the behavior. If she won't come to you while enthralled in the self-reinforcing behavior, you have a problem. You will need to control the environment to avoid regular deposits to the self-reinforcing account and increase *your* bank account balance in that context.

My Border Collie Nicki developed the self-reinforcing behavior of spinning the toy around herself. I trained Nicki to "kill the toy" when cued and now I can call her out of the behavior.

Photo by Suzanne Rider

If your dog is off chasing a squirrel, can you call her off that squirrel?  While it may take months to build up a strong enough reinforcement history in that context, it is still important for safety and to have reliable responses on the agility field.

**Three Types of Games**
There are three types of games you can play with your dog.  Games that involve food, toy games and games that don't involve either.  All three have strengths and weaknesses.

*Food Games*
As much fun as food games can be, it is risky to rely on them exclusively.  Food reinforcers trigger food behavior motor patterns.  These include sniffing, pouncing, hunting, chasing and so on.  In agility training, none of these motor patterns are useful and most are incompatible with what we want.  Agility is about fast, focused and happy movement.  That is more consistent with play behavior systems.  Because of this, play is an ideal reinforcer for agility.

*Toy Games*
A potential problem with toy games is your dog may lock onto one specific toy.  Then this one toy must be present to get your dog's best work.  Without the toy, your dog will display a decrease in motivation.  Just as you can get a food dependency problem, when the dog will only work if food is present, dogs can become dependent on a certain toy.

To prevent your dog locking in on one toy, use a variety of toys in the games you play.  If your dog really loves Frisbees, stop playing with the Frisbee for a while — instead play with a ball on a rope.  When your dog loves the ball on a rope, switch to a fleece tug toy, and so on.  By alternating toys, you are making sure that playing with you is the fun part and the toy is secondary.

*No Food or Toy Games*
This is my favorite category.  No-food or toy games are the Cadillac of dog games.  These games will never create a dependency on food or toys.  No need to carry food or toys, these games are always with you!

## Become a Kid Again
Learning how to play with your dog is all about being imaginative.  A dog that does not want to play, presents the trainer with a puzzle.  All puzzles have a solution.  The solution will come when you find the activities this particular dog enjoys.

## Creativity Guide
To discover what your dog likes, you need to be creative.  Here are some ideas to assist you.

1.  Rid yourself of self-imposed limitations.  Who says you can't be silly or act crazy?  Your dog may love it!
2.  Be motivated.  If you are frustrated or in a bad mood, don't even try to get your dog to play.  Remember dogs are truth detectors.
3.  Be persistent.  When teaching a dog to play, it is easy to give up.  Be persistent.  Make it a fun project.
4.  Observe the dog.  What makes your dog smile?  What makes your dog's eyes light up?  Watch and learn.
5.  Build on what you already have.  If your dog won't play with a toy, but likes to playfully bark at you, start with that.
6.  Follow your hunches.  If you think a real squirrel may do it, get a taxidermy squirrel or squirrel skin.
7.  Break out of your established patterns.  Change what you are doing.  Try different toys, different body postures, etc., experiment!

8. Be both teacher and pupil.  Allow the process of learning to teach your dog to play educate you. Then use what you learn to educate your dog.

If your dog is food motivated but does not play, you can use food to teach your dog to play.  One way to do this is to take a toy and stuff food inside of it.  Many dog-training supply businesses sell toys that include food pouches. Next, follow these simple steps (or be creative and make up your own).

Toss the food-stuffed toy on the ground, and click your dog for glancing at it.  Open the pouch and let her eat a tiny piece of food!  Wait for your dog to approach or sniff the toy.  Click and reinforce with food from the pouch. Continue this until your dog is picking up the toy.  Begin tossing the toy.  Click the dog for running after the toy. Use this game to train a retrieve (more on this below) and to get your dog to play tug with you.

**A Note on Safety**
The games described in this chapter are designed for agility dogs.  The assumption is that these dogs have been properly socialized and handled.  If the dog you are playing with is fearful or has aggression issues, adjust the games accordingly.  Even playfully reaching for fearful dogs may cause the dog to bite.  Exercise caution and consult a clicker trainer who specializes in aggression for assistance.

**Teaching Your Dog to Toggle Between Food and Toys**
Many dogs are more food motivated than toy motivated. This may lead the dog to lock in on food over playing with toys.  If you are playing tug, then stop and feed the dog, she may not want to tug again because she prefers the food to tugging.

To teach this dog to toggle between food and toys, pair the toy with food.  Interaction with the toy earns a click and food treat.  This means that the toy becomes a signal to the dog that food is coming.  Sniffing the toy predicts click and food.  Putting teeth on the toy, equals click and food.  Grabbing the toy, causes click and food.  The dog learns that interactions with the toy earn clicks and food.  Eventually, via classical conditioning, the toy itself will become reinforcing.  Finally, the dog's fun trigger is tripped and you have taught her to play!

**Click and Play!**
After your dog discovers that playing with the toy is fun, pair the clicker with the toy.  Previously, the dog only associated the clicker with food.  Now she will learn that a click can also mean that the toy is coming.  Just as you loaded the clicker by pairing it with food, load the clicker with the toy by clicking and playing five times.  After this, your dog will understand that a "click" can signal either food or a game.

Some dogs prefer toys to food.  My dog Nicki was not focused on food when I began training her as a pup.  Whenever Nicki was highly aroused and I offered her food, she would spit it out and return to the game we were playing.  I paired food with toys, so she learned that she only got to play with the toy once she ate the food.  Now Nicki loves food.  Remind me sometime to tell you how much she loved my rotisserie chicken dinner.

I used to think that you had to have both food and toys to train a top agility dog.  However, I have seen dogs that are amazing at agility and only work for food.  And I have seen dogs that are amazing at agility and only work for toys.  It is possible to achieve your dreams using only one or the other, but it is fun to be able to use both.

**Six Categories of Games**
The games have been put into six categories, according to their purpose.

1.  Motivational games.

2. Self-control games.
3. Recall and safety games.  (Recall is considered a safety issue as an agility dog competes and trains off lead.  An excellent recall is necessary.)
4. Mental stimulation and cross training.
5. Foundation games.
6. Retrieving games.

**Motivational Games**
Games which help build motivation and speed.

*Tug Game*
You can teach the dog that many things in the environment are potentially a toy.  For a dog that loves to play tug, use her leash as a toy.  Leashes are everywhere at an agility trial, so you will always have a toy.

Tug is a great game to use as a reinforcer, to read your dog (more below) and to warm you both up.  You can make it last as long or as short as you want.  A dog cannot tug by herself so tugging with you is a great way to teach the dog that you are fun.

Kay Laurence recommends using tug as a tool for conditioning your dog to use her hind end.

By gently pulling up, Angelica is lifting Zoomie's front end off the ground encouraging him to use and tug with his hind end.  By teaching the dog to tug using the hind end, you help condition the dog's rear.

Photo by Suzanne Rider

*Teaching Your Dog to Tug*
As mentioned earlier, you can use a food stuffed toy to teach your dog to retrieve.  Assuming you have played that game, use the same toy to teach your dog to tug.  The first step requires that the dog put her mouth on the toy while

you hold it.  When she does, click and feed.  Build up to longer holds.  Then, when your dog puts her mouth on the toy, experiment with what gets her in a playful mood.  If you pull the toy away, see if she comes after it.  If so, click and reinforce.  Avoid shoving the toy into her mouth; instead move it away enticing her to keep moving toward the toy.

At the first sign of a tiny tug, click, jackpot and end the session making a big deal about putting the toy away.  The idea is to leave the dog wanting more.  Gradually build up the game from one second of tug, to two seconds to more until you have the desired duration.

*Tug Safety*
In her best-selling book *Culture Clash*, Jean Donaldson cites research (Borchelt and Goodloe), which reports that playing tug with your dog doesn't cause aggression.  It is a common misconception that growls and other noises made by a playing dog are expressions of aggression.  They aren't; they are playful vocalizations that are music to an agility trainer's ears.

While playing tug with your dog, you must feel safe.  If you think your dog is too big and powerful for you to play tug with, don't play tug.  You can play many other games.  If tugging causes you physical pain, don't play tug.  A medium sized dog can put a lot of torque on a person's upper back and arms, giving quite a "chiropractic adjustment."  To be effective a game must be fun for both you and your dog.

If you don't feel in control when playing tug, stop immediately.  Any instance of dog teeth touching skin is a signal to stop the game.  Even if the dog's teeth *accidentally* touch your skin, the game of tug IMMEDIATELY stops.  Wait about three seconds, and begin playing tug again.  If you try to stop tugging, but the dog won't let go of the toy, Dee Ganley recommends gently taking the dog by the collar and holding the toy in the dog's mouth so that there is no pressure on it. The toy is dead and eventually the dog will spit it out.

Ideally stop playing tug before the dog gets too aroused and is tempted to mouth you. A dog that lacks the self-control to play tug has a training issue. Slowly build up the game to expose the dog to more and more arousal. This way the dog has the opportunity to learn how to handle all the excitement the game creates. Once the dog is consistently tugging, put it on cue. I use the cue "get it." "Get it" starts the game of tug and "give" ends it. Below you will find a description of how to teach the dog to give the tug toy. The tug release cue helps the trainer control the dog's arousal. If the arousal gets too high the trainer cues "give" and ends the game.

To keep the game of tug safe for the dog, avoid lifting the entire dog off the ground by the toy, this can damage teeth. Also, be aware of how hard you pull back on the toy. It is better to let the dog drag you than to accidentally injure your dog.

*Teaching the Dog to "Give"*
Teach your dog to "give" by gently taking her by the collar and holding the tug toy that is in her mouth, so there is no tension. The toy is now boring. Eventually the dog will release the toy. When she does, click and reinforce with the toy! Doggie Zen: you give up the toy, you get the toy! Trying to teach a dog to give by continuing to tug, while repeating, "drop it" or by prying the dog's teeth off does not teach the dog to release the toy. Rather it reinforces the behavior of hanging on.

Once the toy goes limp, the dog's release of the toy makes you click and bring the toy back to life. When the dog consistently lets go of the toy, add the cue, "give." Once the give-up behavior is reliably on cue, be sure to maintain the behavior by periodically reinforcing with game re-initiation (or food).

*Proper Tugging Technique*
When playing tug, keep moving backward away from the dog.  Some people try to get a dog excited about tugging by pushing the toy in the dog's mouth and moving toward the dog.  However, most dogs find it more fun if the trainer moves away and pretends to be keeping the toy away from the dog.

Suzanne sets the stage for the keep away game by holding Rev back as she teases him with the toy.

Photos by Angelica Steinker

Now she begins hiding the toy as Rev tries to make a dive for it!

*Wind and Unwind Game*
This game is a form of tug.  While you are playing tug with your dog, use the toy to gently spin your dog in both directions.  Imagine that you are winding up the dog and unwinding the dog.  The purpose of this game is fun and if your dog likes it, it can build motivation.  It's also a good way to warm your dog up before an agility run.  A variation is to grab at your dog while you "wind and unwind" her.  This teaches the dog that being grabbed is fun.  This is important for safety reasons and can also help with vet

visits.  It also prepares your dog for accidental contact that may occur while you are on the agility course.

*Grab the Dog's Bottom Game*
Introduced to me by Pati and Stuart Mah, this is a fun game involving the trainer grabbing the dog's bottom.  To teach your dog the game, playfully reach for her bottom and then toss a toy.  Do this a few times then delay the toy toss.  When your dog scoots forward anticipating the toy toss, click and toss the toy.  Your grabbing at the dog's bottom has become a cue to scoot away from you and a signal for play.  In agility there are times when you may want the dog to move ahead of you or to have a more playful attitude.  You can use this game to prompt both.

*Doggie Soccer*
Dee Zurburg, competition obedience genius, invented this game in which you roll a ball toward your dog. If you get the ball between all four of your dog's legs, you get four points. If you get the ball between two legs, you get two points and so on. Dogs don't know about the points, but it adds fun to the game for the trainer. Dogs will learn to block the ball by crouching down or slamming their legs together in an attempt to stop the ball. Dogs can also grab the ball with their mouth to prevent a goal.

To begin playing this game slowly roll a ball toward your dog so she can see it coming.  She may stop it with her mouth, front legs or by lying down.  Click and reinforce by rolling the ball and letting her chase.

As the dog learns the game, increase the ball's speed. This game is a fun activity for a rainy day, or can be used as a reinforcer.

Arnie has successfully prevented a goal by blocking the ball using his mouth.

Photos by Angelica Steinker

A variation of doggie soccer is nose boxing.

Arnie uses his nose to box the ball back to his play partner. Some dogs naturally nose box toys.  To clicker train nose boxing, click and reinforce the dog for nose targeting the ball and put this behavior on cue.  Next roll the ball on the ground toward the dog while giving the nose targeting cue. Eventually toss the ball at the dog's nose while giving the cue.

*Jump for Food Game*
In this game, you cue the dog to jump up and grab a treat out of your hand which is held directly above her head. Jumping for food, is a great way to get a dog into a happy mood by saying, "okay, get it" and then delivering the food up high so that the dog jumps.

To teach your dog to jump for food, sit your dog next to you in heel position.  Release her with an excited "okay" then click the happy release and deliver the food up high over the dog's head.  Use the delivery to encourage the behavior of getting up on her hind feet or even leaping a little.  Once she has the idea and begins hopping up when released, add the new stacked cues of "okay-get it."  "Get it" will indicate to the dog that it is okay to leap and grab the treat out of your hand.  Of course, you can play the same game with a toy.

If your dog is suffering from the delusion that she is starving to death and likes to take your hand with the treat, you may not want to play this game.  Alternately, you can play the two treats game to teach your dog to take it nicely.  Put on a gardening glove to protect your hand.  Pinch a treat between your thumb and forefinger and hold on tightly.  Don't release the treat until the dog tries to take it nicely, when she does click and toss her a second treat.

Brenna Fender and her Whippet Payton demonstrating the jump for food game.

Photo Angelica Steinker

*Tie Your Dog to Your Waist Game*
Not only is this game a great way to manage puppies for housetraining, it is a way for you to teach your dog to follow you around the house.  Part of the fun is that the leash also doubles as a toy.  By keeping the dog tied to

you, the opportunities to build reinforcement history increase.  For dogs easily distracted while playing agility this game will help create a follow your trainer behavior, which is incompatible with running off!

*Suddenly Appearing Toy Game*
Elicia Calhoun has a fun suggestion to create more drive for recalls.  Call your dog and when she is running full speed, click and suddenly produce a toy (hidden behind your back) and drop it down in between your legs.  The advantage to this game is that the reinforcer is a surprise.

Photo by Suzanne Rider

As the dog approaches, click and drop the toy from behind your back, between your legs.  Most dogs love surprises and find them motivating.

**Self-Control Games**
These games help your dog build self-control.  For agility, this translates to your start line stay, contact stops and table performance.

*Catch Game*
This game proofs the sit position.  Ask your dog to sit and then toss a soft piece of food at her mouth.  Mini marshmallows are a great choice, because they are small and easily swallowed by most dogs.  If the dog catches the food, great!  Uncaught food is off limits.  Make sure you are close by so that she does not grab the food before you can get it.

This game teaches the dog self-control in two ways.  First, you are asking your dog to maintain the sit position while you throw food at her mouth.  Two, the game has a built-in proofing element because even when your aim is poor, she is required to hold the sit and wait for you to pick up the treat and toss it again.  If the dog gets up to help herself, grab the treat before she does.  Set your dog up for success by beginning with very short tosses, directly at her mouth.  If you miss, click the dog for holding position after the treat hits the ground, then pick up the treat and reinforce her.

*The Water Hose Game*
If your dog loves to bite at the water hose spray, use it to reinforce her for an exceptional performance or training session.  Use her excitement and motivation about the hose for a lesson on self-control.  Can you sit while I squirt the hose?  Can you down while I squirt the hose?  The great thing is that you can use the nozzle to control the spray, so start with a trickle aimed at the ground and slowly build up to full stream.  Evaluate whether your dog likes to chase the spray or be squirted by the spray and gradually build up to the more exciting game as reinforcement for demonstrating self-control.

The hose game can also be used to train your dog to run a course despite distractions.  Ask a friend to splash around with a hose while you run a segment.  The key to teaching your dog to ignore the hose is to increase the level of distraction gradually, always building on success.  Begin with the hose turned off and lying on the ground.  If your dog ignores the hose and performs her cues well, click and dash over to the hose to play.  Reinforce her focus by squirting the hose and allowing her to bite into the stream of water.

*Doggie Zen Game*
Deborah Jones teaches this game.  To begin, hold a treat in your hand pinching the treat between your thumb and fingers.  Offer it to the dog.  She will mouth at the treat, lick and paw at your hand.  Ignore all of these behaviors. When the dog backs off and "gives up," click and reinforce.

The dog learns that in order to get the treat, she must give up the treat.  This game can be helpful with demanding and pushy dogs.  Once the dog learns that she is being clicked for backing away from the treat, move the treat around in circles to make the game a little harder.  If she tries to snatch the treat, quickly pull it up and away.  If she demonstrates self-control, click and reinforce with the treat in your hand.

As long as Zoomie remains sitting, the food is moved closer to his mouth.  If he moves to grab it, it is pulled away.

Photo by Suzanne Rider

*Go Wild and Freeze*
This game was created by author and trainer September Morn and emphasizes self-control.  On the cue "go wild" you and your dog both go crazy, leaping, dancing, tugging and going nuts.  A simple task if you have a dog that is easily aroused.  If your dog is laid-back, find something that gets her really excited.  Once your dog is excited, on your cue "sit" or "down," you both stop all movement.  If the dog doesn't stop decrease the intensity of the game to set up for success.  As with the hose game, begin with mild arousal and build up to frenzy-level arousal.  This game will teach your dog to sit or down even when highly aroused.  This is important for your table and start line performances.  For the advanced version of this game, cue sit or down and keep going crazy while your dog holds the sit or down position.

*Hide the Toy Game*
Julie Weir invented this game.  Ask the dog to sit or down, then hide her favorite toy.  At first, make it an easy hiding place, close by and visible to the dog.  If she holds the sit, click and release with an "okay-find-it," to the toy.  When she returns with the toy, celebrate and play with it together.  If she breaks the sit, try again, but make it easier by clicking and feeding the dog for holding position while you place the toy.  Then send her to find it.  This game teaches self-control for duration behaviors.  It can also teach the dog to hold the sit or down if you are out of sight, since at times you will go out of sight to hide the toy.

**Recall and Safety Games**
Coming when called (the recall) is an extremely important cue for safety.  These games either teach or incorporate the recall.  The other games that follow focus on physical handling, including the 'emergency grab.'

*Restrained Recall Game*
One of my personal favorites, this game requires a second person to hold your dog while you run away from her and eventually call her.  Variations include pumping your dog up by gently thumping on her chest and shoving her away from you toward the person holding her to make her eager to come to you.  Of course, this needs to be adjusted for fearful dogs.  Always do what is fun to the individual dog.  If your dog becomes frightened when she's restrained, gradually desensitize her.  In an advanced restrained recall, the person restraining the dog holds on one or two seconds longer, causing the dog to strain against the hold.  When released she will fly toward you and can be clicked and reinforced with an intense game of tug or food.

This game teaches your dog to drive hard toward you.  Be sure to play variations where you change your body position when you recall your dog.  You want speed regardless of whether you are standing, running, walking, sitting or lying on the ground.  Use the same word and tone when calling your dog.  This is your emergency recall and you need it to be the most rehearsed behavior.

When playing the restrained recall game, it is important to signal which side of your body you want the dog to come to.

Photo by Angelica Steinker

In the photo left, Suzanne had dropped her left hand to signal to Sprint to come to that side of her body.  After Sprint committed to running to Suzanne's hand, she clicked and lowered the toy.  The hand targeting game teaches your dog to stay on one side of your body.  The hand targeting game is described in the Ground Games Chapter.  In agility, the dog must not change sides unless signaled to do so.  If your dog comes to the incorrect side don't click or reinforce.  Try again.

*Run and Hide Game*
If your dog gets distracted or does not respond to your first cue for attention, hide as quickly as you can.  This is actually a form of negative punishment.  You remove the reinforcement of your presence for failure to immediately respond to your cue.  If you play this game well, your dog will stick to you like glue and never let you out of her sight.

In order for this game to work, you must have established enough of a reinforcement history for your dog to play this game.  Start with hiding a very short distance away and lavishly reinforcing the dog when she finds you.

A variation of this game is to have a friend distract your dog while you hide.  Your dog learns that if she takes her eyes off you, you may disappear!  This game teaches most dogs to stay focused on their trainers rather than on distractions in their environment.

*Hide and Seek*
Have your dog sit-stay, then walk away and hide from her view.  Release with "okay" and call her name.  Use her name, not your recall cue as it may take her a few minutes to find you, and you don't want a delayed response for your recall cue.  When she finds you, click and reinforce by playing a wild game.  Gradually build up to hiding in places that are harder and harder to find.

This game teaches your dog to find you even when you are not visible and to persist in her search.  It will help strengthen your reinforcement history and turn finding you into a game.

*Popcorn Game*
Clicker trainer Diane Conroy teaches her students the following recall game.  Throw a piece of popcorn across the room.  When your dog has eaten it, call the dog back and click and reinforce the recall with a piece of meat.  An advanced version of this game is to recall the dog before she gets to the popcorn.  The aim is to teach the dog to come even with distractions present.  The game works if your dog likes meat more than pop corn: you pay more for coming and less for moving away.  Use any two foods, as long as the dog values one more highly than the other.  This is a great game to play on a rainy day.  It is useful for strengthening recalls in young puppies.

*Collar Game*
"I'm gonna get your collar" is another way to add some fun to a game of tug.  While tugging, cue your dog to "give" and then tell the dog, "I'm gonna get your collar" as you playfully reach for her collar.  This game will teach your dog that grabbing the collar is fun.  Having her collar grabbed predicts a game of tug.  In an emergency, your dog may need to be grabbed by the collar.  Making it a

game prevents your dog from being fearful or defensive when her collar is grabbed.  If your dog doesn't tug, pair collar grabbing with food.

*Rubs and Scratching Game*
A great no-food, no-toy game is already attached to your body.  Your hands are great tools in playing with your dog.  Your voice is also a wonderful source of fun for your dog.  Petting and rubbing your dog is a fun way to reinforce.  As you continue to play this game, your dog may begin to enjoy it more and more so it becomes a training tool.  You may be able to use clicks followed by rubs and scratches as a reinforcer.  One of my staff has a dog that works for licking.  Kat can ask her dog to perform a behavior, click, and let Tali lick her as a reinforcement.  Be creative and discover what type of touch your dog likes.

Most dog bites occur to hands.  Teach your dog that hands are the source of good things.  Never hit a dog as this teaches that hands are the source of pain.

**Mental Stimulation and Cross Training Games**
Agility dogs are usually active and prefer to be busy, rather than permanently hanging out on the couch.  Of course agility dogs need down time, but too much is usually not good.  For the times you can't run your dog, use these games to keep her mentally stimulated.

*Trick Training Games*
In her book *Agility Tricks*, Donna Duford describes using the food in hand method to teach a dog a paw trick.  Rather than ignoring the dog pawing at your hand to get the cookie, click and treat from your opened hand to reinforce the pawing.  This paw lift can become a wave or a shake trick.  Training tricks is a great way to play and have fun.  Performing trained tricks can also be used to keep your dog focused outside the agility ring while you are waiting your turn.

Junior doing "hoop." Teaching your dog to jump through your arms can help you warm up your dog for the agility ring.

Photo by Suzanne Rider

*Musical Freestyle Games*
Musical freestyle is a mix of obedience heeling and trick training done to music.  While musical freestyle is complex, requiring precision heeling and movements, just playfully dabbling in it can be a great way to offer your agility dog a variety of activities.  To learn more about the game of musical freestyle, consult Kay Laurence's book, *Dances with Dogs*.

Leg weaving, a musical freestyle move, is a fun way to warm up your dog for agility.  During this move, the dog passes between the trainer's legs with each step the trainer takes.

Photo by Suzanne Rider

*Tracking Games*
The sport of tracking, following a scent path, is a fun game for your dog.  To learn more about the game of tracking run, don't walk, to a Steve White seminar and consult the appendix for resources.

*Searching Games*
"Find it" games are a great way to stimulate your dog's brain.  Stuff a Kong® toy with cheese or peanut butter and hide it in a spot where your dog will easily find it.

Bogie playing with a Kong®, positioned on her left front paw. This beehive shaped toy can be stuffed and given to dogs for chewing fun.

Photo by Suzanne Rider

Gradually build up to more difficult hiding places.  Add the "find it" cue.  This game is ideal for preventing boredom and helping the dog develop an interest in the Kong® toy. The Kong® toy can be used as a 'canine binky' (comfort toy) and provide something to mouth.  It can be left with your dog when you leave, to prevent boredom and destructive behavior.  Kongs® can be stuffed with low fat yogurt, low fat cheese, human grade dog treats, pasta (unless your dog is on Atkins), veggies and anything else that is part of your dog's normal diet.  You can even freeze the food stuffed Kong® so that it will take longer for your dog to get all the food from it.

**Foundation Games**
These games help train or maintain behaviors that are part of your play training pyramid.

*Monkey in the Middle Game*
This game invented by Sue Ailsby requires a group of people, enough chairs for everyone and the dog, a.k.a. monkey.  Each person sits on a chair and scoots in tight to

form a circle around the dog.  There should be no gaps between humans and chairs so the dog can't slip out from the center of the circle.  All participants, except the dog's handler, ignore the dog.  Every time the dog voluntarily pays attention to the handler, the handler clicks and reinforces the dog.  The dog learns that good stuff, clicks and treats, only come from the handler and attempting to interact with anyone else gets her nothing.

A variation of this game is great for owners of shy dogs.  In this case, the handler is the only person *ignoring* the dog and the dog is only clicked and fed by the "strangers."  Don't play this game if the dog is stressed by being in the presence of strangers.  Avoid flooding (going too far) as it creates setbacks.

*Over and Under Game*
Sally Treat developed a game in which you sit on the ground with your legs bent and cue your dog to jump over your bent legs and then immediately crawl underneath your bent legs.  This is an activity that most dogs find fun and it can be used as a warm up or reinforcer.  It is especially good for small dogs or larger ones if you have very long legs.

*Are You Tough Enough? Game*
Top agility competitor Rhonda Carter recommends that soft dogs (dogs who are sensitive to touch) learn to be "tougher" by playing tug games that include light smacks on their sides, slaps to their chest and gentle foot nudges.  Carter calls this the 'Are-you-tough-enough-game.'  By exposing your dog to rough housing play while tugging, you can create an association for the dog that bumps and smacks are all part of the fun.  If you and your dog accidentally make contact during an agility run, your dog will view it as a game rather than fall apart or become worried.

While playing tug with Sprint, Suzanne smacks Sprint's sides, which helps her get used to physical contact and intensifies the tug game.

Photo by Angelica Steinker

*Throw a Blanket On the Dog and Beat Her! Game*
Rhonda Carter also recommends tossing a blanket on your dog either covering her or letting her head stick out, whichever the dog prefers, then grabbing and playfully slapping her. As with the tough-enough-game, this will teach your dog that bumps, grabs and slaps are all fun. As always consider each dog's personality and fear issues. If you think your dog won't like a game, skip it.

*The Claw Game*
In the movie "Liar, Liar" Jim Carrey plays "the claw" game with his character's son. The claw is your hand shaped like a claw ready to nail its target: your dog. Once the claw reaches its target, it tickles and grabs. If your dog likes this game, you have another reinforcer.

Suzanne is teaching the claw game by pairing it with a tug (toy not shown). Being "clawed" predicts a fun game.

Photo by Angelica Steinker

*I'm Gonna Get Your Foot Game*
This is a variation of the claw. The trainer attempts to grab the dog's foot playfully while the dog tries to escape. A variation is "I'm gonna get your elbows," invented by agility trainer Brenna Fender, who observed that her dogs appeared to bite at each other's elbows during play. When Fender grabbed at her dogs' elbows, it triggered a fun game. This game can help pass time while you are waiting to go in the ring. And it can help a soft dog physically toughen, and become a reinforcer you can use in training.

Arnie hiding his foot, while playing "I'm gonna get your foot."

Photo by Suzanne Rider

*Spin and Twist Game*
For many dogs, the activity of spinning and twisting (turning circles in both directions) is highly reinforcing. If this is true of your dog, put these behaviors on cue and use them as reinforcers. Spinning and twisting can also be a fun way to warm up. If your dog likes it, use it to prompt a happy emotional state.

*Shove Away Game*
The shove away game can be a wonderful way to get a dog excited about interacting with you. To play "shove away" gently push your dog away when she approaches you. Usually this will trigger the opposition reflex, which will cause the dog to move toward you. Gently shove her away and begin the game again. This game can be used to teach your dog to jump into your lap or arms, if your dog has a strong opposition reflex. Having your dog jump into your arms on cue is a great way to leave the agility ring. The dog is clearly under your control and safe.

*Get Me Game*
Dee Zurburg recommends teaching your dog to "get me."
On the cue "get me," the dog races toward you and targets
you with both front paws hitting your lower leg (small dog)
or upper leg (bigger dog). Lynn Sickinger, one of Dee's
students, taught her dog to "get Greg" – Lynn's husband.
"Get Greg" means to run as fast as she can, play growl
and jump at Greg. Lynn's dog will work very hard for an
opportunity to play a game of "get Greg." To make the
game even more fun, Lynn has added significant distance
to the game. This way she can send her dog from several
hundred feet away to "get Greg." Teaching your dog to get
you or another person is a great way to vary your
reinforcers and keep training fun.

To teach the game both you and the target person need to
have a reinforcer. Previously you have already taught the
dog the actual target behavior, such as jumping on you
with both front feet. I call this "go say hi". Begin with one
person holding the dog and the second person only a few
feet away. Release the dog with your cue "go say hi" and
when your dog reaches the target person, he can click and
reinforce the dog. Continue this game, sending the dog
back and forth between both of you, as you gradually add
distance. For an agility dog, this game can help prompt a
happy emotional state, and can help her generalize
working at a distance.

Advanced versions of the game are to send the dog
around objects or to a hidden person.

*Boing Game*
On the cue "boing," your dog springs straight up in front of
you. This game can really get your dog charged up. To
teach this behavior simply use your hand target. Slowly
raise the hand target until the dog is hopping up into the
air. Click and reinforce the dog for hopping, and name the
behavior when you have the height that you desire.

My Border Collie Stevie really loves this game and gets especially revved up if I clap my hands in addition to cueing "boing." Again, this game can be used to warm up, and to elicit a good attitude

Photo by Suzanne Rider

### Retrieving Games
These fun games can help you keep your dog exercised while on the road to a dog camp or trial. Retrieving games are any game involving you and the dog playing fetch with a toy.

*Fetch Game*
An oldie but goodie is the game of fetch. Playing fetch is a great way to reinforce and exercise your agility dog. Many people expect dogs to play fetch without training. When their dog doesn't they get discouraged. Don't give up. You *can* teach your dog to play this game!

For some dogs, playing keep-the-toy-away-from-the-human is very reinforcing. This game involves the human chasing the dog, while the dog holds the toy in her mouth. A fun game for the dog, and a frustrating one for the human!

One way to maintain control during this game is to tie a cord to the toy. Toss the toy for the dog and gently reel both the toy and the dog back to you. The dog may then turn this game into another modified keep away game (tug).  Anticipate this and only use this approach if your dog has an excellent "give" cue.  If you prefer not to use the cord, toss the toy to the end of an enclosed hallway where the dog can't possibly escape with the toy.  Click and reinforce the dog for bringing the toy back to you.  As your dog succeeds increase the distance of the toss and then move to playing the game outside.  Use a fence line and an exercise pen to create a hallway outside, if needed.  Ultimately, you will have the dog consistently bringing you the toy.  Intermittent use of a click and toy toss will help you maintain the retrieving behavior.

*Hot Toy Cold Toy Game*
Grab two toys of equal value, and place them on the ground in front of you and your dog.  Decide which one will be the 'hot' toy, and which will be the 'cold' toy.  Play with your dog only when she shows interest in the hot toy.  If she plays with the second toy, she gets no reaction from you.  After a few minutes, switch and have the hot toy turn cold and vice versa.  The advanced version adds more cold toys so the dog has to hunt for the "hot" toy.  Be sure to put this game on cue by asking the dog "which one is it?"  Only when your dog 'finds' the hot toy, does the game begin!

Another variation is to use scent.  The 'hot' toy smells like you.  The 'cold' toy is unscented.  Jones has written a great little booklet on how to train this, information on how to get it is provided in the appendix.  Again, you can make this game more challenging by adding more cold (unscented) toys.

**Play is Always with You!**
Who needs toys?  Who needs food?  If you teach your dog to play all three types of games — food games, toy games and no food or toy games — you can **click and play** even when you don't have food or toys.

A dog with a loaded bank account, one with whom a person has built a strong reinforcement history, sees no difference between doing agility and play.  And this is as it should be!  After all, agility is a game we play with our dogs.  Playing agility and the games described in this chapter, makes you the most exciting source of fun in your dog's life!  If you regularly play a variety of favorite games with your dog, your games will be more fascinating than a rat to a terrier, smells to a Beagle or sheep to a Sheltie.

Games will help you increase your dog's motivation, teach her self-control, establish and maintain behaviors you need for safety and create foundation agility behaviors.  Playing will help trigger play behavior motor patterns (moving quickly and running) which is ideal for agility.  Play will help you and your dog be the best team you can be.

# Chapter 6 Click! Ground Games

Ground games are interactive games you play with your dog on the flat ground either without agility obstacles or with bars on the ground.  These games also include interactions in your home, on walks or while exercising.  Every interaction is part of your agility team performance.

Agility ground games help isolate the movements of the dog between the obstacles.  This enables you to successfully guide your dog from one obstacle to another.  Each ground game in this chapter has a description of how to teach it, and how it relates to agility.  The games are a fun way to train if you don't have access to agility equipment, and a way to warm up before doing agility.  They are also an effective way to prepare a puppy for an agility career without risking injury to the pup's growth plates, since you are not asking the puppy to jump or perform any of the obstacles other than bars on the ground.

**Sit Game**
Sit is a behavior critical to agility.  Dogs are asked to sit on the table in AKC competitions, and it is the position most handlers choose to use at the start line.

Sit is a duration behavior that begins with the cue "sit" and ends with the cue "okay."  Your sit cue is like a light switch; when turned on your dog sits and holds that position.  When turned off with "okay," the dog is free to move.

To teach your dog to sit on cue, use your clicker to capture your dog moving into a sit.  A dog will often sit if you are clicking and reinforcing for eye contact.  Click and reinforce the moment she sits.  The behavior of sitting will increase.  Add the cue when you can predict the sit will happen.

To add duration to the sit, begin playing proofing games asking the dog questions like, "Can you sit while I move my arm?" Then continue clicking and reinforcing the dog as long as she holds the sit position. If she gets up, simply move to another spot and try again. You are moving to a fresh spot so that you don't create a behavior chain of: dog sits, gets up, sits again, gets up, sniffs and sits again. This is *not* a duration sit. You want your dog to hold the sit position until you release her.

When first training sit, use food. A toy reinforcer could encourage movement, which, of course, is not desired. Deliver the food while the dog is still sitting as it is the sit that you want to reinforce, not getting up. Only click if you have your food ready to be delivered. If you click and the dog moves, feed anyway. Make sure you are in a better position for the next try, so you can click and feed while the dog is still sitting.

As with all behaviors, proof the sit. Suggestions for proofs are, "Can you hold the sit while I drop a rock on the ground?" "Can you hold the sit while I do a jumping jack?" Training this way is a blast and creates very solid sit duration. Even young puppies can be proofed and will catch on very quickly. Playing fun proofing games makes the activity of holding a sit fun, rather than aversive, as it can be to some dogs. What is aversive depends on the dog; some dogs dislike holding still. If that is the case, you can make holding still fun by playing proofing games. This keeps the dog mentally busy and makes holding still a game.

**Okay! Game**
It is important to have a release word, whether it is "okay" or another word of your choice. A release cue is the off switch for any behavior that the dog is required to hold. Your release cue is the only word that releases your dog from the start line, off the contact obstacle or the table. Avoid using the next obstacle cue as a release word,

156

because a dog's learning is based on anticipation and the next obstacle cue may start with a variety of sounds.  This means that if the timer asks you a question while your dog is on the start line (which happens all the time) your response to the question may accidentally release the dog.  To avoid this problem, have one clear release word.

To teach your dog the release word, attach it to her movement out of position.  For example, a puppy learning to sit will only sit for one or two seconds, so cue the dog with "okay" before she moves.  Click and reinforce the movement out of position.  This captures the release.  You can also prompt the release by tossing a toy.  This is a great way to teach a dog to blast out of a duration position, saving precious split seconds in the competition ring.

In order to train effectively, the behavior that you require must be clearly defined.  Your dog needs to have complete clarity about when to sit and when she can get up.  Without this consistency, you will probably face challenges with duration behaviors.

**Down Game**
In agility, we need a fast down.  If your dog downs slowly on the table, time will be lost.  Ideally, both the chest and the rear of the dog drop simultaneously, like a sack of potatoes.

One way to attain this fast down is to teach your dog to down from the stand position.  Downing from a sit eats up valuable seconds, because two positions (sit and down) are required.  You can shape, prompt or capture the down behavior.  If your dog understands shaping and your timing with the clicker is good, shaping the down is simple.  Just click and reinforce your dog for lowering her chin, then her chest, then a bow and then the down.

You can prompt a dog to down by using a food lure or target.  Hold the target to the dog's nose and then lower it to the ground.  Ideally, the dog lowers the chest and the rear simultaneously or follows the target into a play bow and then a down.  Click when your dog moves into the down position and reinforce.

You can also capture the down by clicking and reinforcing the dog every time you see her move into a down.  Your dog will then begin to offer downs.  Once the $100 bet is certain (the dog is going to down), add the cue and when she downs, click and reinforce.

Regardless of the method, be sure your dog drops the moment you say "down."  To get fast downs, only reinforce those downs that the dog does very quickly.  Slow downs don't pay money.  This is differential reinforcement of excellent behavior (DRE).  Play proofing games involving your position.  Ask your dog to down when you are sitting in a chair, or even lying on the ground.  Build up to these body positions gradually to set your dog up for success.  Play additional proofing games with toys and food.

Remember to add the cue only when you are certain you are going to get the behavior.  Slip the cue in just before the behavior happens.  If you add your cue and wait several seconds and the dog finally lies down, you are going to have a hard time turning that cue into a fast down.  To that dog, the cue "down" means down eventually.  You may find it necessary to retrain the down so that it happens quickly and then rename the cue "drop."

If your dog fails a proof, don't repeat the cue.  You want your dog to respond to the first cue, not the second.  Training is about success, so whatever caused the dog to fail, make it 50% easier.  Move to a fresh spot and try again.  The art of training is making judgment calls about what the dog offers you.  If you do a challenging proof and on the first response the dog offers a slow down, clicking and reinforcing is probably appropriate, but then immediately raise criteria asking the dog "now can you do the same proof with a faster response?"

*Training the Start Line Sit*
Sit your dog on the agility field away from the obstacles. Take one-step away from her and click while you are moving, then reinforce while the dog is sitting. Begin asking the dog questions like, "Can you sit in front of one jump while I dance around? While I move in a circle around you?" Start with easy questions and ping pong your way to harder ones.

Steps for Teaching a Great Start Line

1. Teach a solid sit and play sit proofing games.
2. Add distance, up to 30-feet or more.
3. Proof the sit by raising the dog's arousal. Start close to the dog and then move farther away.
4. Proof with food. Find ways to set the dog up to succeed, and build up to tougher questions.
5. Proof with toys. Remember, set the dog up to succeed.

Photo by Suzanne Rider

6. Gradually combine distance, arousal and proofing games.
7. Add agility obstacles.

159

Photo by Suzanne Rider

8.  Play proofing games again.

To set up for success, maintain a high rate of reinforcement.  The harder the proof, the more money it pays after the click.  For most dogs that enjoy moving, clicks and reinforcements are given for holding the sit. Sporadically click and reinforce the dog for releasing on cue.  Balance the reinforcement history of the sit and the release in a way that your dog will sit but also will blast forward when released.  If you *only* click and reinforce the dog for sit, the dog may not want to get up out of the sit when you release.

A fun proofing game is to sit or down your dog in front of a jump and lead out to the other side.  Once on the other side of the jump, try to tempt your dog to get up by asking a challenging question.  Every time you tempt the dog and she holds position, click and run back to reinforce her self-control.  If at any point during the proofing the dog breaks the sit, try again, but make the next proof 50% easier. Click and reinforce the dog's success.

Time spent training a superb sit is a worthy investment. Training duration behaviors may not be as exciting as teaching your dog a sequence of obstacles, but it is a sit that usually starts the agility game.  Make sure that the first behavior your dog will ever perform in the agility ring is trained to the best of your ability.

*The Set-Up Game*
Every time you prepare to run your dog over a sequence or a course and place the dog in a sit you are "setting up" your dog.  Trainer Dee Zurburg suggests paying close attention to your set up and turning it into a game.  By creating a set-up game and using that game to prompt a happy emotional state and predictable sequence of events for your dog you are setting her up for success.

One set up game involves heeling your dog to the set up spot so that the dog is facing the same direction as you and is automatically at the correct angle.

Photo by Suzanne Rider

Stevie has been heeled into the ideal position in front of the first jump.

Another variation is to stand with your back to the first obstacle and then set your dog up by asking her to come to front position.  Front position is pictured below.  The dog and you are facing each other while you stand and the dog sits.

Photo by Suzanne Rider

Stevie is in an ideal set up position. The trainer used the front position to align him.

*Small Dog Set Up Game*
It is common for small dogs to be carried into the ring by their handlers. When the handler places the dog on the ground some dogs consider this a cue to sniff and wander. Teach your small dog that being set on the ground is a cue for attention. Set the dog on the ground while using the dog's name to get her attention, click and reinforce. Repeat this in various environments and with various distractions.

*Proofing "Okay"*
It is easy to inadvertently release your dog with physical movement rather than the release word. A hand movement or starting to run releases most dogs unless you have proofed the release.

In training, consistently use your verbal release *prior* to moving. This is a great way to test whether your dog really understands the release. If you ask your dog to sit, and then say, "Okay" while standing perfectly still, will she release? If she does, then you have trained what you need.

Alternately, ask your dog to down on the table and begin walking away from her. While you are walking, release the dog with "okay." This is a fun proof to see if your dog is able to release while you are moving. Some courses may require you to move to a strategic position while the dog is on the table.

Proof words other than "okay." The goal is for your dog to only release when you say the word "okay". To help your dog understand this, begin leading out and saying very softly and quietly, "jump, tunnel, tire." While your dog continues to sit, click and race back to reinforce her. Gradually increase the volume of your voice until you can clearly shout the cues and your dog will not release. You can play this proofing game with many other words, but not words starting with "O," because you want your dog to blast off the line, table or contact on the "O" of okay.

Finally, proof handler body movements while your dog waits at the start line. What if you trip as you walk to your lead out spot? Or if you need to use your arm to signal the scribe or timer? Will your dog hold position? You don't want your dog to release on body movements that are not intended to cue her, so prepare for this.

**Does the Click End the Behavior?**
The click is not a release for your dog to get up from the sit position. When you are training a duration behavior or a behavior chain, your click marks the desired behavior, but it does not end it. Only your "okay" cue signals the dog to release.

**Finishing Touches on the Lead-Out Game**
Add different angles and distances until you can lead out across an entire agility field. Build your confidence and your dog's confidence by over-preparing. Watch for signs of stress (dog disconnecting, wandering and sniffing) and if you see any, raise your rate of reinforcement by lowering your criteria until the dog appears more confident. You can lower criteria by reducing the distance of the lead out, by lowering the jumps or both. If you want a two-obstacle lead-out in the ring, make sure you have at least a four-obstacle lead-out in training.

**The Start Line Challenge**
Can your dog stay at the line even when you scream and jump up and down?  Or, if you take off running as fast as you can without saying the release word?  Or while a friend throws toys near your dog?  What if the friend throws the toys away from the dog, out toward the agility field?  Can your dog release off the start line even if you place a hot dog next to her?  Pretend you are a canine Freddie Kruegger and dream up your Nightmare-on-Elm-Street-proof, and then build your dog up to being able to handle it. Imagine the confidence you will have after "Nightmare" proof training.

Whatever you say is impossible is what you must strive to train.  If you think your food motivated dog can't release off the line with a full dinner plate next to her, then train that. You can do it, all you need to do is to find your dog's success point and build on it.

**Start Line in the Ring**
Once you enter an actual competition, everything changes for both of you.  No matter how many matches you attend, your dog can tell something is different about this environment.  Certainly, you will be different.  The most important thing is for you to maintain your criteria in this setting.  Dogs are superb at discriminating different situations or environments and it is very easy for them to learn two sets of criteria.  One for practice (hold the sit) and one for trials (run like heck the moment he turns his back).  If your dog does not hold her start line, you will need to calmly approach the dog and ask the dog to sit. Obvious training is not permitted in competition, so going back and maintaining your criteria will probably cost you your run, but for the sake of your dog's training it is worth it.

Make it a habit to put your dog's training ahead of your competition goals.  Focus on the long term instead of the one run right now.  One lost run means nothing compared to inconsistencies in the competition ring costing you a career of non-qualifying runs.

I once spoke to a competitor puzzled that her lovely fast dog consistently performed the criteria she had trained at home, but in competition raced around the course at top speed out of control.  The fact is the first time this competitor *allowed* the dog to run out of control in the competition ring, she began training that behavior.  After ten times, the behavior was well trained.  Her dog had learned that at home you do fast competitive agility under control, and in the competition ring you run and do whatever you want.  This dog was not being stubborn or difficult; she was doing exactly what she had been trained to do in each environment.  Dogs are sensitive to context so think long term and stick to your criteria in the competition ring.

If you get behavior that does not meet criteria while in the competition ring, a lie down to help the dog calm or a three-second pause is enough to let the dog know a lower arousal state is needed.

**Target Stick Game**
Similar to a lure, the dog learns to follow a target stick, so you can teach other behaviors like stand, left, right and heeling, all of which are important in agility training.

Kicker touches her nose to the tip of the target stick.

Photo by Suzanne Rider

To teach your dog the target stick game, present the stick and click and reinforce when she investigates it.  Raise your criteria until she only touches the tip of the stick with her nose.  Play many 'touch the tip of the stick' games before beginning to move the target stick.  It is common for trainers to rush the process by starting to move the stick before the dog has fully learned to focus on the tip.  If you start moving the stick too soon, you may lose precise behavior prompting ability or even lose stick touching.  So before moving the stick and asking your dog to follow the tip, be sure she will touch the tip when it is above her, to the right, to the left and below her head.

Move the target stick, click and reinforce your dog for following it.  Ideally, she will follow the stick smoothly, without biting or leaping at it.  If she bites it, click and reinforce earlier while her nose approaches the stick and before the biting begins.

Play the target stick game until you have smooth target stick performances with the dog on either side or in front of your body, and with the stick held in either hand.  Seeing the stick is the cue for your dog to touch it.  If you are not actively using the target stick, hold it behind your back.

**Stand Game**
A dog is required to stand still to be measured for her proper jump height in agility.  To shape a stand, sit quietly and observe your dog's movements.  (The trainer sitting in a chair is a cue to the dog that the game of free shaping is about to start.)  The dog is likely to offer a sit.  When she sits, begin observing her hind legs.  When she rises from the sit by moving her hind feet, click and reinforce that movement.  Repeat several times.  Once sit to stands are fluent, change locations, and your body position.  Practice some more before putting the behavior on cue.  Once it is on cue, use fun proofing games to build duration in the stand position.

You can also train stand using your target stick.

Allison uses the target stick to pull Kicker forward out of a sit into the stand position.

Photo by Suzanne Rider

Ask the dog to sit.  Hold the stick to the dog's nose, and release with "okay" while moving the stick slightly forward. This will pull the dog forward and lift the hind legs out of the sit into a stand position.  Click and reinforce the movement.  Repeat a half dozen times then change context and your body position, put on cue, fade the stick and play proofing games.

Target sticks are easy to fade because they disappear into themselves like antennas.  This makes it easy to shorten them until they disappear.  As with any prompt, fade the target stick as soon as possible so the behavior does not become dependent on the stick.  After you shorten the stick begin adding a hand signal (this shifts the dog's focus up the ever smaller stick and on to the hand holding it) or use only a verbal cue.  When fading a prompt present the new cue for the behavior, "stand," prior to the old cue of the target stick.

New cue → old cue → behavior → click → reinforce

**Hand Targeting Game**
In agility, hand signals are often used as cues to direct the dog around the course.  Maybe that is why it is called 'handling.'  Hand targeting creates a foundation for that system.

Photo by Angelica Steinker

Hand targeting also helps when setting the dog up to begin an agility run. Use it to bring your dog to either the left or the right side of your body and to face the dog precisely in the direction you want. Hand targeting also indicates which side of your body the dog should be on during an agility sequence. Usually you will signal with the hand that is closest to your dog.

To teach your dog to hand target, hide your hand behind your back, then pull it out and hold it in front of your dog. She will likely sniff or move toward your hand to investigate. Click and reinforce.

You can also shape hand targeting. Every tiny movement of the dog toward your hand is clicked and reinforced until you achieve the goal behavior of the dog pushing her nose into the palm of your hand.

Play this game with both hands and both the palm and back of your hand. Feed the dog on top of the hand that she just touched. This will help you train a solid touch rather than a dart. Also, teach your dog to target the back of your hand. In agility handling, you will mostly be using the back of your hand to indicate the direction of the dog's path. Ideally, you want a dog that dives for your hand.

Once the dog finds and touches your hand (either side of the hand and on either side of your body), experiment to see if she can target your hand when it is above her head, below her nose and to the left or right of her.  When she can do this 90% of the time, you can consider the hand targeting trained.  Most dogs have no problem using the same cue for both the palm and backside of the hand.

Make sure your dog understands to follow your hand as you move it around your body.  Turn hand targeting into a game.  On the cue of "nose," you want your dog scrambling to jam her nose on your hand.  You now have a new game, the "nose game."

**Running Side by Side Game**
One way to teach your dog handling moves is to begin on the ground without any obstacles.  You will learn more about handling in a later chapter, but to establish a foundation, play the running side-by-side game.

The idea of this game is to simulate agility without any obstacles.  It is like an informal running heel position.  The dog is watching you with her peripheral vision.  Running and staring at you at the same time would cause the dog to curl toward you and maybe even trip you, which you don't want.

To begin run in a circle in either direction.  Play this game off both sides of your body so your dog learns to run on your left and right side.  Circle both clockwise and counterclockwise.  At this stage keep the dog on the outside of the circle.  The dog is faster than you in agility so you will usually strategically place yourself on the inside of the turns. Dogs have a natural tendency to turn toward their handlers.  By steering from the inside of the circles, you are taking advantage of this natural tendency.  If you place yourself on the outside of circles you will have to either run like Olympic champion Carl Lewis or may watch your dog run a different path from what you intended.

However, to proof the behavior of the dog staying on the side you put her on, occasionally run a circle with you on the outside (as pictured below on the right).  Click and reinforce your dog for staying on the side you put her on.  She needs to understand that whatever side you put her on is the side she stays on.  If your dog has trouble, start by running only a few feet before clicking and reinforcing and then gradually build up from there.

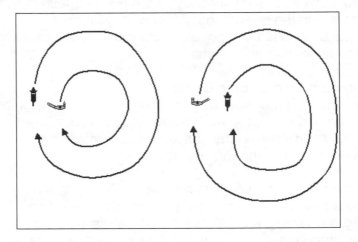

Pictured on the left is the running side-by-side game using the natural flow of the dog.  Going with this flow is the best way to play this game most of the time.  Going against the flow, pictured on the right, is for proofing purposes.  Just in case you ever find yourself out of position and have to run on the outside.  Another way to think about this, on the left side the handler is *pulling* the dog.  On the right side, the handler is *pushing* the dog.  Pushing usually slows the dog down, a reason to avoid it.  Observe your dog as you perform both of the above exercises and you will notice how the dog is faster when she is on the outside.

Click and reinforce her for staying on the side of your body you asked for.  If she needs help, use a target stick to guide her.  As she is successful, fade the target stick by shortening it, and gradually replacing it with a hand signal or verbal cue.  If your dog changes sides without being cued, stop the game, start over and next time reinforce earlier before she changes sides.

Once running next to you is fluent, begin playing this game around agility equipment.  On the agility field, click and reinforce your dog for staying with you and not taking obstacles.  You are creating handler-focus.  Handler-focus is a phrase coined by Pati Hatfield-Mah that refers to the dog focusing on the handler rather than the obstacles. More discussion of handler and obstacle-focus can be found in the handling chapter.

**Magic Flashlight Game**
Pretend the tips of your fingers have the ability to project light.  This light indicates the path that you want the dog to take.  Ultimately, when running a course you will use your arm's magic flashlight to signal about six inches ahead of your dog's nose indicating the path you want her to take. Begin practicing this on the flat without any obstacles and you are playing the magic flashlight game.  The flashlight is magic because where ever you shine it is where your dog will run.  But there are a couple of rules.  In order for it to work, you can't shine it too far ahead of your dog or shine it where your dog has already been.

Agility great Elicia Calhoun running her amazing dog Suni with a perfect magic flashlight. Suni is driving forward because she is absolutely confident where she is going.

Photo by Joe Canova

The magic flashlight gives you a tremendous feeling of unity with your dog.  When you are shining your flashlight just right, you and your dog become one.  Practice this

171

game on the flat and experiment with creating differently shaped paths for your dog.  Once you have learned the moves described in the handling chapter you will be able to create any shape with the dog's path you want.

### Name Game
In agility training, you want fast responses when your dog hears her name.  This may prevent a wrong course. Teach your dog to respond to her name by pairing her name with a click and a reinforcer, ideally food or tug, so that she moves into you.  Say her name with excitement in your voice.  As she snaps her head toward you, click and reinforce with food or tug.  Add distance to the game and ask your dog to run toward you when you say her name. You can also use part of the dog's name to turn her head so that she does not see an incorrect obstacle.  My dog Stevie will recall if I say his entire name, but if I just say "Beep" (the shortened version) he will head check.

### Forklift Game
Clicker trainer Sally Treat invented a game that helps prepare dogs for the height of the contact obstacles.  While your dog is standing pick her up like a forklift would, one arm under the belly one in front of the front legs.

Lifting your dog will help her get more comfortable being up high. If you ever need to lift your dog to place her on the contacts or carry her in an emergency, she will be used to being lifted.

Photo by Angelica Steinker

### Jump in Chair Game
Another way to help your dog to learn to be up high is to teach her to jump in a chair.  Not only does this make for a

cute trick, it habituates your dog to being above the
ground.

**Left and Right Game**
To teach left and right directionals, begin with the dog on
your right.  Place your target stick in front of her and move
the stick around in an upside down U-turn shape, turning
her away from you.  If you have been playing your target
stick game, your dog will follow the stick and make an
upside down U-turn to her right.  Click the dog for turning
away from you and reinforce with food or tug.  If the dog
does not follow the stick, play more target stick games and
then try again.

Allison uses the target stick
to turn Kicker right.


Photo by Suzanne Rider

As soon as your dog catches on to the target stick turning
her in an upside down U shape, raise criteria by moving
the stick faster.  You want this upside down U-turn to
happen quickly!  Add the cue to the behavior then begin
fading the stick by shortening it.  Have your verbal cue
precede the physical cue, so ultimately the entire behavior
will be on verbal cue.

Proof for body position so that your dog performs "right"
regardless of whether she is next to you, in front of you,
behind you or on the opposite side.  Proof by gradually

shifting the dog's position.  The goal is to have her turn to her right regardless of where she is in relation to you.

Repeat the same steps with the dog on the left side of your body, naming that behavior "left."  Again, this cue must be independent of where you are or what you are doing.  Your dog should be able to turn left even if you are turning right.

You can teach both left and right at the same time.  In learning theory, this is called simultaneous discrimination training and it is a fun way to train.

Once you have your 90% success rate at the left and right game, use differential reinforcement of excellent behavior (DRE) to click and reinforce for tight fast turns only.  Gradually raise criteria until you have your dog performing rights and lefts as she is walking next to you and eventually while running next to you.

**Out Game**
In agility, the judge may design a course that requires the dog to move laterally away from you to reach the ideal path for the next obstacle.  Lateral distance refers to a situation where both you and the dog are facing and traveling in the same direction but the dog is required to move away from you.  The out game teaches this lateral movement.

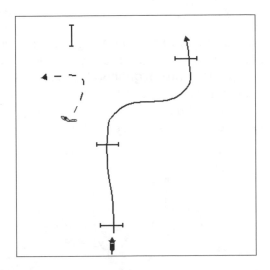

Pictured above is a scenario where the handler used the out cue to kink the dog's path away from the handler to help the dog reach a jump. The handler gave the out cue as the dog landed from the second jump.

Stand next to your dog, both facing the same way. You can prompt and capture the out very easily by tossing a toy away from you laterally. Toss the toy three times, then pretend you are tossing the toy. Once the dog will move away from you laterally, click that movement and reinforce by tossing the toy.

Photo by Suzanne Rider

Use the cue "out" as long as you are getting the behavior. Out is in relation to the handler's body and will be accompanied by your arm signaling the dog's path, so the handler needs to be in proper position for the out cue to be successful. Above you can see Brenna tossing the bait bag for Payton to prompt out over a jump.

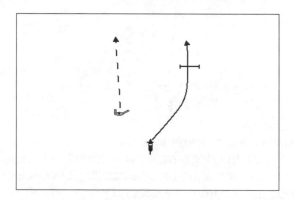

The out cue will be useful when running agility courses that require your dog to move away from you laterally.

Help your dog generalize this cue to various environments and pieces of agility equipment by asking your dog to "out" to each agility obstacle off either side of your body. When she moves out away from you and commits to the obstacle, click and reinforce by tossing your toy or food tube.

Proof the cue by asking the dog to out while your training partner creates a distraction. If the dog succeeds, click for going out, and reinforce by tossing the food tube or toy away from you. If the dog doesn't succeed, just make the distraction easier and try again.

Always reinforce the out game with a toss of the food tube or toy. If the dog must come back to you for reinforcement, she may not want to move away from you and out.

When playing the out game, gradually increase the distance you ask your dog to move away.  Ultimately, you want her to be able to out at least 30-feet laterally away from you.  This will enable you to send your dog out to an obstacle leaving enough room to layer a second obstacle between you and the dog's path.

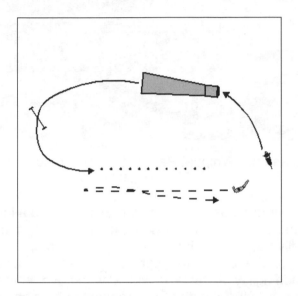

In the diagram above, the handler is layering the weave poles between her handling path and the path of the dog.

## Go Game

The go cue asks the dog to execute a line of obstacles ahead of her.  Unlike out which means a lateral movement away from you, go means "keep going straight until you get another cue from me."  The go cue is usually stacked with the obstacle that you are sending the dog to.  Go-jump would indicate that you want the dog to go ahead of you and take a jump.  Go is relative to the position of the dog (take what is in front of you).

To prompt the go, take the food tube or toy and throw it straight out ahead of you and your dog.  Do this a few times.  Your dog will start to anticipate the toss and start darting out ahead of you.  Click and reinforce this darting movement and then toss the reinforcement forward to encourage continued forward movement.  Once this behavior is consistent, add the verbal cue "go."

Photo by Suzanne Rider

Brenna and her Whippet Payton prompting "go" over a jump.

When your dog has a success rate of 90%, add a jump with a bar on the ground, and stack your cues "go-jump." Gradually back up adding distance, and build up to more obstacles.  The goal is for your dog to move ahead of you over each agility obstacle individually and over entire sequences.  Click the dog for committing to the obstacle, i.e., she has two feet in the air or in/on the obstacle, and toss your reinforcer.

Since go is not dependent on your body position, once the dog understands the task, teach her to go straight even if you are facing a different direction.  To see if your dog can go regardless of your position, set up the following exercise.

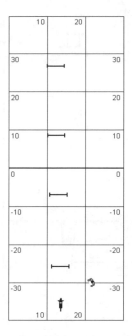

Set your dog so that she is facing the line of jumps, but vary your body position.  Can your dog go without your body indicating the direction?  If she can complete this challenge, with you facing in various directions, set up the same exercise with different obstacles.

Click your dog for moving straight over the line of jumps and have your training partner toss the toy straight forward after the last jump.  If you don't have a training partner, place the toy under a bucket at the end of the line of jumps.  The bucket is your assistant and if the dog is successful, you can click, run out, tip over the bucket and reinforce with the toy.  If you have one of those crafty dogs that figures out how to tip over the bucket, place a brick on it.

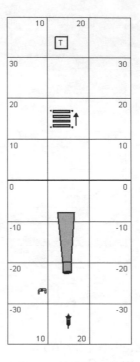

As when training "out," your "area of reinforcement" is at the end of the go sequence.  This way your dog will run hard when you cue her to "go."  Here the handler is actually turned in the opposite direction from the dog to proof "go."

When playing the go game, you are working obstacle-focus.  Another Pati Hatfield-Mah term is "obstacle-focus," which refers to a dog that has a strong reinforcement history for performing obstacles.

**Balancing Handler and Obstacle-Focus**
It is critical to balance handler-focus and obstacle-focus. Some dogs naturally love performing the obstacles so much that they are prone to taking obstacles even when not cued.  Other dogs are so focused on their handlers that they run past obstacles.  To be maximally effective as an agility team you need your dog's reinforcement history of handler and obstacle-focus to be balanced.  This means

that you, the handler, click and reinforce the dog alternately for handler and obstacle-focus.  Playing games such as the running side-by-side and magic flashlight build handler-focus reinforcement history.  Clicking and reinforcing body independent obstacle performance builds obstacle reinforcement history.

**Body Position Recall Game**
In agility training lead-outs or front crosses are performed when you are ahead of your dog.  If you have played the restrained recall game, your dog will drive toward you as fast as she can.  For this reason, it is important to build a strong reinforcement history with the restrained recall game.

While playing the restrained recall game and when using handling moves that put you ahead of your dog be aware of what trainer Chris Bach calls social pressure.  Social pressure is like an invisible force field pushing your dog away from you.  This is caused by the same dynamic that causes us to move away from a person that has stepped into our space.  If the trainer bends at the waist, a dog may be reluctant to approach or will arc, circle around and approach indirectly from the side rather than directly, straight on.  If the handler hovers too close to the weave poles social pressure can cause the dog to run past the poles rather than weave.  Every dog's "space" is different so observe your dog to learn what creates social pressure for her.

Social pressure can also wreak havoc on your recalls.  Facing your dog while calling her to you, can put social pressure on her.  Generally, it is much easier to call your dog to you when you are turned sideways or have your back to your dog.  Be aware of social pressure and train your dog to accept your proximity and different positions.  Do this by gradually increasing social pressure and pairing this increase with clicks and reinforcements.

Because of social pressure, changing your body positions is a great way to proof your recall. Prepare for emergencies by teaching your dog to recall if you are sitting in a chair or lying on the ground. You never know where you'll be or what you'll be doing when you need your dog to recall. Most agility competitors can tell you at least one funny story about when they slipped and fell on course. Recently, I bit the dust while running Stevie on an excellent jumpers with weaves course designed and judged by John Senger. Senger is one of my favorite people to run under, so I was a bit horrified to find myself face to face with the grass I had just a moment ago been running on. Lucky for me, Stevie was in a tunnel while I was inspecting the dirt and he came flying out at just the right angle to take the next obstacle, a triple. I jumped to my feet, resumed handling, and completed the run. The run was clean and a first place. This story would not have had the same successful conclusion if I had not been able to get up. Stevie is not fond of other dogs and it would have been critical for me to call him to me had I been unable to continue. For reasons like this, practice your recalls while you are lying on the ground. It is well worth it to prepare for the time you may fall on course.

**Back Game**
Teaching your dog the game of backing up on cue is important in agility training. This seems to make no sense. Why teach a dog that you want to run full speed, to walk backwards? Because moving backwards helps dogs gain awareness of their hind ends. When a dog backs up, she has to steer with her hind legs. This can only occur if she is aware of what her hind legs are doing. Most dogs have good awareness of their front paws and their nose, but the awareness abruptly ends below their waistline. (Very different from some humans, who seem to only have awareness below their waistlines.)

Teaching back is one of my favorite things. Grab your clicker, treats and a chair. Place two objects on the floor (bricks work well) on both sides of where your dog will stand, then sit in the chair facing your dog.

Photo by Suzanne Rider

I am using Kay Laurence's method of teaching back. Two cinderblocks create a channel to help Zoomie back up straight. As Zoomie progresses to more steps, I move further and further away from the blocks, requiring Zoomie to take more steps back.

Stand your dog between the bricks to create a dog sandwich, one brick to the left of the dog's ribs and one to the right. The bricks create a channel to keep the dog straight and help you prompt only forward and backward movement. Observe the rear feet and when the dog shifts weight backwards as if she is going to back up, click and reinforce. Be aware that one of the biggest mistakes people make playing the shaping game, is expecting too much. The trainer looks for a step rather than reinforcing even a slight weight shift backwards. Kay Laurence calls the process of clicking and reinforcing tiny approximations micro-shaping. Skilled micro-shaping enables trainers to shape behaviors with a high rate of reinforcement and minimal frustration for the dog.

Gradually build up your micro-shaping until the dog is taking a step backwards. Click and reinforce. Continue this process until you have several steps backward.  It may seem tedious to shape with such tiny approximations but according to Laurence's informal research, dogs micro-shaped generally learn faster and seem to retain what they learn better.  I think the day will come when the clicker world will make fun of when we didn't all micro-shape.

Once the dog is consistently backing up several steps, place the behavior on cue.  As with all behaviors train the dog to generalize the cue so that you can change position.  Ask your dog fun proofing questions like, "Can you back up while I am moving away from you?"  And so on.

If you want a challenge, use the back cue to teach your dog to walk backwards over cavaletti (tiny jumps).  This is a great way for your dog to learn hind leg awareness.

Suzanne cueing Blink to back over the cavaletti.

Photo by Angelica Steinker

Teaching your dog to back will also help you teach her lateral movements (sideways movements), because it helps create rear leg awareness in the dog.

Nicki's hind feet cross as her front feet spread apart, moving her side ways.

Photo by Suzanne Rider

Lateral movements also help to develop rear leg awareness and jumping skills.  Use the game below to start working on lateral movements.

### Turn on Forehand Game

Kay Laurence uses a brick to help "lock down" a dog's front end so that the dog's hind end travels in a circle.  Shape the dog to place both front feet on the cinder block, then click and reinforce the dog for rear end movement in a counter clockwise direction.  Put this movement on cue, and then shape movement in the other direction.  Always use your micro-shaping skills.

Photos by Suzanne Rider

Zoomie begins the counter-clockwise turn.

His front feet are stationary on the cinder block while his hind feet travel counter-clockwise.

Still turning!

Zoomie having turned 180-degrees using his hind legs.  Notice he is smiling, he loves this game!

**Look Game**
Sometimes the dog may need to look behind herself to see a specific obstacle. Cueing the obstacle would be useless, unless you can ask her to look behind her, as the dog would not see it. Precious seconds would be lost as she scans the field to find the obstacle, or she could mistakenly take an incorrect obstacle. "Look," signals your dog to turn and look 180-degrees behind her.

Photo by Angelica Steinker

Pictured above, the start position for the look game.

Photo by Angelica Steinker

On Suzanne's cue "look," Rev spins around 180-degrees. No magic involved regarding Suzanne's clothing, the pictures were taken on different days.

Train look by playing keep away with your dog with a food tube or toy. Really encourage the dog to try to get the toy, but don't let her actually grab hold of it.

Take the toy you just teased her with, and ask your dog to sit and hold position.  Toss the toy over the dog's head behind her.  Release with "okay-get it."  This will prompt her to whirl around 180-degrees and look behind her.  Click this behavior and then reinforce your dog with a game of tug with the toy.  Add the new cue (look) before the old cue (okay-get it), fade the old cue, fade the toy, proof, and ta da!  Another fun ground game has been born.

**Self-Control Games**
Agility competition demands that your dog perform a variety of behaviors in the presence of distractions, which requires excellent self-control.  The following games help teach your dog self-control:

**The Leave It and Get It Game**
"Leave it," asks your dog to stop interacting with dogs, people, objects or pieces of food and turn her attention to you.  Leave it is an extremely important cue for agility training because it can save a run.  At an agility trial, if your dog starts sniffing or darts off to investigate a piece of trash, a good leave it cue can help you recover and complete your run.

While training the leave it cue, don't allow your dog to get the "leave it" object.  If she gets it you are training get it, not leave it.  Take ownership of the "leave it" before giving it to your dog or swapping it for something better.  If you reinforce your dog with a cookie that you previously told her to leave alone, you must pick it up first.

"Get it" is the cue that signals your dog to grab the toy or piece of food in her line of vision.  A toy lying on the ground is a proof, not to be played with, unless you give the "get it" cue.  In some venues, you can send your dog to her leash and use it as a toy as you exit the ring.  In other venues, it is forbidden and can get you disqualified.  By putting the behavior on cue, you can control whether or not the dog goes to grab her leash.

To teach your dog to "get it," lay a toy on the ground and shape her to interact with it. Click and reinforce your dog for looking at the toy, then for approaching, then for pawing, or sniffing, then ultimately when she picks up the toy. Once you get her picking up the toy, continue to click and reinforce that behavior. Add the cue "get it" when you are certain the dog will pick up the toy. Use the cue, whenever you invite your dog to play with a toy.

*The Horror of Eating Off the Floor*
Consider training your dog to ignore treats on the floor unless you hand them to her. Allowing a dog to eat food off the floor may teach the dog that food on the floor is available to her. This may create sniffing or interrupt the flow of your cues and responses.

Use the following steps to teach your dog the "leave it" cue. Lay a rock on the ground. While your dog is on leash, walk her past the rock lying on the ground. If your dog chooses to investigate the rock, fine, let her, but the moment she turns away from it and looks at you, click and reinforce.

Add a second rock, next to the first one. Again, if your dog wants to investigate allow it, but the moment she turns away from the rocks and looks at you, click and reinforce! Continue to add rocks until your dog shows no interest in the pile. Click and reinforce the lack of interest and add a tiny dry treat to the pile. Click and reinforce with a moist treat. Continue to add treats to the pile until the dog is consistently successful. If at any point your dog attempts to eat a treat from the pile, limit her options by gently restricting her movement with the leash. The moment she turns away from the rocks and toward you, click and reinforce.

188

Raise criteria by holding a rock in your hand as you walk by the pile of rocks and treats. Toss the rock onto the pile and click and reinforce your dog for turning back to look at you after the toss. Continue this process until you can toss treats onto the pile and your dog still looks at you. Once you have consistent success, add the cue "leave it" to the behavior of turning away from the pile and looking at you.

Generalize the cue by asking your dog to "leave it" in different locations and with different handler body positions. Use different targets like food, toys, people and other dogs.

Finally, remove the leash. Have an assistant stand next to the leave it treat (or toy) ready to cover the treat with his foot if the dog darts for it. Begin walking the dog past the leave it object, and click and reinforce your dog for moving away from it and looking at you on cue!

Remember to click and reinforce your dog for every successful "leave it." Eventually you will only click and reinforce the best leave its, using differential reinforcement of excellent behavior (DRE).

*Fried Chicken Leave it Challenge*
Say, "leave it" and drop fried chicken on the floor. If the dog leaves it, click, reinforce and celebrate! Your training has passed the leave-it-challenge-monster proof! It's your training that passed and not the dog that passed, because the dog is always right. If she had eaten the fried chicken, it only would have been information that your training had not prepared her for the monster of all proofs.

Develop your own leave it challenges. If food distractions are more challenging for your dog, then start with toy distractions. Build your dog a path for success. A solid "leave it" opens up a new world of proofing games to you.

**Competition Obedience**

Competition obedience will create a wonderful foundation for your agility dog's career. Exercises like heeling can be helpful in teaching the dog how to learn precise behaviors and to work close to you. Both competition obedience and agility require dogs to perform cues fluently and accurately. Learning competition obedience footwork helps agility handling, which has its own footwork.

*Heeling*
Heeling is when your left leg and your dog's right shoulder are in alignment as you and the dog move at the same speed. It is considered flashy for the dog to give the handler attention while the handler looks where he is traveling. Obedience folks don't look at their dogs while heeling. This keeps their shoulders straight and is an excellent way to practice using peripheral vision, an essential skill in steering a dog around an agility course. I can understand why top obedience competitors who cross over to agility tend to do well. There is a lot of common ground between the two sports.

Heeling with attention also teaches your dog to focus even when distractions such as food and toys are lying around. This is always a good game to play, as it teaches the dog self-control. No matter which competition obedience exercise you choose to play, it is a great self-control game. When I started working with dogs, I was a force trainer. I forced my Jack Russell to heel by yanking on his choke chain. For years I associated obedience with force and avoided it. I made a commitment to obedience, when I was forced to retire another dog from agility. My Nicki was injured (her calf muscle was torn off the back of her knee) in a roll over car crash preventing her from performing agility. Soon we were playing all our favorite games doing obedience exercises. Within a few months Nicki began to love obedience as much as she had loved agility. It isn't the game we play, it's how we play it. You can make obedience fun. If I can do it, you can do it. All you need to do is make every obedience exercise a fun game.

*Offside Heeling*
Play the heeling game off both sides of your body.  This will help keep your dog's muscles balanced.

Kay Laurence has developed an ideal way to teach a dog both onside and offside heeling.  The process begins with a four-foot target stick, which you use to prompt the dog to perform an extended trot.  An extended trot is similar to the type of trot the judges like to see in the show ring — long effortless strides that cover a lot of ground.  The handler will need to jog next to a medium sized dog to help prompt the extended trot

Do this for several weeks until the dog is confidently driving toward the tip of the stick and consistently and rhythmically extending her trot.  Then lift the stick.  The energy the dog was using to drive forward toward the stick will create a paddling gait when you hold the stick above her head.

Here I have lifted the stick prompting Stevie to paddle with his front feet.

Photo by Suzanne Rider

Since the dog is accustomed to performing the extended trot, she will continue to bring her rear underneath her but in order to continue targeting will paddle upwards with the front end.  Paddling means the dog will engage in a very flashy trot that looks similar to a passage in a horse.  This paddling trot is then put on cue, and the target stick faded.  Train on both sides of your body, so that the dog develops even muscle tone.  Once the trot is on cue, teach heel position as a separate exercise, ultimately combining both behaviors.

*Swing!*
To properly heel, an obedience dog needs to know how to swing her rear into alignment with the trainer.  For competition agility, lateral movement ability will help increase hind leg awareness and is a great thing to teach a young dog while you are waiting for growth plates to close.  The turn on the forehand game is the swing behavior.  Once you have "swing" on cue and fade the brick, you can move out of the chair and step in front of the dog and then cue the dog to swing into heel position.  You had used the brick as a target for the dog's front feet, to enable you to click and reinforce rear leg movement.

Suzanne is standing where the brick used to be.  On her cue of "swing" Rev starts out in front of her and using his rear rotates until he is parallel with her.

Photos by Angelica Steinker

*Half Game*

"Half" refers to the dog sidestepping to her right. The other direction is called "pass." I took the words "half" and "pass" from horse training, where half pass refers to a horse's sidestepping. To teach your dog the "half" cue ask her to stand in front facing you. Very slowly take a tiny step to your left. If the dog has played the back and turn on forehand games she will shift her weight and prepare a side step right to follow you. Click and reinforce. Use micro-shaping to build the behavior from there. Once the behavior is consistent, place it on cue.

*Pass Game*

"Pass" is the same behavior as "half" but in the other direction. All of your training will be the same except the tiny steps will be to your right and your dog's weight will shift to her left.

**Behavior Problems**

Every interaction with your dog is training. In fact everything your dog does is part of agility training. Can you tell I am obsessed with this sport? All day my dogs' activities make me ask myself, "Is this supporting our training?" My goal is to be consistent with my dogs and to avoid setting them up for failure. *Anything* done without agility obstacles is a ground game, including the behaviors your dog practices in your home.

All dogs have behaviors that are normal for them, but we consider problems. Dogs are perfect at being dogs. They bark, they dig and they chew. No matter what the issue, loose leash walking, shyness, resource guarding, housetraining, mouthing, urine marking, barking, jumping on people or destructiveness, they can be modified using clicker training. Don't let anyone tell you it is necessary to hit, spray or frighten a dog out of engaging in behaviors. The most powerful way to modify behavior is by using positive reinforcement. Negative reinforcement and positive punishment are not only less powerful means of modifying behavior, they are also unkind.

Without modification unwanted behaviors may haunt you in the agility ring.  Of all the behavior challenges, the most serious is aggression.  Owners of aggressive dogs should run, not walk, to a Dee Ganley seminar!  Outstanding books by James O'Heare and Jean Donaldson and others are listed in the appendix.

**Agility Specific Behavior Challenges**
The two most common behavior problems that crop up in agility are sniffing and the dog leaving the handler during a performance.

*Sniffing*
To teach your dog to focus on you rather than sniff and explore the environment, shape the absence of sniffing. Shape it in combination with the clean behavior cues game (described in Chapter 1).  This means that whenever your dog is *not* sniffing and responds to a cue, click and reinforce.  If the dog sniffs before performing a behavior or while performing it, the dog loses the opportunity for a click and reinforcement.  In order to earn reinforcement, behaviors can't be accompanied by sniffing, even air scenting (when a dog sniffs the air).  Avoid training sniffing problems.  If your dog performs a behavior and sniffs at the same time, it is the same as the dog not performing the behavior.

Evaluate what might be triggering sniffing during your training sessions.  When does your dog tend to start sniffing?  When was the last time you reinforced your dog?  If you have not reinforced in a while your rate of reinforcement may be too low, accidentally causing stress. Sniffing can be a sign of stress and you can't shape the absence of sniffing very well if your training is causing it. Click and reinforce your dog for not sniffing, and then increase your rate of reinforcement to prevent triggering stress sniffing in the future.  Some dogs sniff as the result of unclear handling or after they fail to gain reinforcement. Teach your dog a bounce back cue such as "nose" for hand targeting.  If either of you make a mistake cue the dog "nose" and then click and reinforce that behavior.  This provides an easy success and prevents sniffing.

*Running Off During Training*
This problem is similar to sniffing.  If you think your dog will leave you in the agility ring, please don't enter a trial.  Go to fun matches because there you can train in the ring.  If you can't find any, create your own.  Once your dog has stayed with you at three fun matches in a row you have a much better chance of her staying with you in the competition ring.

Coming up next: agility contact obstacle training.  Fasten your seat belt, things are getting serious!

# Chapter 7 Click! Contacts

The contact obstacles — dog walk, A-frame and teeter — are so called because of the yellow 'contact' zones painted on the up and down ramps.  To prevent dogs from swan diving off the obstacles and injuring themselves, most agility organizations require the dog to place at least part of a paw on the contact zone for safety reasons.  This presents the trainer with the challenge of training these obstacles to be performed both quickly and accurately.

So what's the big deal?  Can't you just teach a dog to jog across a contact obstacle plank?  Sure, but this may not get you the consistent contact zone accuracy that you want and need to qualify in competition.  Any medium or large dog is likely to miss the zone by striding over it.  The natural stride length of these dogs carries them over the yellow without even leaping off the obstacle.

The A-frame.

Photo by Suzanne Rider

Photo by Suzanne Rider

The dog walk is the longest of all the obstacles.

197

The teeter is the only contact obstacle that moves.  Dogs are challenged to negotiate a narrow board as it tips forward.

Pictured at left is Terry Smorch's phenomenal Remy.  The teeter is the only obstacle that moves while the dog is performing it.  Because of the movement and noise, it can take longer to train.

Photo by Todd Van Buren

Trainers have been working to solve the puzzle of how to have both blazingly fast *and* accurate contact obstacle performances since the beginning of the sport.  It will be fascinating to see what new methods trainers develop in the next decade.

Top agility trainer Stacy Peardot-Goudy had the brilliant idea of teaching the dog a concrete behavior that would enable the dog to understand what the trainer wanted.  The dog stops with her two front feet on the ground while her two hind feet remain on the contact obstacle.  This method was named two on and two off (2O2O).

The 2O2O method has evolved and trainers have built upon Peardot-Goudy's idea.  Susan Garrett added a nose touch.  The nose touch enables the dog to slide into the 2O2O position with weight shifted to her rear end.  In this chapter, I will describe the two feet on the contact two feet off the contact with a nose touch (2O2ONT) which we teach at my school.

With the nose lowered, Riggs is encouraged to maintain a crouch position.

Photo by Suzanne Rider

Although there is no specific research on the topic, agility competitors assume this type of position causes less physical strain on the dog's body. With weight shifted to the back legs strain is minimized on the dog's shoulders. However some dogs get sore in the quadriceps if contacts are physically over trained (too much training for the physical condition of the dog). Massage and feel your dog's body on a daily basis to monitor soreness. It is easy to physically over train your dog, especially if you have constant access to equipment, are a perfectionist and obsessive in nature.

**Different Strokes for Different Folks**
The running contact is the fastest way to perform the contact obstacles. The dog runs full speed up, over and down the obstacle while still touching the yellow contact zones. French agility competitor Christine Carpentier won the world agility championships two years in a row with her brilliant Border Collie Mac. Mac has an amazing running contact over the dog walk. Mac flies up the first ramp, increases speed as he dashes across the center plank and accelerates through the yellow of the descending plank. It is fair to say that his dog walk performance is everyone's dream. The problem is that Mac only hits the downside of the yellow contact zone about 50% of the time. In Europe handlers are reinforced for winning so 50% works. In North America, both accuracy and speed are emphasized, so only fast and accurate agility teams advance.

The great agility minds of the world continue to puzzle over how one can achieve blazingly fast and near 100%

accurate contact obstacle performance.  Many trainers with small dogs have the running contact behavior.  Others with medium or even large dogs have it, but no one consistent method is named as *the* means of attaining the running contact.  Some competitors explain that their dog naturally offered a stride that carried them through the yellow so they captured and maintained the behavior.  If you opt to experiment with a running contact, consider teaching the 2O2ONT behavior concurrently with a different cue so you have something to fall back on.

Currently one of the more successful approaches to a running contact is to train the 2O2ONT behavior, but eventually move to an early release so the dog does not stop but breaks stride just long enough to touch the yellow. I did this with my Border Collie Nicki and it opened a can of worms.  Nicki is a thinking type of dog.  She wants everything in triplicate so she can be sure she is getting it right.  You know the type-A, overachiever, first-born personality.  Once I moved to an early release with Nicki, she started creeping on the down side of the contact experimenting to see which of her steps would trigger the release.  I had muddied the waters and boy was I going to pay for it.  Every time she would creep down a dog walk plank, I found myself mentally slapping myself for even considering the early release.

However, my Border Collie Stevie has done fine toggling back and forth between early release and 2O2ONT.  He is more of a doer and less of a thinker.  When in doubt he does something really fast, then asks questions.  Stevie is easier to train, but I have learned more from Nicki.

If you choose to train for an early release, you also run the risk that your dog will learn two sets of criteria, stop for training and yahoo-leap-off in the competition ring.  Avoid this by being unpredictable about how long you hold your contacts in either environment.  If in both environments you sometimes do an early release and other times hold, your dog will not be able to predict what is required each time. Another possibility is to use two separate cues, given as the dog approaches the contact obstacle, one for the new running behavior and one for the 2O2ONT behavior.

Some trainers pattern train a running contact.  Pattern training is when you ask the dog to perform the same movements repeatedly.  The idea is to ingrain the proper striding over the contact obstacles using stride regulators attached to a lowered contact obstacle which is very gradually raised.  Although some dogs stride in a certain way and have a structure that fits pattern training a running contact, this method does not work for most dogs and the method usually can't predict which dog will be successful.

Another concern is that the dog's angle of approach to the contact obstacle affects whether she is able to execute the proper striding.  The dog's stride is also affected by which obstacle precedes the contact obstacle.  A tunnel before the A-frame will create a longer stride than a triple before the A-frame.  The spacing between the obstacles also affects striding.  USDAA has an average of 18-feet between obstacles, but the AKC averages 15-feet, three feet can make a difference to how many strides a dog takes.  Finally, the surface the dog is running on, and the speed with which she is running also affect her striding and may or may not cause her to hit the yellow.  It requires a tremendous amount of training to control all of these variables and it appears that it may be impossible to control all variables for most dogs.

Toy breeds may be able to consistently run the contact without leaping.  If your dog is tiny and cleanly runs the contact, count your blessings because you just saved many months of training.  Very large dogs such as Great Danes can learn the 2O2ONT position, however their natural stance can span above and below the yellow.  A running contact with these dogs may be a better strategy. Other options include one rear foot on, as developed by

Agility great Linda Mecklenburg. This method makes use of a stop but the dog stops with one rear foot on the contact. Some trainers have a verbal "lie down" cue that teaches the dog to break stride at the yellow. Another option is to consistently stop the dog with all four feet on the ground. This may cause the dog to break stride enough to run through the yellow. Eventually the stop is faded and the dog would be patterned to run to the bottom of the obstacle.

If you think your dog is an ideal candidate for a running contact, because of the dog's size or type of stride, try it. Find out what works for you and your dog. Some day, someone will develop a perfect running contact method that will be the result of experimentation. All of us benefit from the few who are brave enough to try new methods. If you are new to the sport, consider leaving the experimentation to those who are more experienced. A less experienced trainer may not be aware of safety concerns or training issues that prevent certain methods from working.

**Making Contact With the Up**
Most of this chapter will discuss the training of the downside contact zone, because it is far more challenging. Dogs that jump 4- to 16-inches in height, can usually stride through the up contact easily touching the yellow. Taller dogs may stride over the up. After a month or two of performing the entire obstacle dogs that initially miss the up contact, often settle into a type of striding pattern that takes them into the up contact zone. This leaves a small remaining percentage, including the giant breeds, which need to train the up contact.

The methods to train the up vary. Two possible solutions are hoop use and foot targeting. In the hoop method the dog learns to run underneath a hoop which is placed on or in front of the contact obstacle prompting the dog to crouch prior to striding onto the obstacle. The hoop must be faded, which can be tricky.  It is common for trainers to lose the crouch behavior once the hoop is not present.  To fade the hoop, gradually move it further away from the up contact so the dog still passes under the hoop, eventually removing it completely.

The foot target may be the better choice for most dogs.  It is easy to shape a dog to touch her foot to a yellow target and then place that target on the contact zone.  You are using a clear target for a nose touch, so use a yellow target for the foot target.  Ultimately, the yellow target is faded.  You can fade the target by making it smaller until it does not matter to the dog whether it is there or not.  The placement of the target will depend on your dog's natural striding.  Place it so that you are not adding strides to the dog's obstacle performance but so that the dog is clearly in the yellow.  Avoid adding a stride to the up side of the contact, since it usually means an added stride on the down side.  More strides mean a longer performance time.  However, increased time is preferable to consistently faulted performances.

There is a product available called the "Hit It Board Contact Trainer" a yellow colored pad that closely resembles the yellow contact zone.  This pad beeps when the dog touches it.  The trainer can pair this beep with food or toys so the beep is like a click of the clicker.  The mat can be used to teach the dog to foot target.  The trainer then transfers this behavior to the contact obstacle.  The "Hit It" can include extra parts that shine a light instead of beeping.  This assists the trainer in fading the pad.  If the dog gets used to hearing the beep, then the foot targeting behavior may become dependent on the feedback of the beep.  No beep, no foot target.  By using a light, you can still reinforce the dog for the proper behavior without the dog hearing the beep.  A similar type of pad is also available as a nose target and can be useful to trainers unable to bend over and see if their dog is hitting the center of the target with her nose or for proofing when you are behind your dog and can't see if she is touching or not. Agility has gone high tech, see the www.nosetouch.com website for more information!

As with all training, rehearse success rather than allowing your dog to practice incorrect performances.  The more times the dog has missed the up, the longer it will take to retrain the ideal behavior.

**Before You Start Contact Training**
Visualize what it is that you want to train.  It is essential to have a clear picture in your mind of the exact contact behavior you want.  You also need to have a clear understanding of how you are going to help the dog get to that end behavior.  Clicker training is highly effective, but it is not magic.  I haven't seen human-to-canine telepathy work, so you need a plan.  (Incidentally, if you figure out how to make the telepathy training work, please contact me immediately.)

My goals for the 2O2ONT, are for the dog to run up and over the contact obstacle as fast as possible and to drive as fast as she can into the 2O2ONT position.  Mentally picture your dog doing this, before you start training.  Then base your plan on the mental picture.  If your dog is doing the "ideal behavior" in your mind, how does the very last part of the behavior look?  Break your visualization into segments so you can be clear what your dog is doing at every split second of the behavior.  Where are her feet? Where is her nose?  Where is her weight shifted?  What is the position of her legs, her feet?  What is the tail doing? Observe dogs at agility trials to help you hone your mental pictures.

If your dog jumps 12-inches or less, you may opt to train a running contact.  This means the dog does not stop and just runs up, over, and down the contact obstacle.  Clearly, this is the fastest way to perform contact obstacles, however as discussed earlier most taller dogs need to learn a 2O2ONT, otherwise they will leap off the obstacle missing the yellow and incur a fault.

**Backchaining the Contact Obstacles**
The more you break a behavior down into separate actions, the higher the quality of the end behavior. Taking the time to break behaviors down takes patience. However, thorough training provides the long-term reinforcement of reliable performances. Rushing to put a dog over the whole obstacle to compete may be reinforcing in the short term but begins a very long run of poor performances and retraining. Over the years, I have found myself becoming obsessed with finding ways to break behaviors down to improve the result. My hope is that this book will inspire agility trainers to find the joy in breaking down behaviors and progressing slowly through each approximation, so that the result can be the precision and speed that you visualized. An approximation is a behavior that resembles the desired end behavior. Each successive approximation should look more and more like the end behavior until you finally reach your goal. The tinier you can make the approximations, the more likely your dog will succeed and the better the result. Play the tiny approximations game and find ways to break behaviors down more. This will ironically create *faster* progress and ultimately provide you and your dog with more fun.

Because the process of training the contact obstacles is lengthy, here is an overview.

1. Fun with flat boards
2. Cavaletti games
3. The nose touch game
4. The position game
5. The hold game
6. Proofing the hold
7. The slide game
8. Slat games
9. Fading the target game

10. Backchaining the A-frame and other contact
    obstacles

The process will conclude with dog walk and teeter prep
games, backchaining the dog walk, teeter prep training
games, teeter training, and contact obstacle proofing
ideas.

*Backchaining*
You will be training your dog to perform the contact
obstacles by using a process called backchaining. This
means that the last part of the behavior is taught first, so
the dog is always going from the new behavior to a familiar
behavior. This builds great confidence and attitude and for
us agility folks that translates to speed! Backchaining also
is a fun way of learning for the dog.

When your dog runs into the 2O2ONT position, she will be
crouching with both her rear and head lowered. This drops
her weight backwards to minimize the risk of damaging her
shoulder assembly.

The training process will begin with the dog in the 2O2ONT
position. Each approximation will add one new step to the
already familiar behaviors. These steps will include
working the dog while you are in front of her, off either side
and behind her. Play this handler position game every
time you raise criteria starting with the position pictured
below.

Photo by Angelica Steinker

The position (left)
showing the handler in
front, puts some social
pressure on the dog that
helps keep her from
coming off the contact
obstacle. The front
position can help you
set your dog up for
success every time you
raise your criteria.

Photo by Angelica Steinker

After your dog is consistently successful in the front position, experiment with stepping into position next to her, while she holds target position. Only accept nose touches between the dog's two front legs.

Play this handler position game with your dog off both your left and right side.

Photo by Angelica Steinker

The final handler position, the handler standing behind the dog. This is the most challenging handler position. It is tempting for the dog to curl toward the handler or to fail to target between her two front feet. Only accept targeting between your dog's two front feet.

Building on success, increase the distance you stand behind your dog until you reach the full length of the contact obstacle. The goal is to create a contact obstacle performance that is independent of the handler's body position.

Okay, now that you have an idea of what the training will look like and how you will train it, we can get started.

### Fun with Flat Boards
To get a dog used to movement under her feet, you can use a Buja board. You can make a Buja board by taking a

2-foot by 2-foot piece of plywood and staple gunning a tennis ball in a sock to the bottom of it.  When the board is placed on the ground a dog can step on it and feel the board wobble.  This helps dogs get used to movement under their feet.  In addition, I like adjustable contact equipment.  You can vary the height so that the obstacle board can be placed flat on the ground and then gradually raise it.

Allow your dog to investigate and become familiarized with the A-frame, teeter and dog walk boards.  After the dog has investigated the boards, use your target stick to help her run across the flat boards on the ground.  Fade the target stick so that she can fully focus on her body rather than on the target stick.  Play these games off both sides of your body until your dog is completely confident running across the boards.  A confident dog is relaxed and happy and will attempt to initiate the game of running across the contacts.

**Cavaletti Games**
Walking, trotting and cantering your dog over cavaletti will help create hind end awareness.  You can make adjustable cavaletti as pictured below that allow you to set them at various heights.

These cavaletti, made by Sam Turner, allow for multiple heights; they have a high, medium and low setting.

Photo by Suzanne Rider

Determine the height of the cavaletti by the size of your dog.  Tiny dogs can even use bars on the ground.  Alternately, small dogs can use the lowest setting, medium dogs the slightly higher setting and large dogs the highest setting.

Set up a minimum of four cavaletti with the appropriate spacing for your dog.  For walking, the spacing is very close together, for trotting a little wider and for cantering even wider.  Observe your dog's gait on the flat to determine the appropriate spacing between the cavaletti.  Or dust a flat surface with some flour and move your dog across the surface to see the actual foot prints.

While walking your dog over the cavaletti, click and reinforce your dog for not ticking any of the bars.  Ticking is when your dog hits the cavaletti with her feet creating a "tick" noise with her toenails.  You are shaping the absence of the ticking.  Once you have successfully achieved this, begin clicking and reinforcing your dog for rhythm.  Toss a toy or food tube in front of your dog when she is straight and facing ahead in the center of the cavaletti.  If you reinforce the dog to the side, towards the handler, you will be teaching the dog to curl.  Ticking and loss of rhythm will then occur.  Repeat the same game at the trot and canter off both sides of your body.  You are done playing this game when your dog generally does not tick the cavaletti and maintains rhythm in all three gaits off both sides of your body.  For dogs with severe jumping problems cavaletti games may need to be part of their maintenance training.

During this training, your dog will be learning to work through the click.  If you click for the first cavaletti, the dog must complete the remaining cavaletti.  The area immediately after the last cavaletti is the area of reinforcement.

Area of reinforcement

Withhold the toy toss until the last cavaletti has been completed. Tossing earlier would prompt the dog to bowl the remaining cavaletti, like a bowling ball, an undesired behavior.

### The Nose Touch Game

Use a clear Plexiglas target for teaching the nose touch behavior.

Photo by Angelica Steinker

To help you see the center you can place a black dot on it with a permanent marker. Use a clear Plexiglas target because it will be easier to fade.

It is recommended that you reinforce with food for the nose touch behavior. It is easier to deliver food above the target using treats.

Photo by Suzanne Rider

210

After your dog has touched the Plexiglas target five times and you have clicked and reinforced this behavior each time, move the target to another location. Once you have consistent nose touches with a success rate of 90% in various locations, put the nose touch behavior on cue. "Touch," "spot" or "bottom" are commonly used cues.

Be sure your click occurs *as* your dog is touching the target. Clicking early may train your dog to stop short of actually touching the target. Clicking late may train your dog to pick up the target with her mouth, another unwanted behavior. Visualize a chicken pecking at the ground. This is the motion you want to create, your dog's head bobbing up and down at the target.

Your food delivery will affect your dog's nose touch behavior. Delivering it in front of the target, will train her to target in a "nose scraping" fashion, moving from the target to the anticipated area of reinforcement. Instead, deliver the food to your dog's mouth as she is touching the center of the target.

Prompting with food by placing it on the target, will get the dog to run to the food, and eat it, but it will not necessarily teach her to touch her nose to the target. Just say no to putting food on the target! If you tap the target with your foot or finger or point at it your dog may become dependant on those cues and they can be difficult to fade so it is best avoided. The moment you are not in position to indicate the target your dog won't know the behavior. Instead of food dependency, you have pointing dependency. This presents a problem since most of us are behind our dogs when they perform the contact obstacle. A huge part of the contact training process involves making it independent of your body. It can be easier to avoid prompting from the beginning than to find yourself unable to fade it later.

The chicken pecking effect is multiple nose touches on one cue. To train this, repeat your cue, "touch," two or three times before clicking and reinforcing. After doing this a few times, fade the additional verbal cues, and your dog will bob repeatedly after only one cue.

The end behavior should look like this:

Trainer: touch!
Dog: bobs and touches, bobs and touches, bobs and touches
Trainer: clicks and reinforces
Trainer: releases with okay!

Since the multiple nose touches create repeated targeting, use your "okay" release. You don't want a nose touch without bobbing because it takes away your dog's ability to counter-balance.

Once you have the nose targeting behavior on cue, calculate your success rate. You want your dog to "touch" on cue at least 90% of the time in various locations before going to the next step. Depending on how many sessions you do per day, this will usually take a few days.

Next, begin playing the race-to-the-target game. Back your dog away from the target a few inches (don't move the target because your dog may not know where you put it) and cue her to touch. You want your dog to drive to the target from 15-20 feet away. Add distance a few inches at a time. As the distance increases, you may want to play the game so that the target is near a chair or other object so that it is easy for your dog to find it. To prevent the dog overshooting the target, place the target in front of a wall. Make sure your dog can touch her target on cue when she is in different environments and in distracting surroundings. Play proofing games and make sure she runs to the target even if you are standing still or running in the opposite direction.

Dogs often lie down while touching their nose to the target. If this occurs, ask yourself what your criteria are: lie down and nose touch the target simultaneously, or nose touch while standing?  Pick one and be consistent. Inconsistency is the enemy of learning.  While many dogs may be able to compensate for their trainers' inconsistencies, it is ideal to avoid confusion.

**The Position Game**
Once you have trained a superb nose touch to the Plexiglas target, take it to the A-frame.  Stand in front of your dog and place her on the A-frame so that her two front feet are on the ground, her two back feet are on the A-frame and roughly 2/3 of her body is on the A-frame. Place the target between her front legs so she can touch it when cued.  Cue her to "sit," click and reinforce that and then cue her to "touch" and click and reinforce again.  You are cueing the dog to sit because you are training a crouch.  Start with the dog in the front position and then move to the side, pictured below, once the dog has the idea of where the target is.  The next approximation is to stand behind the dog.

Zoomie is ready to be cued to touch his target. To make the game more fun I am restraining him from reaching for his target until I cue him.

Photo by Suzanne Rider

You can gently pick your dog up and place her on the contact, or you can ask her to jump up from the side. Whatever method you use, read your dog's body language and choose one that is fun to her.  If your dog dislikes being picked up you can either avoid doing it or teach her to enjoy it.  To countercondition her worry about being picked up, click and treat when you bend over her.  Then for reaching over her, then for picking her up only a half inch from the ground, and so on, until your dog thinks that being picked up is a fun game.  If your dog is too big to pick up, place a table next to the contact and ask her to jump on that and get on the contact from there.

Suzanne had Rev hop on the table and from there onto the contact to avoid having to pick him up.

Photo by Angelica Steinker

Okay, so you have your dog in the 2O2ONT position. Yippee!  Ignore any touches without rear lowered.  A touch is only clicked and reinforced if the rear is lowered at the same time.  The lowered rear will help ensure that you get the slide that you want.  If her rear is in the air and her back arched she is more likely to pop.  Sliding and popping are explained in detail below.

The dog should look like the one pictured below.

Keegan demonstrates a straight spine and beautiful nose touch position. Notice both the rear and head are lowered. That is exactly what you want to click and reinforce!

Photo by Allison Marsh

You are creating the ideal position that you ultimately want your dog to reach at the end of the A-frame.

*Curling Isn't Cute*
Curling occurs when the dog's front end is off to the side, not in alignment with her hips. Her spine is curved, rather than straight.

Photo by Suzanne Rider

Curling can be accidentally trained. The dog curls and the trainer doesn't notice and accidentally clicks and reinforces it. Riggs is curling both his hind end and his head toward the handler. His nose touch is not between his front feet — don't click and reinforce this.

215

Feeding your dog facing toward the trainer rather than with her head down and forward will also cause curling.  For training (consistency) and health reasons we don't want the dog to curl her spine.  Curling is not the behavior you originally started to train.  While we don't know for sure, agility trainers assume that a curled spine may pull muscles or otherwise injure the dog.  So keep your eyes peeled for curling and if you see it, remember, it isn't cute.  Click and reinforce your dog when her spine is straight.

*Dangling Leg Syndrome*
Another consideration while playing the position game is the location of the dog's hind legs.  Both hind legs need to be neatly tucked under the dog's body.  Both the dog walk and teeter are narrower than the A-frame.  You don't want to train dangling leg syndrome.  Medium or large sized dogs especially can have a problem holding their hind legs on the narrow dog walk or teeter boards and may allow one leg to slip off the plank and dangle.

This commonly happens if the dog's normal stride is wider than the board of the dog walk or teeter. It may not seem like a big deal for one leg to be dangling off the side of the plank, but keep in mind that any deviation from your desired behavior can cause the dog to become confused.

Photo by Suzanne Rider

It is easy to fix dangling leg syndrome by shaping its absence.  Don't click and reinforce your dog if her leg is dangling off the dog walk or teeter board.  You will need a second person to watch the dog's legs on the side opposite you.  If there is no second person available, consider using a prompt like a cone or other object to keep her from dangling a leg.  If you use a prompt, you will need

to fade it.  Move it away from the bottom of the contact a
few inches at a time.

**The Hold Game**
At this point, you have trained your dog to nose touch the
target repeatedly on the cue "touch."  You have introduced
her to the 2O2ONT position with her hind feet actually on
the A-frame and her rear lowered.  Now you are ready to
begin teaching your dog to hold the 2O2ONT position.

To teach the hold, play the fun proofing game you did for
the ground games sit and down.  Ask your dog a question.
Can you hold this position for one second while I move my
foot?  Can you hold the position while I bend over, or place
a toy on the ground?  Click and reinforce while your dog
holds her position.  She will quickly figure out that
maintaining the 2O2ONT position pays.  Ping-pong the
level of difficulty of the questions asked.  This will keep it
fun and interesting for her.  When playing the hold game,
deliver all reinforcement between the dog's two front legs
with her head down, so her spine is straight.  Feeding her
in proper position will strengthen the hold behavior.

*Okay Game*
Now that you and your dog know how to play the hold
game, you can play another game.  Whenever you are
ready to release your dog from the 2O2ONT position, say
"okay," click and toss your toy or food tube ahead of her as
hard and fast as you can.  This teaches your dog to blast
off the contact quickly.  Keep your reinforcement history of
hold and release balanced.  If you click and reinforce
holding and never click and reinforce releasing, you may
get a dog that does not want to release.  If you click and
reinforce only the release, you probably won't have a hold
for very long.  For most dogs, it is much more fun to run
than to hold a position.  If your dog is one of those,
reinforce holding more than releasing.  Releasing is its own
reinforcement for these dogs.

The release game also needs to be independent of your body position, so your dog releases on the verbal okay, not on body movement.  Here are some fun proofing games to make sure you and your dog are on the right track.  Can your dog hold the 2O2ONT position and *release* on okay as you run past her?  Can your dog hold the 2O2ONT position and *release* on okay and blast forward if you stand absolutely still behind her?

Both questions will be asked in the ring.  You may have to run ahead of your dog to a strategic position and release her while you are running.  Most of us are definitely behind our dogs as they go into position and we are still behind as we release our dogs.  We need to have verbal control of the release so our dogs aren't looking at us or self-releasing.

Some people worry that holding position is punishing to their dog.  My Border Collie Nicki agrees.  She hated holding position.  Many people told me to hold my Border Collie for a long time in the competition ring.  I did and with my long 3-4 second holds I saw my dog's motivation to do the contacts decline.  I had made a critical mistake.  I had not made training the hold fun, the fun was in the release.  If your dog does not enjoy the hold, make holding so much fun that she is begging you to play the game some more.  Be unpredictable.  Vary the length of your holds to keep the game fun and interesting for your dog.

**Proofing the Hold**
To proof your dog holding in 2O2ONT position, begin by asking the dog questions.  At first ask easy questions like, can you hold this position while I take a step away from you?  Gradually build up to harder questions until your dog can hold position while you run past her, stand behind her, sit on the floor, lie on the ground and anything else you can think of.

Make proofing exercises fun games that involve your body, toys, food, arousal and even your facial expressions.  If your dog can hold position during all five categories of proofing then you have an excellent chance of being successful in the competition ring.  Playing the proofing games at every stage of the contact training is important.  You can't be sure the behavior is really learned until you proof it.

*The Goal of Proofing the Hold*
Ultimately, while your dog holds the 2O2ONT position, you will need to be able to:

1. Run past your dog.
2. Run toward your dog.
3. Throw toys.
4. Toss food.
5. Stand in front of your dog.
6. Stand behind your dog.
7. Be laterally away from your dog.
8. Cue your dog to nose touch while you are standing 10-feet behind her.
9. Anything else you can think of that proves that your dog really truly understands the behavior and can do it regardless of what you are doing or where you are located.

When you have accomplished all this, you are ready to back the dog up to the first slat (or lower if you suspect popping tendencies; popping is explained in detail below).

**The Slide Game**
To get the ultimate contact performance, your dog's weight needs to shift back onto her rear end so that she slides into the 2O2ONT position.  If most of her weight is forward, she is more likely to become injured, or to pop the contact.

*Popping the Contact*

Popping is when a dog's center of gravity is so far forward that she either leaps from the down plank of the contact obstacle to the 2O2ONT position, or pops her front end forward off the base of the contact into position. I accidentally taught my Border Collie Nicki to pop by clicking and reinforcing for only her two front feet touching the ground without the nose touch. This created more of a jerking motion than a slide, not the ideal.

Notice that in the picture at left Turbo's hind legs are actually a few inches above the A-frame board. Turbo is built squarely (think cube). Because of this, it was more challenging to teach him to slide. A cube is more likely to tumble forward versus a rectangle which can more easily slide.

Photo by Suzanne Rider

Turbo's center of gravity is higher than a longer backed dog, so he tends to pop forward off the obstacle onto his front feet rather than slide his feet down to the ground even when his head is low. Dogs built like Turbo have a harder time getting into a crouch. Even when crouching, because he is so small, he still has to hop over the slats, which interferes with his ability to slide. Over time and with consistent training, Turbo has learned to stay low as he performs his 2O2ONT.

Some dogs are more than capable of shifting their weight back, but resist the process because of hip, knee or some other pain. These dogs commonly arch their backs to avoid putting the weight on their hind ends or will assume a frog leg position, splaying their legs out to the side.

This dog has severe hip dysplasia. You can see she carries a lot of her weight on her front legs. This dog also has difficulty bringing her rear under her when jumping. Most veterinary surgeons recommend that dogs with hip dysplasia continue to play agility to keep their muscles strong to help support the arthritic joint.

Photo by Tony Rider

Adjustments to training and common sense must be implemented when running a dog with hip dysplasia. If your dog resists the 2O2ONT position, explore the possibility of a physical problem.

*Sliding versus Popping*
To see if your dog is sliding versus popping, focus on the nose touch. Closely watch what your dog's nose is doing before it reaches the ground. If your dog's nose and front feet are not moving toward the ground in unison then she isn't sliding and is likely to pop, so withhold your click and reinforcement. Moving both legs together is also faster than stepping down one foot at a time. If your dog is truly sliding, you will see her front feet slide together down the contact before she reaches 2O2ONT position. The dog can't slide from higher up because she would jam her toes and injure herself. In addition, if she lowers her head for the nose touch too soon, she may tumble head over heels down the A-frame.

When backchaining, begin with the first slat (closest to the ground) and count slats up toward the apex.

Turbo's hind feet are below the second slat and his front feet are below the first slat.

Photo by Suzanne Rider

Going to large regional or national competitions will allow you to observe dogs performing the contact obstacles. To hone your observation skills watch a different body part for each ten dogs you watch. As the first ten dogs run past, observe the dog's nose during the entire contact obstacle performance. The next ten dogs, observe the right rear leg. Continue this game, until you have identified patterns of performance. Use this information to form your mental picture of how you want your dog to perform her 2O2ONT behavior.

*Preventing Popping*
To prevent your dog from popping, look for the dog's head and rear to be low as she goes into position. During the process of backchaining the contacts, ask the dog to sit before cueing her to "touch."

Photo by Suzanne Rider

Before cueing Payton to touch, Brenna makes sure that her rear is lowered by asking her to sit. Brenna is gently supporting Payton by her chest, as she cues "touch," Brenna will simultaneously remove her hand.

222

Click and reinforce only when both her rear and her nose are lowered into position.

When you begin to backchain the A-frame, physically place your dog on the A-frame only one or two inches above the ground. This will help prevent popping because there is less downward distance for your dog to travel. Progress slowly and be sure that her front feet and her nose are moving toward the ground together. Sounds tedious, but the result will be beautiful.

Performing the contacts with a 2O2ONT is not a natural behavior. My Border Collie Stevie naturally popped so I spent six months training him below the first slat making sure he was sliding not popping. It was worth it. Today every time he slides into position, it makes me smile.

Stevie, sliding on the teeter. I'm smiling, are you?

Photo by Spot Shots

The patience required to train the contacts to the highest level is significant. At a Kay Laurence seminar, Laurence explained that to teach a dog to 'passage' (a high stepping prance) takes about a year. My first thought was, "why would anyone take that long to train a behavior?" I then realized that my young Border Collie, at 16-months old, was still working 5-7 slats from the ground on all of his contacts. At a year and a half, he had never done an entire contact obstacle. Ultimately, he will have been trained for longer than a year before he ever does an entire contact obstacle. Contact training takes time, as passage training does, because the dog has to develop strength for the proper biomechanics.

To me the process of slowly training my dogs is not something that requires patience; it is self-reinforcing because every time my dog performs a contact I will have the joy of seeing my training just as I had visualized it.  To the obsessed, there is no more powerful reinforcement.

Breeds such as Border Collies are generally at an advantage when training a slide type 2O2ONT position.  Other breeds such as Corgis and Bully breeds may be too heavy-chested to use this method and running the contact may be a better option for them.  Very long-legged dogs, such as sighthounds, can learn the 2O2ONT position, but may not slide.  Get a videotape of a dog that is the same breed or type as yours performing at the speed and skill level that you desire.  Watch this videotape to get ideas for creating your own dog's personalized training plan.

If your dog is physically able to slide, but pops most of the time in training, try backchaining on a slatless teeter (like a regular teeter without slates) locked into place so it won't move.  By eliminating the slats, it is easier to get the dog to slide.  Once the sliding behavior is fully established on the teeter, go back to the A-frame and dog walk and proceed with your training plan.

You may have a gorgeous slide from below the first slat, but if you move the dog up to the third slat from the ground, your dog may stop sliding and start popping.  If this happens don't panic, just return to her success point and back up one-inch at a time.  And of course only click and reinforce sliding.

If at any point your dog starts to pop, withhold the click and reinforcement, and go back to half the distance to get sliding again.  Find your dog's success point and build on it.

**Slat Games**

You have backchained the A-frame below the first slat and reached the first slat.  Be sure your frame is set at 5-feet 6-inches.  Then set your dog's front feet on the first slat and ask her to find the 2O2ONT position by cueing, "touch".  Be patient and give her time to think as this is a challenging question.  When she finds the position click and reinforce.  If she doesn't, no big deal, just try again from half a slat off the ground and build from there.  Once you have her sliding to the target position from the first slat, begin all your proofing games again.  Then back up another slat or half slat.

As you move your dog up the individual A-frame slats, your opportunities for proofing your body position increase.  Take advantage of that.  One of the more challenging handler proofs is to walk in the opposite direction the dog is traveling, while the dog moves forward to the target position, pictured below.

All approximations will need to be done off both your left and right sides.  You can't be sure your dog understands the behavior unless she can do it independent of your body position or movement.

Photo by Suzanne Rider

225

The handler needs the dog to find the 2O2ONT position while he stands at or moves around to all the various locations pictured in the diagram above. Changing handler positions, as shown above, is called moving "around the clock."

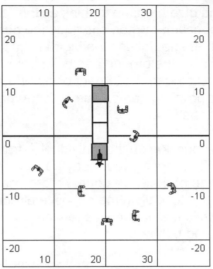

In this diagram, the handler positions are more challenging to the dog's ability to find and hold the 2O2ONT position. In addition to altering the location of the handler, the movement of the handler is also changed. Sit or lie on the ground, run and even pretend you are falling.

**Fading the Target Game**
When you reach the third slat, fade the target. To do this, ask your dog to "touch," click and reinforce when she does. As you reinforce your dog, use your other hand to pick up the target. Immediately ask her to touch again. When your dog touches the space where the target was, click and reinforce. Now you know why clear Plexiglas is the way to go, it is easy to fade. During the next few sessions, place the target in position at the beginning of the session, but after a few nose touches fade it again. Continue this game until the target is no longer necessary.

If you are having trouble getting speed, go back to playing race games to the target on the flat.  Make sure your dog can race to the target regardless of your position.  You want her to race to the target while you are running with her, standing still and not moving, moving backwards in the opposite direction the dog is traveling, at a lateral distance up to 30-feet, and to recall to the target.  Target games to play are:

- o   Race game to target with handler behind the dog.
- o   Race game with lateral distance between dog and handler.
- o   Handler standing next to the target in various positions.

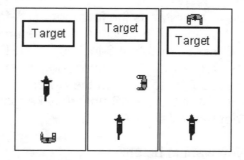

From left to right, sending your dog ahead to the target, cuing your dog to target and move past you to the target, and recalling your dog to the target.

*The Fourth Slat and Beyond*
The training process should now become a smooth routine.  Whenever you have 90% success, move one slat or half slat up until the dog is covering the entire downside of the A-frame.

*The Apex*
Backchaining always stops at the apex, because it is unsafe to place your dog on the up ramp and expect her to safely get to her target position.  Instead lower the A-frame to four feet tall.  Dogs started on a taller A-frame may jump

high onto it as if they are attempting to hurdle the entire obstacle. By starting lower you are setting the scene for more ideal striding instead.

Since you have played the proofing games and have the 2O2ONT behavior regardless of where your body position is, you will be able to quickly backchain your dog at this lower height from the first slat up until she reaches the apex again. When she does, ask her to perform the entire up side and then cue her to touch once she reaches the apex. Give her two chances to get the behavior, if she doesn't get it, go back to backchaining. Proof and take your body out of the behavior. If she is successful, click, go nuts and throw a reinforcement party for her.

Once your dog understands the four foot tall A-frame, begin raising the apex a few inches at a time until you reach 5-feet 6-inches or 6-feet 3-inches. In USDAA, United States Dog Agility Association, dogs that jump over 16-inches are required to perform the A-frame with the apex at the height of 6'3". AKC uniformly keeps the A-frame at 5-feet 6-inches.

Ultimately, you want to be able to:

- o   Send your dog to the touch position while standing 10-feet behind the A-frame.
- o   Recall her to the touch position while you stand 10-feet in front of the bottom of the A-frame.
- o   Have her "touch" while you run alongside the A-frame and past her as she slides into position.
- o   Have her "touch" and hold while you are out of her sight.
- o   Ask her to "touch" while you throw toys.
- o   Ask her to "touch" while you toss food.
- o   See if she can "touch" while you do jumping jacks.
- o   Cue her to "touch" when you have her cranked up to her highest arousal level.

A-frame performance depends on your competition goals. Top agility competitor Kathy Keats says that nationally competitive times for an A-frame are around 1.5 to 1.7 seconds.  This means from the moment your dog hits the A-frame to the moment she slides into the 2O2ONT position will take around 1.5 to 1.7 seconds.  A world class A-frame performance will be around 1.2 to 1.4 seconds. For small dogs, any A-frame performance under 1.7 seconds would be considered very good.  The surface the dog is running on and the approach angle will affect the dog's speed over the A-frame, so your dog's time for the A-frame will vary.

If you are new to agility and these times seem blazing fast, don't worry, be happy.  Most dogs in North America perform their A-frames much slower than these top times. Your dog does not need to complete the A-frame in less than two seconds to qualify or to make standard course time.  A four-second A-frame is competitive and will enable you to have lots of fun!

*Proofing Games for the A-frame*
Here are some ideas for A-frame proofing.  Can your dog do the A-frame if:

- o   You run past the contact like a screaming maniac.
- o   You run and stop short while your dog completes the contact.
- o   You stand still behind your dog while she does the contact.
- o   Other dogs are running loose.
- o   Toys are flying all around.
- o   Your friend is rolling a ball in the grass near the down side of the contact.
- o   Food is lying all over the floor.
- o   You trip and fall.

Proofing games will always be part of your training so make them fun for both you and your dog!

*Take Time*
Training the A-frame is a lengthy process. Taking your time to get the behavior with the right attitude will be worth it. A rough estimate of the time it will take is one month per slat with daily sessions. There are many variables: the dog, the number of sessions and the precision of your training. If your dog shows a lack of interest in the contact training games, shorten your sessions and go to every other day or even less. Keeping it fun for the dog is the most important part of any training.

*Dog Walk and Teeter Prep Games*
The dog walk and teeter have narrower planks than the A-frame. Your dog will need to be aware of her hind feet and be able to travel in a straight line to stay on the narrower boards and avoid falling off. Teaching your dog the cavaletti games, back game and turn on the forehand games will help her be aware of her hind feet. Cavaletti games are described in the jumping chapter and the back, turn on the forehand and side stepping are explained in the ground games chapter.

*Training the Dog Walk*
You can begin training the dog walk soon after you start backward chaining the A-frame. Since both you and your dog are now familiar with the basics for training the A-frame, backchaining the dog walk will be easier.

*Position Game*
So the games begin again, starting with the position game. Once your dog has generalized the 2O2ONT position to the downside of the dog walk, proceed to the hold games and then to the slat games. Use your target and once you get consistent nose touches fade it. Place your dog below the first slat and ask her to touch. As with the A-frame, require your dog to slide into position.

Change your body positions.  This obstacle will be the most difficult to proof for the handler's body position, because it is the longest of the obstacles.  Take your time with this process.  Be sure to work lots of sending to the 2O2ONT position.  At every approximation, play proofing games.  Have fun, training your dog is the best part of your day.

Back up a slat, or half slat, only when you have the speed, accuracy and the 2O2ONT position that you want.  Attitude is everything.  This process seems tedious, but it is exciting to watch your dog learn and slowly create the exact behavior you want.

*Top Speed for the Dog Walk*
Kathy Keats says that any dog walk performance around 1.5 to 1.6 seconds is world class.  Nationally competitive dog walk performances are around 1.8 to 2.2 seconds.  For small dogs, any dog walk under three seconds is very good.  A four to six second dog walk will be fast enough to make time (run the course in the time the judge allowed), have fun and qualify.

*Training the Teeter*
The teeter is the smallest of the three contact obstacles yet it can present big training challenges.  For one, the teeter MOVES!  Imagine running down a sidewalk to suddenly discover it's moving under you.  As if this horrific experience were not enough, the movement is accompanied by a loud BANG, followed by a short rebound.  Most of us would rather have our teeth drilled than to run down that sidewalk.

To avoid creating teeter problems, train each part of the teeter separately before asking your dog to do the entire obstacle.

Resist the temptation to rush or pressure your dog in the process of learning the teeter.  This one obstacle requires your dog to learn more things than any other obstacle. Your dog will need to adjust to:

- o   Height.
- o   Balancing on the plank while it moves.
- o   Noise.
- o   Shifting her center of gravity.
- o   The force of the board hitting the ground.
- o   The board rebounding after it hits the ground.
- o   The variable speed with which each teeter tips (every teeter is a little different.)

Ultimately, you want your dog to confidently run past the teeter's pivot point, ride the plank down and slide into position.  First see it in your mind, then train it, then see your own dog do it.  For a trainer, one of the best reinforcements is seeing the result of your training in real life just as you had envisioned it.

At every step of the training process, progress only when your dog is running through the movement of the teeter without hesitation to the 2O2ONT position.  Hesitation indicates a lack of confidence.

There are several effective methods for getting a dog to run past the pivot point.  One makes use of placing a jump bar under the teeter to prevent it from pivoting.  I prefer allowing the dog to experience the pivot using an adjustable teeter.

This teeter is on the lowest setting, allowing the dog to experience almost imperceptible movement.

Photo by Suzanne Rider

232

*The Buja Board Game*
The Buja Board, invented by clicker trainer Brenda Buja, is a brilliant training approximation for the teeter. All you need is a two-foot square piece of plywood, a tennis ball, a sock and a staple gun. Place the ball inside the sock and staple gun the sock to the center of the board. Turn it over and place the board on the ground with the ball underneath. The ball unbalances the board so it tips and moves just like the teeter.

Use this mini-teeter to teach your dog and even your puppy that movement under her feet is fun. Shape your dog to walk across and eventually run across the Buja Board and click and reinforce.

The young puppy at left already loves the Buja Board as it has been associated with lots of food and fun games. The trainer is using her foot to manipulate the board so that it wobbles even more.

Photo by Angelica Steinker

Karen Pryor suggests to get your dog over the fear of the movement of the Buja Board by asking your dog to bark or perform a favorite trick while she is on the board. This method helps shift the dog's attitude from worried to fun! One of my clients, Sharon Loftly, taught her Corgi Bernard lefts and rights on the Buja Board. This game was very successful in teaching Bernard to love movement and the teeter ended up being his favorite obstacle. Another option is to play tug with your dog while she is on the Buja Board.

If your dog is too fearful to touch the Buja Board, play with her near it. Gradually play closer and closer to the board. Remember that getting on the board has to be the dog's choice, otherwise you are not teaching the dog confidence. You need to find your dog's success point, and build on it.

Use the Buja Board to help your dog accept the rebound effect the teeter has when it hits the ground. Have your dog run across it and simultaneously manipulate the board with one foot to make it bounce a second smaller bounce. Click and reinforce confident responses. If the dog is fearful of this game, go back to just playing near the Buja Board, then build up to having the dog on it and then back to playing the rebound game.

*The Bang Noise Game*
To teach your dog that the bang of the teeter is fun, use classical conditioning. Pair the noise with something your dog really likes. If your dog is food motivated, bang the teeter and feed her. If your dog is toy obsessed, bang the teeter and play with her.

Some dogs, especially herding breeds, can be noise sensitive. These dogs may require very light initial bangs of the teeter. To soften the bang, place towels underneath the upside and downside of the teeter. Pair the soft bang with food or toys. Gradually build up to louder bangs by unfolding the towels until they are completely faded. Eventually, even a loud bang will signal good stuff to your dog.

Pots and pans can be great agility training tools. Banging on a pot and then feeding your dog dinner can be a great way to teach her that loud bangs are nothing to fear. Gauge what your dog can handle and work within her comfort zone. If your dog is very afraid of loud noises, or has thunderstorm phobia proceed very slowly. If you accidentally frighten her, stop and next time pair special reinforcers, like steak, with a quieter bang game. Gradually exposing a dog to her fears is a better approach than flooding. Flooding is when the dog is forced to confront her fear, overwhelming her with anxiety with the trainer hoping the dog will be able to adjust.  Most of the time dog's can't adjust and flooding backfires.

Another great game is to have someone else bang the teeter while you play with your dog.  (Greg Derrett shows how to do this in his *"Agility Foundation Training"* video.)  Again, the process is a gradual one.  Start far enough away from the teeter so that your dog isn't afraid of the noise, gradually move closer as she habituates.  A fun variation is to increase the intensity of the tug game, as you get closer to the banging teeter.  According to Pam Reid, a dog is capable of eating food and still being afraid, but play is much less compatible with fear.

You can also record the banging noise of various teeters and play the recording at home while your dog eats or plays.  Begin playing the recording at a very low volume and gradually build up over many weeks to higher volume settings.

Musical freestyle trainer Carolyn Scott has some great advice on working through stress.  If your dog is stressed by either the movement of the Buja Board or the noise of the teeter, keep her moving!  A dog is less likely to feel stressed when moving, usually a stressed dog moves slowly or stops moving all together.

*The Real Thing*
After your dog is comfortable with the movement of the Buja Board and the bang noises of the teeter, you are ready for the next step, backchain the teeter without any movement or bang noises.  Adjust the teeter so it is flat on the ground.  Place your dog on the downside of the teeter, and play your 2O2ONT position and hold games.

Next, move your dog back to the first slat or equivalent if you have a slatless teeter.  Once you reach the beginning of the teeter, raise the height of the teeter one chain link at a time.  Most adjustable teeters have chains that allow you to adjust the height.  Don't proceed to the next chain link until your dog is supremely confident at the current height. Each time you raise the teeter height by one chain link, start the backchaining process over.

Once your dog is fully accustomed to the movement of the full sized teeter, and has a 90% success rate, begin varying the pivot point.  Adjust the height or duct tape sand bags to the bottom side of the teeterboard; this will allow control of when the teeter tips.  Your dog must be accustomed to a variety of tipping points, because every teeter is different.

Play proofing games to be sure that your dog's 2O2ONT position is straight and that she will release on "okay". Then you can begin raising criteria to gain speed.

Rev blasting over the teeter and into position.

Photo by Tony Rider

*Speed Teeter*
In Kathy Keats' opinion, a nationally competitive teeter is under 1.0 second, though very good teeters are anything up to 1.5 seconds.  Dogs that weigh less than 10 pounds will have slower times, depending on how fast the teeter tips.  Any time under 2.5 seconds would be considered very good for small dogs.  The speed of the teeter performance will also depend on the ground surface the dog is running on and the approach angle to the teeter.  If

your dog performs the teeter anywhere from 3 seconds to 4 seconds, you are doing great and will have lots of fun. To speed up your dog's teeter performance play the extreme teeter game. Rev your dog up and ask her to do the teeter. To quicken the drop, gently hit the board with your hand as she runs along it. Play this game with caution, use common sense and highly valued reinforcers. Adjust the pressure you are using to tip the teeter according to the dog you are working with. The idea is to over prepare your dog for an extremely fast individual teeter and eliminate any concerns about the teeter's movement. The goal is to avoid problems, not create them!

Angelica leans forward and hits the board of the teeter to make it drop faster as part of extreme teeter training.

Photo by Suzanne Rider

Another way to get and maintain speed on the teeter is to periodically return to backchaining the last part of the teeter. This will help remind your dog that the "sweet spot" is the 2O2ONT position.

*The Best Teeter You Can Train*
Train the teeter to the highest level. You can be completely confident that your dog understands how to perform the teeter when:

- o You can send your dog the full length of the teeter without moving and she performs the teeter quickly driving into and holding the 2O2ONT position.

- o You can stand still and recall your dog the full length of the teeter.  Your dog performs the teeter quickly, goes into and holds position.
- o You can be laterally at least 10-feet away from your dog while she performs the teeter, goes into and holds position.

Depending on your goals, work up to a distance of 30-feet between dog and handler on all contact obstacles.  The ADCH title (agility dog championship) from USDAA requires your dog to perform contact obstacles, as part of sequences, from 30-feet away.  This distance training includes sending, recalling and lateral distance off both sides of your body.

**Contact Obstacle Proofing Games**
Make it a habit to play proofing games with one of the contact obstacles on a monthly basis.  Every three months each contact obstacle will be proofed, which helps maintain your training.  January is A-frame month, February is dog walk month, March is teeter month and then April is back to the A-frame for the next cycle.

Use the checklist below for proofing ideas.  Your dog must be able to perform all the contact obstacles, get into position and hold the position even if you:

- o Are running past her.
- o Ask your dog to perform all three contact obstacles three times in a row without clicking and reinforcing.
- o Are doing Jumping Jacks.
- o Move slowly or not at all.
- o Run next to the contact and suddenly stop.
- o Increase your lateral distance (moving parallel to your dog.)
- o Decrease your lateral distance by converging toward your dog (while moving parallel to her.)
- o Move away at a sharp angle.
- o Throw food tubes or toys.

- o   Wave a toy in your hand while your dog performs the obstacle and goes into position.
- o   Leave toys lying around at the end of the contact.
- o   Put a tunnel right in front of the end of a contact.

Use a sheet of paper to create your own proofing ideas.  If you teach classes, you can host "proofing parties" during which each student creates a distraction for classmates.

**Click Speed Over the Contact Obstacles**
Once you have trained the contact obstacles to the level described above and you have proofed your dog's performance, you can play some fun games to help her gain speed.

I asked behavior analyst Jesús Rosales-Ruiz what he thought of games that rev the dog up before asking for a behavior.  Some trainers think that these games are a dangerous form of prompting, dangerous because these people fear the behavior will become dependent on the revving.  Jesús said that ideally cues and prompts are given in a way that is "fun to the dog."  I loved this response.  Agility is a game we play with our dogs, and if your dog likes it when you shout your cues, shout them from mountaintops.  "Whatever the dog thinks is fun" is the best training advice I ever received.

Rhonda Carter recommends two fun games to increase speed on the contact obstacles.  The first is called the flyball start game.  Flyball is a dog relay race game that gets dogs very excited.  One of the fun components of the game is the dog is restrained before her turn to dash out to the box.  Since you have already played the restrained recall game, your dog should get excited when restrained by someone while you walk or run away from her.
Transfer this game to the contact obstacles.  Have a friend hold your dog while you lead out, all the while revving her up with your voice.  On your contact obstacle cue, your friend releases the dog.  She flies over the obstacle and

races into the 2O2ONT position.  Click her for getting into
position, dash in to reinforce and very quickly release with
"okay."

The second game that Carter recommends is the target-to-
target game.  This game creates anticipation of a fun
release to a toy, so the dog rushes to get into the 2O2ONT
position.  To play the game, place a toy 20-feet from the
bottom of the contact obstacle and ask your dog to perform
the obstacle.  The moment she drives into the 2O2ONT
position, release her with "okay," and send her to the toy.
Vary your click point during this game, sometimes click for
a fast 2O2ONT position, feed in position and release the
dog to the second target, the toy.  Other times when your
dog completes the obstacle and is in the 2O2ONT position,
say "okay," click a fast release and send the dog to the toy
and play.

Photos by Suzanne Rider

**What Part Was Excellent?**
You can also use your clicker to communicate exactly
which part of the contact obstacle was performed in an
excellent way.  If your dog has a rocket approach to the
dog walk, click it, then reinforce when she gets into her
2O2ONT position.  Likewise, you can click the dog for
jumping the apex of the A-frame, and then reinforce when
she gets into the 2O2ONT position.

**What If?**
What if your dog does not get into the 2O2ONT position?
Stop and think about why.  Did you present your dog with a
challenge she was not ready for?  Is a tunnel suddenly
stuffed under the A-frame, and your dog has never seen
that before?  Are you in a different environment from
usual?  Different equipment?  Evaluate what may have
caused her to not get into the 2O2ONTposition and make
changes in your training program to proof the problem.

Any behavior that is not reinforced will eventually
extinguish, unless of course it is self-reinforcing.  Stopping
at the bottom of a contact is not self-reinforcing to most
dogs.  This means that as long as you want to maintain the
2O2ONT position you will need to periodically reinforce it.

**Reactive Dogs and the 2O2ONT Position**
If a dog is very reactive (impulsive and prone to doing
everything quickly) it is a good idea to ask her to hold the
2O2ONT position for a few seconds in the competition ring
for about the first year of trialing.  This will help cement the
2O2ONT position criteria in a trial environment.  If your dog
is the thinking type or not extremely motivated to run
agility, don't ask her to hold position for two seconds in the
ring.  It is likely to be a motivation killer.

Consider that holding still is punishing for most active
dogs.  A dog that wants to move and run is not happy
about staying still.  Offset this by bringing lots of
reinforcement to the 2O2ONT position.  Verbally praise
your dog for it in the ring.  And remember to ping-pong the
duration of the hold, so that she is not always anticipating
a long boring wait.

**Converting 2O2ONT Into a Running Contact**
After the first year of 2O2ONT performance, you can opt to
release the dog as soon as she is in the yellow.  Many top
competitors use this early release to get a very competitive
contact obstacle performance.  However, this early release

is not consistent with the criteria you created.  It can lead to slow creeping contacts because it is no longer clear to the dog what you want.  It can also lead to a 'leave when you want' behavior.  These dogs sometimes choose to leave the obstacle *before* the yellow contact zone.  Converting the 2O2ONT to a running contact comes with some risk, so consider it carefully before doing it.

**Contact Obstacles in Competition**
Competition can change us.  The quiet subdued handler gets frantic.  The frantic handler becomes quiet, and so on.  To our dogs with our demeanor everything changes.

*The Alien*
Consider that once you go into the competition ring, your facial expression and everything about you may change.  The fact that you are being watched, judged and that you want to do well may cause you to behave differently.  Your dog will know it, and have her own stress about experiencing the "real" thing.  No matter how hard you try to make training like competition, and competition like day-to-day training, it will be different for both of you when you step into that ring for the first time.  Your dog will read the stress in your body language, smell your stress and think you've turned into an alien.  Whether your dog experiences stress will depend on her sensitivity or resilience.

You may suddenly get competitive and begin counting the seconds.  The temptation can be to let your criteria slide, to save time and maybe win.  Contact training is especially sensitive to the alien phenomenon.  In that competitive moment, the dog being 'almost in position' will be good enough.  You will be focusing on the next obstacle, relieved the current one has nearly been completed, and let a poor 2O2ONT position go.  If your dog shows confusion by slowly creeping down the contact, the alien will command you, "release her the moment she creeps into the yellow."  Alien takeovers endanger your training.  Nothing affects training more negatively than letting criteria slide in the competition ring.  Rare dogs may compensate for their handlers and perform correctly anyway, but most dogs' behaviors will degrade if the trainer is not consistent nearly 100% of the time.

Beware of the alien!  Prepare for ring pressures ahead of time.  Familiarize yourself with writings on sport psychology and gather information from your past.  In previous competitive circumstances, did you want to win?  In the past, how have you responded to being judged?  Understanding your own personality and its response to competition stress will help you prepare so that you can keep your alien transformation in check!

Quiet moments, like Candace and Henri are having, can help you stay centered and prevent alien takeovers!

Photo by Pet Action Shots

*What Face to Wear?*
If your dog is sensitive to your facial expressions, be prepared to make that part of your proofing games.  Use clicker training to teach your dog that you are especially fun when you wear the 'don't mess with me face.'

Observe the facial expressions top competitors wear when they are competing.  For some it is a serious intense expression, for others a smile.  They wear this mask when they train and compete.  This is the expression their dog is accustomed to seeing.  If you look intense when you train and in the ring, your expression doesn't change so it can't cause problems.

## Time Out
If an otherwise consistent dog (90% or higher success rate) misses the 2O2ONT position at a trial consider timing her out (taking the dog out of the ring) for not going into position or self-releasing.  This means that you stop your agility run and take the dog out of the ring.  Not an easy thing to do for most agility addicts.  Time outs should be used sparingly if at all.  Excellent training focuses on minimal errors while the dog is learning and doesn't make use of time out.  Before using time out, explore physical causes for both not going into position or holding.  If you don't have at least 90% 2O2ONT performances in the competition ring, your dog needs more training, not a time out.

## Maintenance Training for Your Contacts
When training, vary the length of time you have your dog hold her 2O2ONT position.  Don't over-control by asking her to hold for too long.  This may cause her to lose attitude.  From the dog's perspective, why rush to the 2O2ONT position if you are going to be held there for a long time?  Alternate quick releases with holds of varying duration.  Keep her guessing.  It is all part of the game!  This is where the art of training comes into play.  The length of time that you ask your dog to hold the 2O2ONT position will depend on the dog's desire to do agility, her ability to withstand a long hold without losing motivation and the reinforcement history that you have created for the behavior.

Half or more of your dog's agility runs will include contact obstacles.  Your training of these three obstacles will be with you for the span of your dog's agility career.  The patience, consistency and time you put into your contact training will be well worth the effort.

# Chapter 8 Click!  Jump Training

Jumping is one of the most important skills you will teach your agility dog.  Without any training, dogs jump on and off the furniture while they zoom around the house, but dogs don't naturally know how to jump well.  For agility, we want our dogs to clear a variety of jumps and to do it consistently, efficiently, quickly and safely.  This takes training.  If you have a young dog only play the cavaletti games.  Once your dog's growth plates have closed you can start jump training.

Help your dog learn how to jump by designing a jumping program specifically for her.  The program described here combines the ideas of Julie Daniels and Chris Zink, authors of *Jumping from A-Z: Teaching Your Dog to Soar*, jumping seminar presenter Susan Salo, world-class agility competitors Pati Hatfield-Mah, Stuart Mah, Rhonda Carter and all the dogs I have learned from.  A most helpful book regarding canine striding and structure is the book *Dogsteps: A New Look* by Rachel Page Elliott.  What teaches a dog to jump effectively is a matter of debate.  One jumping expert will argue one strategy and another will argue the opposite.  Probably both are correct, ideally with all training the method used depends on the dog.

Most of the obstacles on an agility course require jumping, yet of all the agility behaviors, jumping usually receives the least training.  One knocked bar can eliminate you from qualifying, so teaching your dog to jump properly is well worth the time.

Many factors, including vision and physical health, influence your dog's ability to jump.  My dog Turbo is blind in his right eye, so he has no depth perception.  This is a handicap for him when jumping, especially when turning to the right.  If your dog consistently knocks bars or has other persistent difficulties when jumping, check with vets who specialize in orthopedic issues, soft tissue, canine athletes

245

and a veterinary ophthalmologist to rule out a physical problem, rather than assuming it is a training issue.

If a dog suddenly starts refusing jumps, or shows resistance to jumping, assume it is a physical problem. Common genetic and physical problems that can cause jumping issues are elbow dysplasia, hip dysplasia, vision problems, back or shoulder problems, luxating patellas, cruciate ligaments, soft tissue injuries and more.

**What Influences a Dog's Ability to Jump?**
A critical factor in jumping is the dog's structure and flexibility.  If a dog has a powerful rear structure but a weak front structure, this will influence her ability to jump.  Such a dog would have the rear strength to jump, but her front end may not create enough lift to consistently clear bars. Dog's front legs are not attached to the body by a joint, but rather with soft tissue only.  A dog landing on a weak front is probably more likely to develop front-end lameness. Likewise, a dog that is stiff through her spine will have a less athletic jumping style; she will be both unable to round her back, which skilled jumping requires and curl her spine to the left and right which is necessary for tight turns. While some dogs learn to compensate for poor structure, well-built dogs usually have fewer challenges.  Short-legged dogs have a tendency to knock bars because they often lack the physical leverage to create enough lift to arc over jumps.  Instead, they jump flat, taking the bars as a result.

**Words of Caution**
Jumping can be dangerous.  Dogs don't have a shoulder joint, so the strain that jumping puts on the front end is great.  Other than weaving, jumping is probably the most strenuous exercise for them.  If your dog slows down, or shows any signs of tiring please stop jump training — ideally, *before* your dog tires.

If your dog is less than 18 months old, save jump training until she's older. Because young dogs have open growth plates in their joints, vets recommend setting jumps no higher than their pastern height until these plates are closed. A dog's pastern, located on the lower front leg, is roughly the equivalent of your ankle. For a medium-sized dog, this generally means jumping the dog at eight inches.

Resist the temptation to use methods that force your dog into a correct jumping position. Placing jumps next to walls to force rounding, using spiked bars, or weighted bars and other such methods can endanger your dog physically and mentally. Staying focused on win/win training will keep you both happy and healthy.

**Introducing Your Dog to the Jump Obstacles**
Before you start jump training, familiarize your dog with all of the jump obstacles. Here are photos and descriptions of the different types of jumps:

Single bar jump. Most of the jumps on an agility course are single bar jumps. The jump has a bar going across the ground and a bar set at the height the dog is jumping.

Photos by Suzanne Rider

Double bar jump. A jump that has two parallel bars, requiring the dog to jump both high and wide. It has no ground bar. A third bar is placed diagonally as a visual cue to the dog.

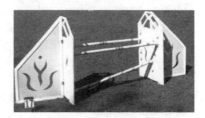

Panel jump. Appropriately named, this obstacle is comprised of panels rather than bars. The panels make it impossible for the dog to see what's on the other side.

Photos by Suzanne Rider

Triple bar jump. A spread hurdle jump that requires the dog to jump both high and wide. It has no ground bar.

Broad jump. Made of wood or PVC panels, this obstacle requires the dog to jump long rather than high. This obstacle used to be rare, but it is very popular in Europe.

With an increased emphasis on international competition in the agility community, it is being used in North America more often.

One bar jump. This jump does not have a ground bar to connect the two uprights. This presents a special challenge for the dog to visually assess her take off point.

Many judges are designing jumpers courses using mostly one bar jumps.

Winged jumps. These jumps have wings made of wood or PVC material attached to jump uprights. This means that the handler cannot run directly next to the dog. Some wings are small, others huge and for a small dog they can present a challenge, since they force the dog to run at a greater distance from the handler. The double, triple and one bar jumps pictured above are winged jumps.

Non-winged jumps. These jumps don't have wings attached to the uprights. They can be harder for a dog to see, especially when traveling at speed.

Jumps can be decorated in unique ways. At agility trials, jumps may have flowers, banners or cameras connected to them. It is important that your dog is familiar with various objects attached to jumps so that she will be unfazed in competition.

Tire jump. A metal or PVC frame holds a "tire" made of PVC tubing. For this jump, it is particularly important to expose your dog to a variety of approach angles because the circular shape of the tire can appear as an oval when approached at an angle.

Photo by Suzanne Rider

Shape your dog to approach and investigate each of these obstacles. Teach her to hop over the bar on the ground by using the 'go' cue (described in the ground games chapter). Raise criteria by adding a variety of approach angles, and if your dog's growth plates are closed, the bar can be raised one notch at a time until your dog's competition jump height has been reached. At each jump height, play the approach angle game so that your dog learns to negotiate the obstacle from various angles.

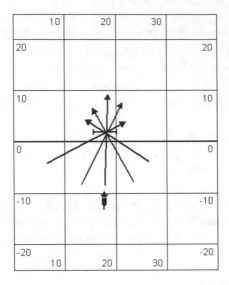

This diagram shows the around the clock game. Teaching your dog various approach angles off both sides of your body is critical. For each jump obstacle, teach your dog to send to, recall over, and work laterally away from you. Be sure your dog can perform the obstacle even if you are not right next to her and independently of what your body is doing.

**Click Commitment**
While playing around the clock with the various jumps, click your dog for committing to the obstacle. This means, clicking when the dog has two feet over the bar and is clearly taking it. Deliver your food or toy reinforcement on the landing side of the jump.

Turbo is committed to this jump. His two front feet are in the air and his two hind feet are pushing off the ground.

Photo by Suzanne Rider

After clicking the commitment point, toss your food tube or toy to the other side to support your dog's forward motion.

**Strides**

Jumping itself isn't the important part of your dog's training, striding is. Striding helps your dog reach the ideal take off point. From the ideal take off point, executing the jump is easy. To be a skilled jumper, your dog needs to either extend (elongate), or collect (shorten) her gait in order to reach an ideal take off point. Teaching a dog to jump is about teaching the dog stride regulation — how to extend and shorten her stride.

Although you will be using your clicker, at no time will you click for bars staying up. The bar won't learn, no matter how many times you click it! Be clear in your mind what *behavior approximation* you are training, i.e. what *behavior* you will be clicking. Once a dog is hanging in the air over a jump, the startle response the clicker creates may cause knocked bars. Consider clicking and reinforcing for ideal striding, rather than clicking while your dog is in mid-air.

A stride is one complete cycle of movement. Dogs have four types of gait. The different gaits are walk, trot, canter and gallop. The slowest gait is a walk. The walk is a four-beat gait, meaning each of the dog's four paws hits the ground individually. Rachel Page Elliott describes the walk as "a slow gait with a regular beat in which the limbs move laterally — left hind, left fore, right hind, right fore." Once this cycle is complete, one stride has occurred.

Riggs is walking, three legs are making contact with the ground one leg is lifted.

Photo by Suzanne Rider

The second, faster, gait is the trot.  It is a two-beat gait, during which the dog alternately moves the left front and the right rear and the right front and left rear in unison; so that two paws hit the ground simultaneously.  This is the type of gait used with show dogs in the conformation ring to help the judge appraise the dog's structure. Conformation judges use the trot to evaluate structure because this symmetrical gait is ideal for observing smoothness of movement, balance and soundness.

Riggs is trotting.

Photo by Suzanne Rider

Turbo cantering, lots of lifting of his front legs.  His gait is influenced by his breed and structure.

Photo by Angelica Steinker

The third gait is the canter.  It is a three-beat gait, which is faster than the walk and trot.  One stride at the canter consists of one leg moving individually then two legs moving together and then one leg moving individually again.  Hence it is three beat.  At the canter, one rear leg hits the ground, the second rear leg and one front leg hit the ground together and finally the remaining front leg makes contact.

If the dog runs faster, the canter becomes a four-beat gait called the gallop.  The gallop is an extended form of the canter.  Each hind leg hits individually, followed by each front leg, creating a four beat gait.

Photo by Suzanne Rider

When a dog is cantering or galloping, one of the dog's two front feet will be leading.  At the canter, if the dog is traveling to the left, the left front leg is usually the lead leg.  If traveling to the right, then the right front leg usually leads.  The dog is said to be on the "right lead" or on the "left lead."

Photo by Suzanne Rider

Riggs on the right lead.

Your ground cues, left and right, prompt your dog to change leads.  In the handling chapter, you will learn handling moves that will cause lead changes and that can manipulate striding.  It is important to understand leads and lead changes for course strategizing.  You don't want to cause your dog to change leads while jumping since it can cause a knocked bar.  Instead, you can use your handling moves to help her change leads on the flat between obstacles.

For agility, the canter and the gallop are the important gaits.  You want your dog to run the course at a canter or gallop, not the trot or walk.  To accomplish this, your dog needs to learn to extend and collect the canter stride. In between "extended" and "collected" is your dog's normal stride. If the judge has not allowed a lot of room between two obstacles your dog may need to collect her normal stride to reach her ideal take off point. If she needs to cover a relatively long distance quickly, she may need to extend her normal stride.

The normal stride will vary from dog to dog. Some dogs naturally collect their stride, other dogs naturally extend. If a dog tends to collect, she may look like she is traveling fast on course while actually not covering much ground. My Jack Russell Moose was like this. He ran as hard as he could and when his time was posted, it was never terribly impressive. His stride was very short so he had to do a lot of striding to cover the same distance as a longer striding dog in his jump height. Moose never learned to extend his stride to cover more ground. Moose and I were blissfully ignorant of his striding problem.

Rachel Page Elliott comments that for a dog to jump well the most important things are "good proportion which will lend to a supple back, which in turn will enable a strong thrust from the dog's rear." She recommends "strong pasterns (the same as human wrists) and thick pads" to reduce the shock of sudden impact. For a top performance dog, she emphasizes the importance of a "firmly muscled" and "flexible back."

**Gait Variations**
The cross canter, which refers to a dog cantering on one lead with the two front legs while on the opposite lead with the hind legs, is considered a normal gait in dogs.

Riggs is cantering on the left lead with his two front legs and his hind legs are on the right lead, this is called a cross canter.

Photo by Suzanne Rider

Cross cantering will not interfere with the dog's ability to perform agility.

Another variation is the counter canter, which is when a dog traveling to the left canters on the right lead or vice versa.

Other variations of gait, such as pacing, may be a sign of a physical problem. Pacing is when a dog's regular four beat walking gait becomes two-sided, the dog moving right front and right hind forward in unison, followed by both the left front and left hind. According to Elliott, this type of gait can be a sign of back or knee problems.

Skipping or bunny hopping are gait variations that can also be a sign of a physical problem. At the canter, if you notice your dog sporadically hopping on one or the other hind leg, this may be a sign of knee issues. A dog hopping with both hind legs simultaneously may have a hip problem. These problems are mostly genetic and unfortunately more common than many people realize. See a veterinarian with a special interest in orthopedics and soft tissue if you notice anything unusual in your dog's gait.

**The Goal of Jump Training**
A dog that jumps seamlessly at the canter will maneuver her legs in a way that make her movements seem effortless. This dog will gently push off her front legs to lift her upper body into the air, and then shift her entire weight to her hind legs as she lifts off. Powerfully pushing off the

255

hind legs to arc over the jump, she then lands on her front feet.  To watch a skillful dog jump is a thing of beauty.

**Potential Challenges**
Below is a list of what the dog does when jumping:

- o   She is required to transition from a three-beat canter or gallop to the foot placement that jumping requires.
- o   She has to gauge if the jump is both tall and wide, just tall or just wide and make decisions accordingly.
- o   She has to pay attention to which lead she is on and what lead she will land on.
- o   She needs to perfectly time her moment of take off.
- o   She needs to adjust for different types of footing, lighting, spacing between obstacles and approach angles to the jumps.

This is why dogs that consistently jump well are called "brilliant."  These dogs truly are brilliant in their ability to assess and adjust for various situations.

**Striding at Top Speed**
When your dog runs an agility course, the fastest way for her to navigate from one obstacle to another is to bounce. This means that your dog gathers herself up and uses one jump stride to clear obstacle #1 and then immediately pushes off and uses a second jump stride to clear obstacle #2.  Your dog jumps, lands and immediately jumps again without taking a ground stride in between.

Photos by Suzanne Rider

In coming!!! Zoomie almost ready to land.

The front feet are making contact.

He brings his rear under himself and immediately pushes off for the next jump.

A dog's ability to bounce depends on the length of her stride and the spacing of the obstacles. Usually fewer strides will equal a faster agility run.

Agility courses present us with the challenge of calculating where to add and where to subtract strides. Ideally, you may want your dog to add a stride in a certain location in order to save several strides later in the course. To play the game of adding and subtracting strides, your dog needs stride training. Before discussing how to teach your dog stride collection and extension, here are a few more terms to throw into the pot.

**Trajectory**

"Trajectory" refers to the dog's flight path from the moment she leaves the ground to the moment she lands. The pictures shown below illustrate the dog's trajectory.

This series of photos shows Payton completing a jump. If you draw a line of her path through the air that is her trajectory.

Photos by Suzanne Rider

The trajectory will depend on various factors. A dog traveling quickly will have a flatter trajectory than a dog jumping from a more collected stride. This is because the faster stride drives the dog forward, flattening the arc, a collected stride drives the dog up, raising the arc. A dog jumping an obstacle on the diagonal rather than straight-on will also have a longer trajectory (see diagram below).

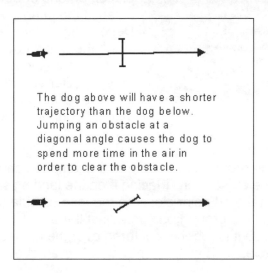

The dog above will have a shorter trajectory than the dog below. Jumping an obstacle at a diagonal angle causes the dog to spend more time in the air in order to clear the obstacle.

Chris Zink and Julie Daniels explain that the flat trajectory is actually the fastest. The flatter the trajectory, the more forward momentum the dog has. Of course, if the dog is too flat, she is likely to knock bars.

The ideal jump trajectory depends on the path the dog will be traveling on course. A twisty-turny segment will require more collection for efficient land and turn movements. Collection leads to rounder jump trajectories. A straight segment is ideally performed with flatter trajectories for optimum speed.

*Take off Where?*
Some dogs don't understand how to find an ideal take off spot to clear jumps. These dogs may consistently take off too soon or too late, or alternate. You can help a dog find a better take off spot by using ground bars. A ground bar is a jump bar placed on the ground in front of the jump, as pictured below.

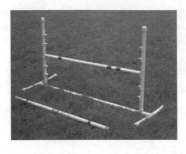

Ground bars can be placed on one or both sides of the jump. Depending on where you place them and how far they are from the jump, they will alter your dog's jumping causing her to take off sooner or later.

Photo by Suzanne Rider

Placing the ground bar in front of the jump will cause the dog to take off sooner. Placing it on the landing side will prompt a take off point closer to the take off side of the jump. Use the ground bars to adjust the arc of the trajectory so it is roughly centered over the highest point of the obstacle, such as Payton's arc pictured above.

Don't place a ground bar where you anticipate your dog will land or take off. Landing on or taking off from the top of a ground bar could injure your dog. Experimentation will tell you exactly where to place the ground bar. If the dog takes off early place the bar on the landing side, for a dog jumping 16-inches roughly 16-inches off the base of the jump on the landing side. If the dog takes off too close to the jump, place the bar as pictured above, using the same approximate formula of same distance as height.

The ground bars act as a prompt, however they are usually easy to fade because the act of jumping from a superior take off point will usually be self-reinforcing to the dog. It seems to feel better to dogs to jump from an ideal take off point than to struggle with incorrect take offs.

If a dog takes off too close to a jump, she will likely knock the bar with her front legs or chest. To help this dog shift her take off point to an earlier spot, place a ground bar in front of the jump, as pictured above, roughly the distance in front of the jump that the bar is set at in height. This formula is only approximate and will require tweaking. Some dogs may need more distance or less, experimentation will show you.  The ground bar works by giving the jump depth.  It turns the jump into an obstacle that is both high and wide, making it easier for the dog to gauge a better take off point.  Dogs that have a tendency to flatten or take off too close to the jump rarely knock the double or triple, because these obstacles give them information about height and width.  The ground bars provide the dog information that generally improves take off points.

If your dog is taking off too early and therefore landing too soon, knocking the jump bars with her hind feet, you can try placing a ground bar after the jump to help her adjust her take off point.  Video is an excellent tool to help you see how ground bar adjustments affect your dog's jumping. Playing the video back in slow motion will help you see exactly what your dog needs in order to reach a better take off spot.

*Over-Jumping*
It is common for some dogs to over-jump.  This means the dog's trajectory over the jump is far higher than necessary to clear the jump.  Generally, an over-jumping dog will lose to a more efficient jumper.  Another problem with over-jumping is that it uses more energy, which could be used to increase speed.  Last but not least, the over-jumping dog is straining her body with more wear and tear.

Suzy consistently over-jumps. Notice how high her front paws are in relation to the jump bar.

Photo by Tony Rider

Turbo consistently over-jumps because he is blind in one eye, causing him to lack depth perception.

Photo by Angelica Steinker

A dog that over-jumps may lack jump chute training to learn to jump more efficiently. A jump chute is a row of jumps spaced in a way that encourages the dog to bounce between jumps. Exposing an over-jumping dog to five minutes of daily jump chute work can help her adjust her take off point and modify over-jumping. A jump chute is a row of five or more jumps that ask the dog to jump land and immediately jump again. This helps dogs learn jumping rhythm and take off points. More to come on jump chutes!

*Crash!*
If your dog lacks conditioning, she will be more likely to crash jumps. If she is fit for jumping and still crashing jumps, a physical problem may be the cause. Jump chute work that gradually builds up the dog's strength is helpful. Dogs that naturally have a long powerful stride are more likely to crash jumps. These dogs usually have a hard time collecting or shortening their strides and find themselves right on top of the jump. They then crash through it with their front legs and/or chest. To teach these dogs to shorten their strides, work them in a jump chute set up to help them bounce. Very gradually, (only a few inches at a time) decrease the spacing between the jumps. Once they can shorten their stride the crashing subsides. This can take many months to years so take patience pills.

*Stutter Stepping*
Some dogs will very briefly shuffle their feet before taking a jump. This stutter step is hard on the dog's body, just as

over-jumping.  Every time the dog stutter steps, she loses her rhythm and momentum thus requiring more energy to fling herself over the next jump.  M. Christine Zink, D.V.M., Ph.D. and Julie Daniels, in *Jumping from A-Z: Teaching Your Dog to Soar*, state that if the stutter step comes on suddenly in an already trained dog, the problem is likely to be physical.  If the dog has always stutter stepped, playing the jump chute game at lower heights will help her gain confidence and begin to resolve the stutter step.  Once she is smooth and confident, raise the height of the very last bar of the jump chute one jump height.  As the dog succeeds gradually, raise the bar on the next jump one bar one jump height at a time, until all the bars are at the dog's full jump height.  Begin with the last bar, then next to last and so on.  Dogs usually jump the last jumps better than the first jumps of the jump chute, having gained momentum and rhythm.  Adjusting the last jump first you are setting her up for success.

**Body Awareness**
Back, turn on the forehand and side stepping (as described in the ground games chapter) are all helpful in jump training.  To jump well your dog must have an awareness of where all four of her feet are.  Generally the more awareness she has the better her jumping.

Kay Laurence recommends creating body awareness by shaping your dog to move one body part at a time, and then putting it on cue.  You can then stack these cues such as nose-paw, where your dog touches her front foot to her nose.

Photo by Suzanne Rider

If you do this with all four feet, your dog will have excellent awareness of where her feet are. You can also name head, ribs, hips, tail and ears. One of our trainers, Suzanne Rider, put ear movement on cue while her dog was relatively immobile after a series of surgeries. You can take the body awareness game further and shape your dog to touch her hip to an object, or to press her ribs against a wall and so on.

**Cavaletti Games**
The best way to prevent jumping problems is to gradually introduce your dog to jumping. A great way to do that is to play some games with cavaletti (a series of very low jumps that prompt the dog to high step or hop over them).

The cavaletti pictured were made by Sam Turner and allow for three heights.

Photo by Suzanne Rider

For small dogs, bars on the ground can be effective. For large and medium sized dogs, actual cavaletti are most useful.  No matter what you use, it must be something that the dog wants to step *over* rather than step *on*.

In horse jump-training cavaletti are used for months to prepare a horse for jumping.  They are also used during the off-season to keep the horse fit and supple.  It is a great idea to make cavaletti games part of your dog's maintenance training.

*How and What to Reinforce During Cavaletti and Jumping Games*
While playing cavaletti and jump games, click and reinforce your dog at various points of each of the exercises.  During the cavaletti games, click and reinforce for approaching the cavaletti, or for rhythmically striding over them but avoid clicking and reinforcing at the same point.  Click your dog and reinforce in the area of reinforcement for a nice rhythm at the third cavaletti, then the first, then the fourth.  Pick only one criterion per session but vary where you click for that criterion.  One session can be spent working on rhythm, the next on committing to jumps and yet another on striding between jumps.

Reinforce your dog in a way that supports the behavior.  For most cavaletti or jumping games, toss toys or a food tube ahead of your dog.  Ideally, click your dog when her head is facing the direction that she is moving.  You don't want to accidentally teach your dog to snap her head around looking for you or for the toss, causing the dog to tick cavaletti or knock bars.

Photo by Angelica Steinker

Notice how Blink is looking straight ahead as he completes the jump chute. This is exactly what you want. When playing cavaletti or jump chute games, your reinforcement delivery is delivered straight ahead of the dog to prompt looking straight ahead.

Begin by placing your cavaletti in a straight line with even spacing to prompt a normal trot. Play around with the spacing until you can find the exact distance that causes your dog to trot at her normal rhythm.

Photo by Angelica Steinker

Blink demonstrates gorgeous foot placement and rhythm while trotting the cavaletti.

Your goal is to have your dog trot rhythmically over the cavaletti with very little or no bar ticking (when a dog's foot makes contact with the pole). If your dog has good rear-leg awareness, very little ticking should occur. If your dog has poor rear-leg awareness, take extra time playing cavaletti games, shaping the absence of the bar ticking behavior. Click your dog for not ticking and reinforce after the last cavaletti. The behavior of not ticking will increase, until your dog is able to do the entire set of cavaletti without ticking.

If you are not able to get your dog to stop ticking on five cavaletti, start with two. Gradually add one cavaletti at a time to raise criteria, until you have reached five. Alternately, take a break from cavaletti games, and focus on some of the other exercises, while your dog matures to a less gangly stage of her development. Either way when your dog has accomplished the straight cavaletti with no ticking 90% of the time, you are ready for the next step.

Space the cavaletti out until your dog is cantering over them. You want one stride over each cavaletti, with the dog bouncing between. Continue this game until you hear little or no ticking. Click and reinforce the dog for bouncing and keeping a nice rhythm. Usually this can be accomplished in a few sessions of a dozen repetitions.

Use differential reinforcement of incompatible behavior (DRI) to shape the absence of bar ticking. DRI means you click and reinforce a behavior that is incompatible with the behavior you are trying to eliminate. To eliminate bar ticking, click and reinforce the dog for rhythmic striding without ticking.

Now the fun can really start! Begin spacing out the cavaletti to help your dog learn how to extend her natural canter stride. If the dog is small, move the cavaletti a few inches at a time and if the dog is medium or large, six-inches at a time.

Photo by Angelica Steinker

Blink cantering over the cavaletti, notice that the spacing has been increased.

To teach your dog to collect her stride, adjust the cavaletti back to the spacing that creates your dog's normal canter stride, and then gradually start shortening the distance between the cavaletti until your dog is collecting her stride. For a small dog, move the cavaletti only an inch at a time. For medium and large sized dogs, three to six-inches is a good starting point.  Look for 90% success before going on to the next step.

Your dog has learned that she can adjust her striding to be longer and shorter.  To extend, lengthening the stride and collect, shortening the stride.  At this point, you are ready for the next game.

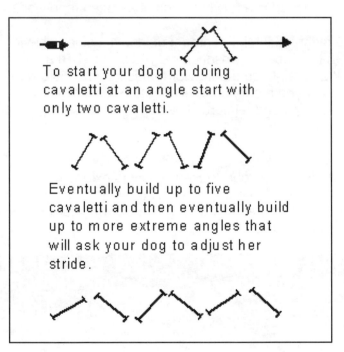

To start your dog on doing cavaletti at an angle start with only two cavaletti.

Eventually build up to five cavaletti and then eventually build up to more extreme angles that will ask your dog to adjust her stride.

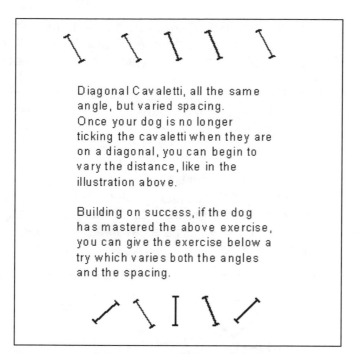

Diagonal Cavaletti, all the same angle, but varied spacing.
Once your dog is no longer ticking the cavaletti when they are on a diagonal, you can begin to vary the distance, like in the illustration above.

Building on success, if the dog has mastered the above exercise, you can give the exercise below a try which varies both the angles and the spacing.

Now that your dog has mastered a straight line of cavaletti at various angles, you can play with your body position and see how your dog responds to your movement. Some reactive dogs are sensitive to the handler's movements. Any fast movement of the handler triggers lots of ticking. If your dog ticks the cavaletti when you begin moving, gradually add your body movement. This will help desensitize your dog to your movement. Set your dog up for success. If adding movement causes ticking go back to the first cavaletti game and gradually build on success from there.

Proofing
Before going on to the next step be sure to evaluate whether your dog is able to play the cavaletti games when you:

   o   Recall her over the entire set of cavaletti. If you
       attempt this and the dog starts ticking, break it

down for her.  Recall over one cavaletti and then gradually build up from there.  Remember to click and reinforce your dog's rhythm when she is not ticking.

o   Send her over the entire set of cavaletti while you stand still.  Again, if the behavior falls apart just break it down for her by starting with one cavaletti and gradually adding one at a time.

o   Run full speed next to your dog while she performs the entire set of cavaletti.  To break this down, start with running only the last cavaletti, then the last two and so on.  Don't progress to the next step, until your dog is rarely ticking a cavaletti.  Click and reinforce success.

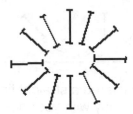

As with all the other cavaletti games, start with only two cavaletti and build up to the full circle in different sessions.

This set of cavaletti games will help prepare your dog for pinwheels, jumping and turning.  Pinwheels are usually groups of three or four jumps placed in a way that requires the dog to turn.  Pinwheels can be found on many courses.

Photo by Angelica Steinker

By placing wings on either side of the cavaletti, you can help your dog get used to winged jumps.

Once your dog confidently plays the cavaletti games, you are ready to move on to the next set of games.

**Jump Chute Games**
The jump chute is a line of jumps equally spaced and at a distance ideally suited for your dog to bounce between every jump. When a dog bounces she is learning the ideal way to jump and push off her rear.

The jump height can be one to two heights lower than what your dog jumps in competition, small dogs can jump bars on the ground. The idea is to teach your dog rhythm and striding. Backchain the jump chute by starting with two jumps. Once your dog is successful, include a third jump. Continue to backchain until your dog is performing the entire row of jumps. Then raise the jump bars, one jump height at a time, starting with the last jump and gradually working your way forward as your dog is successful.

As with the cavaletti games, jump chute games have many variations. Here are additional ideas for games to play.

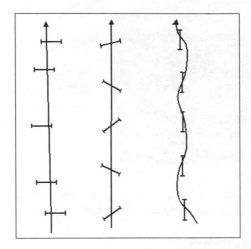

The jump chute on the left has varied spacing between the jumps and the jumps themselves are off set. Begin with one variation, either varied spacing or off set jumps. If your dog is successful combine them. By putting your dog through this jump chute, she learns to find straight lines even when they don't appear obvious. The jump chute in the center allows the dog to practice jumping on the diagonal. The last jump chute on the right is an extreme example of diagonal jumping, in this case one where your dog is working the jump chute as a serpentine. This jump chute game will teach your dog to identify serpentine patterns, which are very commonly used. In addition, it will teach her to jump on an extreme diagonal.

Once you have consistent success, you can further vary the jump chute games by varying the spacing between the jumps. The cavaletti games you played earlier taught the skill of collecting and extending, which you are now generalizing to the jump chute.

When you have completed the jump chute games, your dog should successfully:

1.  Be sent the entire length of the jump chute.

2. Do a recall down the entire length of the jump chute.
3. Perform the entire jump chute with you running next to her as fast as you can.
4. Perform the jump chute with varied spacing.
5. Perform the jump chute while you laterally move away from her.

*Sending*

To teach your dog a send down the entire jump chute is fun and easy. All you need is a toy that you can toss ahead of your dog, or a friend that tosses the toy for you. Starting with the last jump of the jump chute, place your dog in a stand at location A marked on the diagram below. Stand next to your dog, hand on chest, and tell her "okay, go" to send her over the jump. When she commits to the jump, two feet in the air, click and toss the toy to the area of reinforcement.

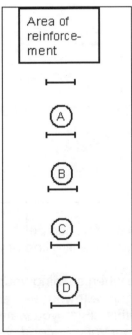

Do this for a few repetitions.  When your dog has a 90% success rate, back up another jump and send her over two (location B).  Click for the last jump and throw your toy to the area of reinforcement.  In this way, you are backchaining the jump chute, and eventually you will be able to send your dog down the entire length.  Avoid clicking for anything but the last jump as the dog may cut out and not complete the remaining jumps.  Repeat the same process off the other side of your body.

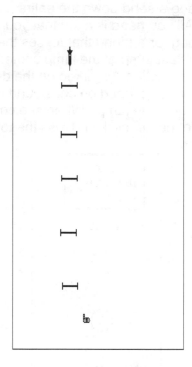

This diagram shows the finished behavior.  The handler has sent the dog over the entire line of jumps.

Be sure not to move when sending your dog forward, keep your feet still and signal with your arm and voice.  There are two reasons for this.  First, you want your dog to learn to move ahead without you.  Second, you want the dog to experience the jump chute without the distraction of your movements. Once the dog is consistently successful, you can gradually add your body movements.

*Recall*
In agility recalling your dog over a jump means that the dog will perform the jump toward the handler and then continue as directed. It does not mean that the dog will stop in front of the handler like in competition obedience. To recall your dog over the entire jump chute, employ the same backchaining method. Again, begin at the last jump. Put your dog in a sit, and walk to the other side of the jump, so that you and your dog are facing the same direction. Once the dog commits to the jump, click and toss your reinforcer in the direction she is moving. As before, toggle back and forth, working your dog off both sides of your body. When she is successful, back her up another jump.

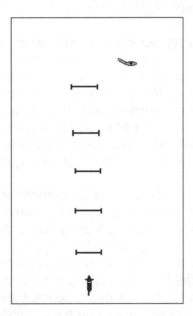

*Anticipation Problems*
While training the jump chute recall game, vary where you click and reinforce your dog. If your dog is reactive and does not want to maintain the sit, then click and reinforce

the sit, instead of clicking her for jumping.  If your dog is more laid back, click and reinforce her for releasing and jumping.  If your behavior chain breaks down, isolate the problem area, train it by itself and then gradually rebuild the chain.  If your dog bypasses a jump, click and reinforce for performing only that one jump, then go back and add a second jump, then a third until you have the entire jump chute rebuilt.

*Running With Your Dog*
Running alongside your dog is a lot of fun and, for most dogs, the easiest variation to teach.  Click and reinforce her for both successfully completing obstacles and for staying on the same side of your body.  Starting with the last jump again, add the other jumps one at a time.  Build on success until you have the dog jumping the jump chute as you run alongside, off both sides of your body.

Reactive dogs may get excited that you are running with them and bars may go flying.  Or she may lose rhythm and start ticking the bars.  If your dog drops bars as you run with her, but keeps the bars up on the send and recall, you have a movement sensitive dog.  Use habituation with tiny approximations to help her learn to keep the bars up.  Start with slow movements while she does one jump and increase to fast jerky movements, building on success.

As the reactive dog habituates, becomes familiar to your body movement and the bars stay up, slowly add jumps. The process will take time, possibly years, and you may find yourself competing while she continues to get used to your body movement.  Since jerky movements will cause knocked bars, the hidden blessing is that you will learn to be a smooth handler.   It is easier to deal with the frustration of knocked bars if you have another dog to compete with simultaneously.

**Jumping and Turning Games**
You have played straight-on jump chute games and diagonal jump chute games, it is time to raise criteria and add turns. Once your dog can successfully play the jump chute games in straight lines and is keeping the bars up at full height, move on to jumping exercises that require the dog to jump and turn at the same time. If the dog has trouble, lower the jump height. As the dog learns to adjust her striding raise the bars up to full height again.

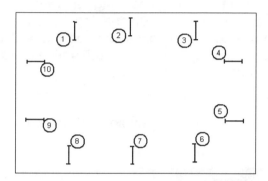

Rhonda Carter was the first person to introduce me to the concept of working jump chutes on curves. Above is an exercise that she recommends to teach a dog to jump and turn at the same time.

*Sidedness*
If your dog prefers to turn in one direction, this is probably an issue of sidedness. Just as humans prefer to write with either the left or right hand, dogs generally prefer turning in one direction. Ideally, your dog should be balanced in both directions. To accomplish this, work your dog twice as much in the direction that she prefers less. Eventually you will find that she is equally apt turning in both directions.

**Preparing for Competition**
By playing the games diagramed below, you are teaching your dog to jump while exposing her to common patterns of course design. You will have completed your jumping games foundation, when your dog is able to fluently

negotiate the sequences below with a variety of approach angles and spacing.  The majority of your dog's jump training should be at a height lower than her competition height, however, prior to competing be sure to expose your dog to all the games below at full competition height.

Regulation spacing in most agility venues is 15 to 18 feet between obstacles.  If the obstacle is a spread hurdle, the spacing is 21-feet on the approach side, to allow for extra room for an obstacle that is both high and wide.  Ideally, play most of these games with spacing that allows your dog to bounce, to ensure that she is rocking back on her rear.  Once bouncing is a strong habit, move on to spacing that is regulation for agility competitions.

*Pinwheel Game*
One of the most common groupings of jumps is a pinwheel.

To start an inexperienced dog on a pinwheel, break it down by backchaining the obstacles.

Photo by Suzanne Rider

To teach your dog a three-obstacle pinwheel, begin with the last jump.  Click and reinforce your dog for performing that jump.  Next, back her up so that she will take both the second and last jump of the pinwheel.  Click and reinforce the successful performance of the two jumps.  Finally add the first jump of the pinwheel, click when the dog commits to the third jump and reinforce after she safely lands.

While playing this game, vary where you click your dog.  Always reinforce after the last jump.  For instance, click the first jump then proceed with the last two, reinforcing after the third, or click and reinforce at the end of the pinwheel. By varying where you click the game is more interesting to the dog.  You are also teaching your dog the skill of working through the click, which is important since you don't want the click to end the sequence or chain.

Play this backchaining the pinwheel game at various jump heights and with different spacing between the jumps.  To work on your dog's jumping style, set the jumps at a distance that encourages her to bounce.

*270 Game*
A variation of the pinwheel game is the more advanced game of 270's.  270's are more advanced because they require the dog to perform two jumps as if they were a pin wheel, with one of the jumps (the center one) missing.

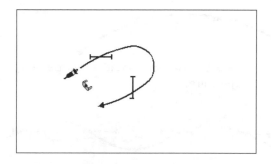

Teach your dog to efficiently wrap the 270.  As with the pinwheel, you can teach the 270 by backchaining the two obstacles.  270 training will not allow your dog to bounce. The objective is efficient wrapping.  Ultimately use differential reinforcement of excellent behavior (DRE) and only click and reinforce the fastest and tightest 270 performances.  Click the optimal path between the first and second jump and reinforce after the second jump.

As with the pinwheel game, begin with the jumps close together.  This will help set your dog up for success and prevent her from cutting in between the two jumps. Gradually spread out the spacing.  The final goal is to be able to handle the 270 at a distance.  At the highest level of competition, this will be required.  By making 270's part of your early jump training, your dog will understand how to recognize and efficiently complete 270's in competition.

*180's and Serpentine Games*
It is common for judges to use 180-degree turns and serpentines in their course design.  A serpentine is when the dog's path curves with two or more 180-degree turns.  Prepare your dog for these obstacle patterns by training 180's and serpentines.  This will help your dog recognize the serpentines and be able to accurately and quickly execute the obstacles.  As with the 270's, most dogs will not be able to bounce 180's and serpentines.

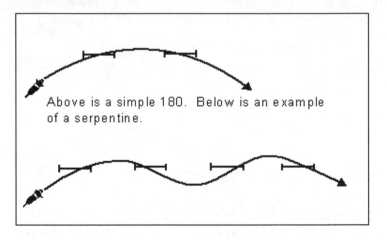

Above is a simple 180.  Below is an example of a serpentine.

Set the jumps in a way to familiarize your dog with both tightly spaced and competition spaced 180's and serpentines.  Note the optimal dog path: line with arrow.

While playing this game, your click and reinforcement points will vary depending on where your dog is having difficulty.  Put your click and reinforcement where your dog needs help.  As always, play these games off both sides of your body.

*Box Games*
Another popular obstacle constellation is a box pictured below left.

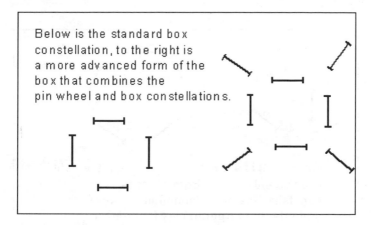

Below is the standard box constellation, to the right is a more advanced form of the box that combines the pin wheel and box constellations.

The box in the above diagram on the right was introduced to me by Elicia Calhoun. It is a fun exercise to use for both jump training (set jumps so that your dog will bounce) and for competition preparation (distance set at 15 to 18 feet). Both these set ups allow for a variety of dog path options, for weeks of fun training exercises.

Boxes can be in a variety of shapes, so it is a good idea to expose your dog to as many as you can think of.

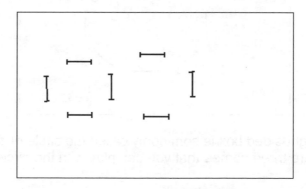

The double box above is a popular exercise used by Greg Derrett. Greg lists exercises that can be done with this set up on his foundation video tape series, listed in the appendix.

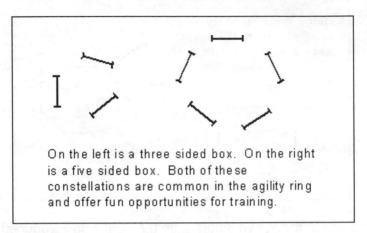

On the left is a three sided box. On the right is a five sided box. Both of these constellations are common in the agility ring and offer fun opportunities for training.

All of these exercises can be used to either practice jumping skills (bounce spacing) or use them to prepare your dog for common patterns she will see in the competition ring (15 to 18-foot spacing).

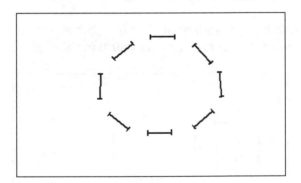

The eight-sided box is commonly called the circle of doom. Here are three games that you can play with the circle of doom.

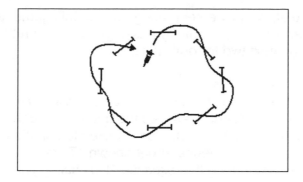

Pictured above is the classic circle of doom exercise.  The dog is asked to serpentine all the jumps on the circle.

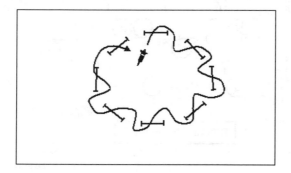

This variation of the circle of doom requires the dog to take the jumps only in one direction.

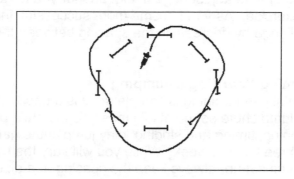

Pictured above is the keep out game.  In this game, the dog is asked to stay "out" by passing one jump and then taking the next two to "out" again.

**Fun Jumping Drills**
Rhonda Carter likes to set up the "S" exercise pictured below.  This sequence teaches the dog how to perform jumps with tight turns.  The dog is asked to complete the obstacles in the numerical order shown.  Take a patience pill before attempting this exercise, it is challenging.

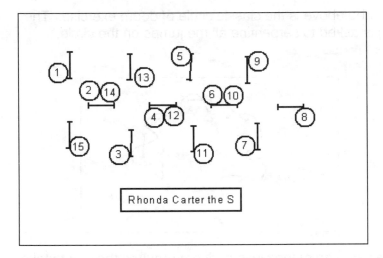

Rhonda Carter the S

In the beginning set up the S with wide spacing to allow your dog time to adjust her striding, and for you to get used to the exercise.  As you become more successful, increase the challenge by decreasing the spacing between the jumps.

**Maintaining Your Dog's Jumping**
After initial jump training is completed, it is a good idea to keep a jump chute set up at all times.  To maintain proper conditioning, timing and striding, play jump chute games two to three times a week.  While you will vary the type of jump chute set up, always keep the spacing at a distance that prompts bouncing.

Jump training guides your dog in the process of where to put her feet and when to take off.  It also exposes her to familiar patterns of obstacles, so that she can learn how to adjust her striding for common jump patterns.  Playing jumping games is reinforcing to the trainer too.  Every time your dog clears a bar you are reinforced for the time and effort you put into teaching her to jump properly!

If you play all the jumping games described, doing five-minute sessions once daily, it will take most dogs about three to six months to complete the program.  The actual time will depend on your dog's natural jumping ability, structure and training challenges you encounter.

# Chapter 9 Click!  Obstacles

During jump training, you exposed your dog to the individual jump obstacles, spread hurdles, broad jump, panel and tire.  The contact obstacles were covered in their own chapter, so that leaves the table, weave poles, tunnel and the chute.  Of these, the greatest training challenge can be the weave poles.  If the timing of your click is not perfect, it will be exposed by training weave poles.  And if your reinforcer delivery is not ideal, the poles are your best training partner, they will tell you how you are doing.

As with jumping, training each individual obstacle taking very small steps and playing proofing games before you do a sequence may seem tedious, but it truly is the most efficient way to train.  Resist the temptation to skip steps (self-control) and be reinforced every time you take your well-trained dog into the ring.

**Obstacles Training Checklist**
Be sure your dog can perform every obstacle you train under almost any circumstance.  The list below will help you verify that your dog knows how to complete each obstacle when highly aroused, with distractions and regardless of where you are positioned.  By training this way, it is highly likely that your dog will perform well in competition.

Use the list below to gauge when your dog has reached maintenance for fluent obstacle training:

1.  Performs obstacle on cue 90% of the time.
2.  Performs obstacle even when highly aroused.
3.  Sends to obstacle from 30-feet away.
4.  Recalls to you over the obstacle while you stand 30-feet ahead.
5.  Performs obstacle while handler is laterally 30-feet away from her.
6.  Performs obstacle while you rear cross.*

287

7.  Performs obstacle while you front cross.*
8.  Performs obstacle while you run next to her at full speed.
9.   Performs obstacle while her most tempting distraction is present (food, toy, etc.).
10. Performs obstacle from any approach angle off either side of your body (for safety, this is modified for the contact obstacles.)  This is the "around the clock" game.

*The rear cross is a handling move during which the handler crosses behind the dog.  The front cross is a handling move where the handler changes sides in front of the dog.  Both will be discussed in detail in the handling chapter.

**Sequencing**
Sequencing is performing two or more agility obstacles in a row.  Wait to sequence your dog until you have trained her obstacle performance to the level described in the above list.  Begin with two or three obstacles.  When your dog is consistently successful at two or three obstacle sequences, add one additional obstacle.  Expose your dog to simple straight-line sequences and twisty, turny obstacle sequences.  As long as the sequence is short and your rate of reinforcement is high, you and your dog will have a blast!

**Wrap!**
Your dog needs to develop the skill of turning tightly, because sequences can be complex with sharp changes of direction.  Rhonda Carter recommends that you teach your dog the game of wrapping a jump.  Wrapping means your dog jumps over the bar and immediately turns 180 degrees around the jump's vertical upright.  The goal is to have your dog wrap the jump's upright as tightly as possible.

Photos by Suzanne Rider

Angelica and Turbo performing the wrap game.  This game teaches the dog that tight turns are clicked and reinforced.

Think of this exercise as a U-turn.  You teach your dog to take the jump, wrap the upright, and speed back to you for a reinforcer.  Click and reinforce for the tightest wraps by using differential reinforcement of excellent behavior (DRE).

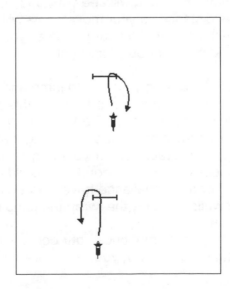

Begin the wrap game using a jump with the bar on the ground.  Sit your dog in front of a jump and release her with "okay – go," sending her over the bar on the ground.  Then direct her with your body to get the 180-degree turn back to you.  You can use your hand-targeting cue to bring your dog around the upright, if necessary.  To help your dog keep the turn tight you can rotate into her, performing a front cross.  If you are not familiar with this move, skip ahead to the handling chapter.  Calling your dog's name as she commits to the obstacle will also help turn her towards you and prompt a tighter turn.  This name calling exercise is a great timing game.  If you call the dog's name too early your dog will likely pull off the jump, click and reinforce your dog and try again.  If you are late calling her name and your dog is already jumping, you may cause the dog to knock the bar.  If this happens, cue the dog to come to you, deliver a reset cookie and try again.

Play this game off both sides of your body, wrapping your dog around both uprights.  Once your dog is doing well up close gradually build up sending distance.  Add a few inches at a time until she can be sent to wrap a jump from 20-30 feet away.  Your dog will see your body language even from this distance so your movements will be the same.  You will notice that the further away you are the harder it is to keep your dog's turn tight.

Proof wrapping by asking your dog to jump and wrap while you have toys lying around, but only begin this game when you have a solid "leave it" cue.  Start by placing just one toy far away from the jump.  Gradually bring that toy closer and closer until it is directly under your dog's feet.  Then repeat the process adding a second toy.  Build up to toys everywhere!  For a big challenge have your training partner throw the toy while you play the 'wrap the jump game.'

Add the cue "hup" or "jump" once your dog is fluent at the wrap jump game.  Ultimately, your dog will know when you

want a wrap and when you want her to move straight
because of your body language and the use of her name.
A front cross or pull turn (a turn during which both you and
your dog turn in the same direction) will signal wrapping
turns, whereas running straight will signal her to continue
moving straight.

Short easy-to-say cues are ideal.  You will be grateful for
this later when running a master's level course and need to
stack many cues on top of each other.

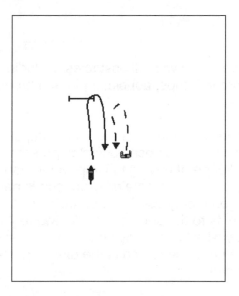

Above, the handler is turning into his dog, a front cross.
Alternately, the handler can also turn with the dog, a pull
turn, pictured in the diagram below.  Again, if you are not
familiar with the handling move, pull turn, skip ahead to the
handling chapter.

Play the wrap game with all obstacles, including the contacts, spread jumps, double, triple and broad jump.

**Big!**
Spread hurdles are double or triple-bar jumps, sometimes referred to as oxers.  These obstacles present your dog with the challenge of having to jump wider than with a regular single bar jump, so a different cue is needed.  The cue "big" is commonly used.  When training, click your dog as she commits to the spread (usually two feet in the air) and reinforce when she lands on the other side.  Tossing the reinforcement ahead and in the direction she is traveling is ideal.

**The Double**
Begin by setting the double to the lowest jump height usually four- or eight-inches.  Face your dog toward the jump from about five-feet away and cue her "okay - go."  Click her for committing to the double jump and reinforce after she lands.  When you have consistent success off both sides of your body and from various angles, raise the bars one notch.  Continue this process until you reach full jump height.

**The Triple**
The process of training the triple is the same as the double. The only difference is that you now have three bars to adjust instead of two. Since the triple is only slightly wider than the double, your dog should learn this obstacle quickly. Again, work both sides of your body and around the clock.

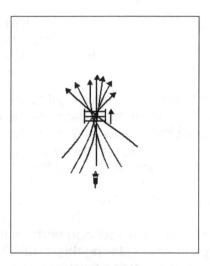

In addition to playing around the clock, remember to play send, recall and lateral distance games.

**Broad Jump**
When clicking your dog's performance of this obstacle, click and reinforce jumping the entire obstacle without any ticking or displacement of the boards. Some dogs try to step on the boards instead of jumping them. If this happens, lower your criteria. Begin with placing a single bar jump in between the uprights of a board jump as pictured below.

Photo by Suzanne Rider

A jump in the middle of the broad jump, can prompt jumping rather than stepping. Click and reinforce this jumping and gradually fade the single bar jump, by first lowering the jump bar, then removing the bar, then finally removing the uprights.

Dogs jump two times their jump height for the broad jump. So, if your dog normally jumps 12-inches the broad jump will be 24-inches wide. If your dog normally jumps 20-inches then the broad jump will be 40-inches wide. Of course, jump heights and widths vary for different organizations, so be sure to check the rulebooks. Gradually build up to the full width.

As with other jumps, have your dog perform the broad and wrap back to you. When playing this game, be sure to allow room for your dog to land. Wrapping your dog too tightly can cause broad jump ticking or panel displacement, which is faulted.

To avoid slicing the broad jump, set your dog up for a straight approach. Slicing is when your dog jumps at an angle, like when you play around the clock. The four corners of the broad jump are usually marked with displaceable corner markers, as shown below. If your dog slices this obstacle, she may actually end up taking it sideways, which would be faulted. See diagram below.

The view of the dog's ideal approach to the broad jump.

Photos by Suzanne Rider

The view of the side approach of the broad jump, it looks similar to the proper approach.  Teach your dog to take this one obstacle straight on and avoid around the clock training.

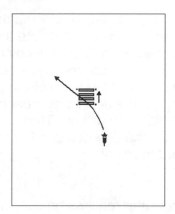

You will also be faulted if your dog passes between the first two corner markers at the front of the obstacle, but not between the last two on the back of the obstacle, as shown in the diagram above.

Unlike the other jumps, give your dog more distance to build up speed for the board jump.  Start training this obstacle by recalling your dog over it, then move to running with her and then finally sending once she understands the striding she needs to clear this obstacle.  As with the other jumps, add the cue once your dog is reliably performing the broad jump 90% of the time.

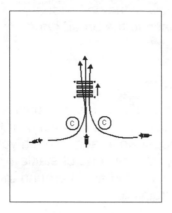

To teach your dog to take the broad jump straight-on rather than at an angle, shape your dog to run out around a cone. Then place the cones in front of the broad jump, as pictured (the circles labeled "C" represent cones).

When cued, your dog will run out to wrap the cone to create a straight approach and complete the broad jump at the appropriate angle.  Fade the cones by removing them after a few repetitions, but use the same body language and verbal cue as if the cones were still in place.  Click and reinforce your dog for the desired approaches.  Don't click and reinforce angled approaches.  Throw your dog's reinforcer forward in the direction she is traveling to encourage forward momentum.

**Panel Jump**
By itself, the panel jump requires no special training.  It looks a little different, and it never has wings attached, but nothing terribly intimidating to your dog.  However, depending on the size of your dog and her approach angle, part or all of the view of the *next* obstacle will be obstructed by the panel jump itself.  This means your dog needs to learn to quickly adjust for whatever follows, so spend extra time sequencing a variety of obstacles with the panel.  Especially tricky can be a challenging weave pole entrance after a panel jump.

**Tire**

The tire offers two challenges.  First, your dog must actually jump through the tire itself, not inside the frame that holds it.  Second, she must be able to jump the tire from various angles.  From straight on the tire looks like a round circle, however at an angle the shape changes to an oval.  This optical illusion can cause refusals.  Train with the goal of your dog doing the tire from any angle.

Photo by Todd Van Buren

To start, lower the tire as close to the ground as possible, usually at the eight-inch setting, sit your dog directly in front of it and stand beside her.  Release your dog "okay - go," click and reinforce for approaching the tire.  If possible, try to toss your reinforcer in a way that prompts your dog to pass through the tire.  Repeat but delay your click until you are actually clicking for going through the tire rather than just approaching.  During this process, your dog may run past the tire.  This is not a problem.  Don't click and reinforce.  You want your dog to learn that only passing through the tire earns a click and reinforcement.

Next, play the around the clock game.  Click just as your dog's torso is passing through the tire.  As usual, be sure that your dog knows how to perform the tire regardless of your location.  Sending your dog ahead of you and recalling her through the tire from various angles is particularly important because the opening appears to be an oval from an angled approach.

297

If your dog seems fearful of the tire, is reluctant to approach or frequently refuses, spend time playing some of her favorite games around it.  Transition to clicking and reinforcing your dog for approaching and staying close to the tire, and then shape the rest from there.

Another way to train the tire is to sit your dog close to the low tire, walk to the other side and recall her through the tire.  If your dog passes by the tire, no click and treat, if she passes through, click and reinforce.  Prompt her to pass through the hoop by using your hand target.  Once she has succeeded several times, fade the hand target.

Add the cue "tire" after your dog is confidently performing the tire 90% of the time.  Common cues for the tire are "hoop," "through" or "tire."  When working the tire click for your dog passing through the hoop, and then toss your toy or food tube to your dog's landing side.

**Table**
The table requires your dog to leap onto it and assume a position for five seconds until released.  You may need to train a table/sit *and* table/down (American Kennel Club), only a table/down (United States Dog Agility Association), a sit, down or stand (International competitions) or no table at all (North American Dog Agility Council).  Your dog needs to maintain the position (sit, down or stand) for the judges' count of "five-four-three-two-one-and-go."  It is important that your dog release off the table only when the judge has completed the count, including the "o" of the go.

Prepare for table training by training fast sits and downs on the flat.  When you have fast sits and downs on grass, and various other surfaces, begin to ask your dog for sits and downs on the table.  The ideal table performance requires your dog to leap on to the table and immediately sit or down, saving precious tenths of seconds.  Kathy Keats says that it should take a dog around .5 seconds to hit the table and lie down or sit.

If you don't have a table, use your bed or an ottoman as a mock table.  Table training can be tricky, because it is the only obstacle that requires 5 seconds of holding still.  All the other obstacles are action oriented.  For dogs that like to move, performing the table can be considered a form of punishment, because stopping isn't fun.  So make table training especially fun!  Lots of playing on the table is a great way to establish a reinforcement history with this obstacle.

Start by placing the tabletop on the ground.  Click and reinforce for approaching the tabletop, then for moving one foot on to the table, then two, and so on, until the entire dog is on the tabletop.  Even if your dog is not afraid of jumping onto raised surfaces, play this game anyway.  You are building reinforcement history.  The table is becoming a fun place to be.

Once your dog is happy to be on the table, only click and reinforce when she stays there.  If she jumps off, no big deal, just no click or reinforcement.  If she gets back on, click and reinforce.  Very quickly, your dog should realize that the fun starts when her feet stay on the table.  Clicking your dog for approaching the table can make for a nice surprise, and prevent the problem of slow approaches to the table.

Using fun games such as the race game (race your dog to the table) to train the table can also help build attitude for this obstacle.  Once your dog is consistently and happily getting on the table, begin adding height.  Start with the short legs and build up to the height that your dog will be required to perform.

When training the table, you are actually teaching your dog that the cue "table" means for her to:

*Run to the table as fast as she can.* — To teach this, use the "okay-go" game. Then shape speed of approach, clicking only fast approaches and tossing your reinforcer just past the table. You are not reinforcing on the table because you are training the approach. Begin this training after your dog is familiar with the table and has fast sits and downs on the flat.

*Jump on the table preparing to down.* — Training fast downs on the flat is the most important skill for training fast downs on the table. Once your dog downs fluently on various flat surfaces, ask her to hop on the table using the cue "go" and then cue "down." All reinforcements now occur on the table. If you are using food, click and feed while she is down. If you are using a toy, click while she is down, say "okay," and play on the table.

*Grip surface of the table to prevent sliding off, if necessary turning her body back in the direction she was coming from.* — Always click your dog for gripping the table and preventing herself from sliding off. This is part of teaching your dog to get on the table. Reinforce while she is on the table as this encourages her to stick to the table surface. (See table torquing exercise p. 317.)

*Hold this position regardless of whether the handler is moving or not.* — Since you have taught your dog that sit and down are duration behaviors and have proofed for your body movements, it should be easy to get her to hold a down on the table. To keep things interesting and unpredictable, vary the amount of time you require her to hold the down position. Balance your reinforcement history: if your dog doesn't enjoy holding still on the table, click and feed while your dog is in the down or sit position. The release will act as its own reinforcement. If your dog loves downing on the table, and is slow to get up, click and reinforce her for a fast release.

*Release on "okay" cue independent of the handler's location or movements.* — Since you practiced this for your start line duration sit, your dog should quickly generalize this behavior to the down on the table. Use food instead of toys because you don't want to pull your dog out of position. Click and reinforce while your dog stays down on the table.

*Explode off the table and proceed to the next obstacle.* — Training this is one of my favorite things. It's fun. Ask your dog to get on the table and lie down. When ready, release your dog with "okay" and blast a toy in the direction she is headed. Once the release is quick, alternate releasing and blasting the toy into the air with releasing your dog to another obstacle.

Sometimes click holding the down and feed while in the down position, sometimes click the release and toss the toy, and sometimes just send her on to the next obstacle. This variety makes training fun for both you and your dog.

Teach a default down on the table. One cue "table" signals the entire chain listed above. It is easy to teach table/down as one behavior, and then to cue your dog "table/sit" if you need a sit. If you cue "table/sit," your dog will adjust in mid air and sit on the table. Proofing games are especially important for the table. Dogs are more prone to notice noises or movement while on the table. Sporadic reinforcement for excellent table performances will help you maintain your table training.

Common cues for the table are "table" and "bench". Add the cue once you have the entire behavior chain fluently trained.

Photo by Spot Shots

Stevie is leaping on the table in a crouch so that he can land in a down, saving time.

*Don't Squish the Dog!*
If your dog does not want to down on the table, or holds her elbows up, avoid pressing down on her back to lower her body. This may hurt her, and the aversive effect of being pressed down will be associated with the table. That is something you definitely don't want to happen! Squishing your dog onto the table or yanking your dog down using a leash may "poison" your table cue/training. This means that the table becomes an icky place to be so the table or cue becomes aversive. This is the exact opposite of what you want. Train the down that you want on the flat. If you notice your dog lifting elbows, you have a doggie push up training challenge.

*The Doggie Push Up*
Some dogs will keep their elbows lifted off the table. Whether these dogs are interested in developing their pectoral muscles, or are anticipating the release is anyone's guess, either way it's a behavior that you don't want. Never click and reinforce a down with raised elbows. If your dog has this tendency, down training should center on your observation of her elbows. If she is small and it is hard to see if the elbows are touching, teach her to touch her chin to the table. This will be easy to see and will ensure she is fully down. Shape your dog to place her chin in your cupped hand, while she is standing, put this behavior on cue, "chin," and then stack the two cues, "down-chin." The chin cue is a duration behavior and your dog should not release from the chin cue until you say "okay." Once your dog has the idea of what you want,

302

transfer the behavior to the table.  Fade your hand by giving your verbal cue before presenting your cupped hand cue.  Click and reinforce the chin on table.

Riggs demonstrating a lowered head to be sure that his elbows are touching.  He has also rolled his hips to his left, which helps ensure a solid down.

Photo by Suzanne Rider

You can teach hip rolling by asking your dog to down, then placing your hand target by your dog's elbow, prompting a hip roll.  Click and reinforce the hip roll, when consistently getting the behavior, name it and fade the hand target.

While playing table games it may seem like a good idea to place food on the table, however this may prompt sniffing.  Remember food lures can be tricky to fade.

Placing food on the table for proofing is a good idea.  Just be sure to pick it up before offering it to your dog.  During training, food is only available to your dog if you place it into her mouth.  If necessary prevent your dog from eating the food by throwing yourself on it like a baseball player throws himself on home plate.  Just kidding — you weren't actually going to do that, were you?

*Slow Downs on the Table*
If you already taught your dog the table and accidentally trained a slow down, there is help!  Go back to training downs on the flat and find a way to get fast downs.  Suddenly cueing "down" while playing will often prompt a fluent response.  Use DRE and only click and reinforce fast responses.  Change to a new cue, which names the fast down rather than the old slow down.  When you are certain

that your dog will consistently drop like a sack of potatoes, take the new cue to the table.

*Table With or Without the Handler*
While doing all your table games, be sure to send, recall, and run with your dog from various approach angles. You want her to learn 'table', regardless of where you are positioned or how you are moving. While playing this game, put your click and reinforcement where your dog needs it the most. If your dog does not want to send, click and reinforce for the first step moving away from you. If your dog does not want to recall toward you and the table, click for tensing her muscles and stepping toward the table.

*Teaching Your Dog to Stick the Table*
A common fault seen in the agility ring is for a dog to hit the table at full speed wowing the crowd, only to dramatically skid across the top of the table and fall off the other side. The table is the only obstacle that requires your dog to put the brakes on by herself, especially at speed, and stick like Velcro.

Elicia Calhoun recommends playing the table torque game to improve sticking. To play this game, ask your dog to jump on the table and immediately rotate your upper body into her.

Photos by Suzanne Rider

Table torquing works, because your dog will follow your shoulders.  Your click point will be the moment when your dog torques, curling her body towards you to stop the forward momentum.  Then reinforce with either food or a game of tug, while your dog is still on the table.

Play the table torque game a few times off both your left and your right.  Now the fun can really start.  Place a jump 18-feet from the table.  Ask your dog to jump, then table and torque.  You are now adding speed into the mix.  If your dog is successful 90% of the time, add a second jump 18-feet away from the first.  Eventually you want your dog to be able to do the sequence below and stick the table.

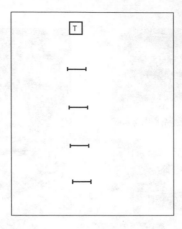

*Table Challenge*
To see if your dog really knows how to stick the table, lower the table at least one jump height from what your dog normally performs. The lower table will make sliding off easier because your dog's trajectory is flatter. Set up a speed line of four jumps to the table, and get ready to click and party when your dog sticks the table. If your dog is not able to meet the challenge, find her success point and back her up one foot at a time until you can include all four jumps. Build on success!

*Proofing the Table*
Wet the table with a hose and ask your dog to down on it. Agility is rain or shine, so it is important to proof for a wet table. For some lighter coated breeds, a cold table is an issue. Place a bag of ice on the table for a few minutes to chill the surface, then ask your dog to hop on the table, click and reinforce with 100% meat baby food or whatever else that your dog rates as a level 10 reinforcer. Build up to sit and then down, on the cold table.

Toys are a great proof for play-crazed dogs. Build up to kicking toys, and eventually tossing them while your dog continues to hold position on the table. Be sure to proof for toys flying through the air.

Proofing games are fun. Can your dog perform the table even with a food bowl on the table? How about four food bowls on the table or on the ground around it? Can your ball-crazed dog perform the table even while a ball rests on the table? How about ten balls lying in the grass all around the table? How about while you throw a ball as hard as you can? When you can say yes to all these questions, your dog is fully prepared to perform the table in the competition ring.

**Weave!**
The perfect weave pole performance begins with your dog racing away from the previous obstacle, full steam toward the weave pole entrance. Briefly adjusting her stride, she nails the entrance, and snakes through the 12 poles in two seconds. Her weaving style is tight to the poles (highly efficient) and her head is low and forward like an arrow. If she is a medium sized dog, her feet are reaching forward one at a time. If she is small, she efficiently hops through the poles one stride for each pole. If she's a very large dog, there will be a fast snaking motion of her entire body that enables her to quickly negotiate the poles.

Kathy Keats says that of all the obstacles, the weave poles are most influenced by the surface your dog is running on. Weaving on grass will consistently yield faster times than weaving on mats or carpet. Sharp approach angles will increase the amount of time your dog spends in the weave poles, because your dog has to turn to enter the poles and immediately dig in hard to wrap the third pole. Turning and digging in add time. World-class times for the weave poles are between 2.2 to 2.4 seconds for 12 poles on grass with a 21-inch gap between the poles. Nationally competitive weave times range from 2.5 to 2.8 seconds. For small dogs, anything under three seconds is very good. Weave pole times increase about 0.5 seconds depending on the surface, pole spacing and the approach angle to the obstacle.

There are many different ways to train the weave poles. Most of the methods can result in fabulous fast weaves. The method I use combines shaping with the channel method. If you are not confident shaping, you can still use this method because you are only shaping three poles.

*Weave Pole Prep Games*
The rough handling games are great for preparing dogs for poles banging against their face and body. Fast weaving dogs will collide with the poles. Be sure that your dog is physically tough enough to handle light slaps to the face, shoulders, side and rump. By making rough contact a game, your dog will assume pole contact is just part of the fun. I failed to do this with my first Border Collie Nicki and it really came back to haunt me. At one trial Nicki was particularly fast heading into the poles coming from a tunnel. She bumped into the first two poles as she was wrapping the entrance. She yelped and it took me months to get her to weave in a trial setting again. Nicki is a very soft dog and one collision (one trial learning) is all it took to convince her that all trial weave poles were evil. I was able to get her to weave again by gradually raising criteria in the ring. I would ask her to weave just the entrance. If she did, I said "yes" and sent her to the next obstacle as reinforcement. If Nicki had not found the next obstacle reinforcing, I would have taken her to different environments and matches and reinforced with a toy or food. Slowly I asked for more and more weaving until ultimately she was weaving again. This was a tough and expensive lesson because all the months I was rebuilding the behavior, she was not qualifying. But it was worth it, to this day she consistently weaves with gorgeous snaking and an intense attitude.

*Attitude is Everything*
Every dog is different. Some dogs don't like the poles when first introduced to them. They just want to run, have fun and not have to think! If your dog shows little interest in doing the weave pole training games, keep your training

time short and fun.  This will mean slow progress, but building and maintaining a good attitude toward the weave poles is worth it.

Focus on getting your dog's attitude before approaching the poles.  Play games next to the poles!  Your dog will think, "Wow, every time we go near these weird poles, great things happen."  Now you can begin your training.

*Shaping Three Poles*
Training the weaves can be more complex than training some of the other obstacles, so always make it a blast for both you and your dog.  To be successful, have a clear mental picture of what each part of your dog's body will be doing while she is weaving.  Observe the weaving style of dogs the same size and build as of your dog.  What are the head, neck, spine, front paws, rear paws and tail doing?

Weaving Observation Notes
Dog Type: Sheltie.
Jump height: 12-inches.
Head: the head is straight and facing the direction she is traveling.
Neck: the neck is mostly straight and pointing forward.
Some curving when entering and exiting the poles, depending on approach and exit angles.
Spine: alternately slightly curving toward the weave poles.
Body: low and forward.
Legs: two front legs reaching forward together as dog canters one stride per pole.
Front feet: front feet moving together, alternately reaching forward and pushing her body forward.
Rear feet: alternately reaching under the dog and pushing off so that they spring out behind the dog.
Tail: the dog uses the tail as a rudder to obtain balance for the low and forward motion; at times the dog uses her tail to push off the poles.

Now you have your mental picture.  You will refer to it frequently while training.  After every session ask yourself did my dog look like my mental picture?  If yes, great!  If no, evaluate what is off, and adjust accordingly.

When shaping your dog to do three poles, you want her to learn to approach the weaves to the *right* of the first pole (the pole will be on her left).  She will then slip between the first two poles, and snake past to the right of the second and to the left of the third pole.  Your dog's path when performing three poles is similar to the shape of macaroni.

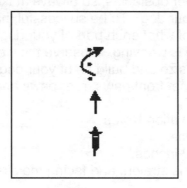

Your dog's path forms a "macaroni," while her head faces straight forward, in line with the poles.  While shaping the three poles, click, and reinforce with food.  Once you have achieved a 90% accuracy rate, switch to reinforcing with toys to increase speed.  Using the toy will increase speed because you can throw the toy ahead of your dog, teaching her to drive forward to the anticipated "area of reinforcement."

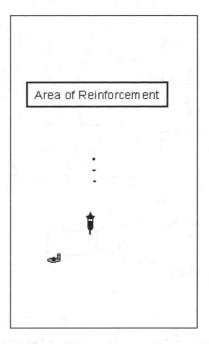

The goal of this training is to get your dog to weave three poles regardless of where you are standing or how you are moving.  Shaping allows you to accomplish this, because you are not prompting.  You are avoiding making the behavior dependent on how you are moving.

Below is a diagram of how the shaping process generally progresses.  During the first step, the trainer is clicking and reinforcing the approach to the poles.  In the second step, the trainer has raised criteria and requires the dog to pass between the first and second poles.  For the third step, the trainer requires a complete "macaroni."  During this process, the trainer only clicks the dog when her head is facing forward and then tosses the reinforcement forward.  The head stays straight even after the click because the click is immediately followed by the toss.

311

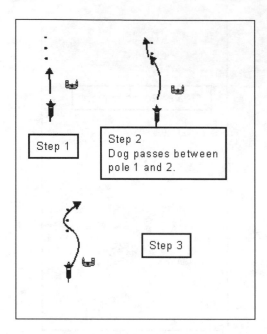

Step 1

Step 2
Dog passes between
pole 1 and 2.

Step 3

Your area of reinforcement will always be after the third pole.  This is important as you want the poles themselves to become cues to continue weaving.  As long as your dog sees another pole, no matter what else is going on, she continues to weave.

Be sure that your dog can recall, send through the three poles and do them off your left and right sides and with lateral distance.  You will only release with "okay-go." Don't use the weave cue yet.

Weaving is strenuous on dogs.  Vets recommend not weaving a dog until her growth plates are closed at approximately 14 to 18 months.  Therefore, if your dog is a puppy your training stops here until the plates are closed.

*No Popping Please*
Popping is the term used to describe the dog leaving the weave poles before completing all of them.  A dog that pops out of the poles in competition, will be faulted a refusal.  Many clicker trainers have allowed the click to end

the behavior rather than using the clicker as a marker signal.  As a result a dog that is clicked in the poles will pop out of the poles looking for her reinforcement.  By teaching a dog to pop out of the poles after a click a trainer is actually rehearsing an undesired behavior.

Once the process of shaping three poles is complete, your click spot will vary.  Sometimes click for the approach to the weaves, sometimes for the entry, sometimes for the third pole.  No matter where you click, your dog must continue to weave and only gets her reinforcement at the end of the three poles.  Teach your dog to work through the click by re-cueing her after you click.  "Okay - go" starts the macaroni, then click for the entrance and immediately say, "go," then reinforce at the end of the poles.  If your dog pops, withhold reinforcement, do a simple behavior like a hand target, click and reinforce for that and try again. At no time should the click end the weaving behavior. Weaving is a duration behavior, just like sit or down. Nothing should interrupt your dog's weaving.  The only thing that will signal that it is time to stop weaving is that there are no more poles.  Kay Laurence and others have been using the area of reinforcement technique for many years, and it has consistently proven successful.

*The Dog That Already Weaves*
If you click your dog for hitting the entrance of 12 poles, your dog should continue to weave the remaining ten poles and be reinforced in the area of reinforcement at the end of the poles.  If you have trained your dog to pop when you click in the poles, follow each click with the cue "weave" and then reinforce at the *end* of the poles.  Most clicker-savvy dogs can make the transition from popping to no popping in a few sessions.  My dogs were retrained within one to three sessions and were happy to keep weaving and get their reinforcer at the end of the 12 poles.

*Why No Popping?*
After learning that the click ends the behavior, my dog Stevie would stop weaving if I used a verbal bridge or he heard any noise resembling a click.  Once I switched to teaching Stevie and my other dogs to work through the click and toward the area of reinforcement, they didn't pop regardless of the noises they heard.  We have been able to duplicate these results with other dogs, so a new method was born.

*Backchaining the Remaining Weaves*
Once you have a three pole macaroni, you are ready to begin the channel weave game.  Channel weaves are specially constructed weaves that pull apart to form a channel.

Photos by Suzanne Rider

The channel weaves opened approximately the width of a medium sized dog.

The channel weaves close once training is complete.

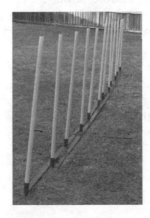

314

Set up the channel weaves so they are as wide as your
dog.  Use hand targeting to guide your dog between the
poles until she is by the 11$^{th}$ pole (second to last pole).
Cue her to "go," then click and reinforce for staying in the
channel until she passes the last pole.  Starting near the
last pole makes success easy and creates a high rate of
reinforcement.  Your dog should quickly catch on to the
idea that being in the channel is a cool thing!  As before,
use your area of reinforcement and toss your toy or food
tube ahead of her.

Once your dog is successful 90% of the time staying in the
channel from the 11$^{th}$ pole, place your dog by the 10$^{th}$ pole,
and then by the ninth, and so on.  Play these games off
both sides of your body, moving with your dog and
standing still.  In this way, you backchain the entire
channel until your dog is able to run the whole set off both
sides of your body and when you move with her or stand
still.

Now the fun can start!  When your dog reaches a 90%
success rate on the entire set of 12 poles, close up the
channel by an inch, or less if your dog is small.  Then
begin backchaining again.  Start at the 11$^{th}$ pole and click
for going forward to the 12$^{th}$ pole, then start the 10$^{th}$ pole,
the 9$^{th}$ and so on.  Work your dog off both sides of your
body.  Practice both moving with your dog and standing
still as she weaves.

Rev has graduated to poles
in a straight line.  Suzanne
uses her hand target cue to
place him at the eleventh
pole so he can be set up for
success.  Building on this,
she will back him up, two
poles at a time.

Photo by Angelica Steinker

315

Each time you complete backchaining the entire set at a
new width, play the fun game of restrained recall down the
center of the channel.  Then play the recall, send and
lateral distance games.  Your goal is to get the behavior of
running through the channel independent of where you are
standing or what side of the poles you are on.  Continue
closing the channel inch by inch proofing each time before
moving it in tighter, until the poles are in a straight line.

Photo by Angelica Steinker

The finished product: a restrained recall through the poles.
Rev, blasting away from Brenna, racing to catch up to
Suzanne.

*When to Add the Weave Cue?*
Add the cue "weave" when your dog is reliably weaving
(90% of the time) six or 12 poles at a good speed.  Don't
name the weave poles if your dog is going significantly
slower than what you want.  Compare your dog to your
mental picture.  If your dog is performing close to your
ideal mental picture, you are ready to name the behavior.

When your dog is able to do the entire set of 12 poles with
the channel completely closed, at the speed and with the
foot placement you want, begin your proofing games.
Don't play toy and food proofing games prior, because you
first must fade the prompt of the channel.  If you don't
rapidly close the channel, you may find your dog is unable
to progress.

316

*Channel Method Challenge*
Some dogs dart in and out of the channel cutting across
the "train tracks" that your dog is meant to run between.  If
this happens, lower your criteria by backchaining the
weave pole channel some more.  Click for being in the
channel and reinforce in the area of reinforcement.

*Around the Clock for Entries*
Use three poles to play the around the clock game with the
weaves.  Click for hitting the entry correctly (to the right of
the first pole) and then reinforce after the last pole.  Once
your dog is successful from various angles, begin adding
other obstacles before the three poles.

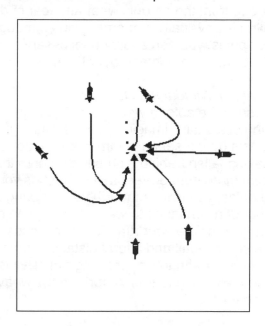

For a fast dog, a straight-on approach can be challenging.
Fast dogs usually don't like putting on the brakes to check
their stride in order to make the entrance, so they are
prone to flying past the entrance.  If your dog is fast, spend
extra time working straight-on entries.  Those entries are
very common at the lower levels of agility.  Another

challenging entry is the 90-degree approach angle.  It can be hard for a dog to decelerate and curl to make a 90-degree entrance.

Slightly less difficult are the 180-degree entrances, because it is usually easy to give dogs a straight approach to the poles, and since they were just turning, you don't have the issue with missing the entrance because of too much speed.

As with all the games, play around the clock off both sides of your body and click for correct approaches, entries or wraps around the second pole.  Then deliver the reinforcer at the end of the poles.  Use only three or four poles to keep your dog from the chronic wear and tear of doing all 12.  Weaving is physically demanding on your dog.  By using fewer poles, you can avoid unnecessary strain that may cause cumulative damage over time.

*Weaving With or Without the Handler*
Your dog should be able to weave when you are next to her or sitting in a chair.  Imagine you are running your dog and she blasts over a series of jumps and out of a straight tunnel.  Having fallen behind, you send her into the weaves from more than 30-feet away.  Just as your dog enters the poles, you trip.  Although you are lying on the ground, your dog continues to weave.  You jump back on your feet and complete your run.  Make this possible by playing the send, recall and lateral distance games off both sides of your body with lots of proofing fun.  By playing these games, your dog learns to perform the weave poles with or without you.

*Send Through the Poles*
Ask your dog to weave and as she approaches the eighth pole, slow down.  Continue slowing and eventually stop as she gets to the 11$^{th}$ pole.  Click for moving ahead of you, and throw your toy ahead of her.

Click as you slow down or stop to let your dog know she is right and to ensure that she continues to the area of reinforcement at the end of the poles.  As your dog learns this game, slow down and stop sooner and sooner until she can be sent through the entire set of poles!

Photo by Suzanne Rider

*Recall Through the Poles*
Begin with a set of six poles.  Stand at the third pole, and call your dog into the poles to weave.  When she reaches the third pole, begin moving with her and complete the rest of the poles together.

Click for performing the first three poles without you, but reinforce when all six poles are completed.  Whether you click for the first, second or third pole is up to you.  Back up one pole at a time until you are recalling your dog through all six poles.

Photo by Suzanne Rider

319

Repeat this process building up the number of poles until you reach twelve. Be sure to play this game off both sides of your body and with varied handler positions.

*Lateral Distance and the Poles*
To get lateral distance while your dog is weaving, use the same concept as was used for the send and recall. Ask your dog to weave and move with her until she reaches the eighth pole. At that point, gradually move away from her laterally. Click your dog for continuing to weave and reinforce after the last pole. Gradually peel off laterally sooner and sooner, until your dog sends from a distance and weaves all 12 poles while you maintain lateral distance.

Photo by Suzanne Rider

Play this game off both sides of your body and vary the lateral distance so that your dog is prepared for you to both peel away while she weaves and to move in towards her while she weaves. This erratic body movement makes for great proofing and if you ever need that kind of body movement in the ring, you will have the confidence to do it.

*Increasing Speed in the Poles*
To train your dog to weave as fast as she can, you need a clear mental picture of what top speed looks like. Having

this clear mental picture before you start speed training enables you to make it real with precise clicking.  Karen Pryor says that the click "speaks" to your dog's muscles.  Observe what your dog's muscles are doing and click and reinforce your dog for duplicating that muscle use.

Photo by Tien Tran

Elicia Calhoun's BreeSea is single-footing the poles, her forward momentum is so powerful she actually had no feet touching the ground when Tien Tran snapped this picture.  The clicker enables you to capture this speed by marking the moment the dog is using her muscles to create the fast forward movement.

Photo by Tien Tran

Jean Lavelly's Taz speeding through the poles.  Small dogs canter the poles, so viewed from the front two feet will alternately appear on either side of the poles.  Tight forward movement can be clicked and that behavior will increase.

No matter what size your dog is, do your speed training on different types of weave poles with different distances between the poles.  NADAC, USDAA and AKC all have different rules regarding the spacing required between each pole.  The distance can be from 18 to 24-inches, with 21-inch spacing being most common.  Keep in mind that the training surface can also influence your dog's speed and performance.  Prepare her for what she may experience in the ring.

*Proofing Handling Moves*
It is extremely important that your dog allows all types of handling moves while she is weaving. Leaving your dog in the poles while executing a handling move will give you strategic advantages.

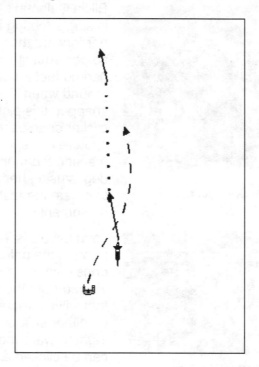

This diagram pictures a handler sending his dog ahead of him into the weaves. The handler then rear crosses while his dog continues to weave.

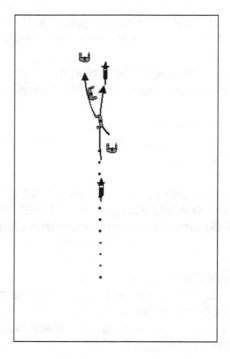

The diagram above depicts the handler running ahead of the weaving dog so that he can cross in front of her. The front cross will be completed by the time the dog exits the weave poles.

*Proofing Games*
To help proof the poles, put a different hat on each weave pole and tape each pole a different color. While your dog is weaving, run and stop abruptly. Can your dog keep weaving? How about if you bend at the waist and clap? Clap loudly with various rhythms? Try clapping and then suddenly stop clapping as she is weaving. If your dog comes out of the weaves while playing any of these proofing games, make the proof easier. Find your dog's success point and build on it.

Make sure your dog can weave while you:

    o   Move in and out laterally.

323

- o Pretend to be a drunken agility handler.
- o Run ahead, do a front cross and continue running hard.
- o Do a poorly timed rear cross.
- o Pretend to be a klutzy handler, trip over the first pole.
- o Do jumping jacks.
- o Run and stop at the third pole.  Act as if you have fallen and can't get up.

All these proofing games will help you sleep at night.  You will never need to worry that you won't be able to get that last Master's Gambler's leg, or to earn that championship title.

*Another Weave Pole Game*
If your dog enjoys playing the race game, teach her to race you to the end of the poles where the toy is lying.  This is a fun game that will help build reinforcement history for performing the weave poles.

For dogs that are food motivated, teach them to race you to a toy that contains food.  If you are concerned that your dog will cheat and attempt to steal the food or toy, use Rhonda Carter's trick of placing the reinforcer under a bucket so that your dog can't play without you.

*Weave Pole Challenges*
Every method has its advantages and disadvantages.  No matter which training method you choose you will encounter training challenges.  They are part of the fun! Here are some ideas for solutions to common weave training challenges.

*Slow Then Really Fast*
Most agility competitors have witnessed dogs that slowly enter the poles, but exit at top speed.  It is important to understand how people accidentally train their dogs to perform the weave poles this way.  If a dog is consistently

reinforced for *completing* a set of twelve poles, some dogs will eventually slow down at the beginning of the poles and then speed up toward the end.  This happens because of something called scalloping.  If you consistently do 12 poles and consistently reinforce after 12 poles you have created a fixed interval reinforcement schedule.  It has become predictable that you will always reinforce after 12 poles.  To avoid scalloping, you want to vary the number of poles after which you click and reinforce.  Ask your dog to weave three, eight, six or two poles.  Reinforce at the end of the poles, but vary when you are clicking, so your dog never knows how many poles are coming or when the click will happen!

Another 12 pole scalloping problem is dogs skipping poles to hurry to the sweet spot after the 12th pole where reinforcement always occurs.  Avoid these challenges by varying the number of poles you play with!  Practice on sets of 3, 6 and 9 poles too.

*Reinforcer Anticipation*
A common weave pole challenge is popping, often at the 10th pole.  This may happen because at that point your dog can get a clear look at what fun obstacle is coming next, is anticipating food delivery and turning her head to see if it is coming, or the handler shifts focus to the next obstacle and your dog follows his body language.  Also, consider a physical problem.  Rule out health issues before addressing training challenges.

If physical problems aren't a factor, use the following fun method to fix the 10th pole popping syndrome.  Place your dog at the tenth pole in a stand.

Suzanne has used her
hand target cue to get Rev
into position at the 10th
pole.  She can then cue
the dog to "weave," so
that he only completes the
last two poles.

Photo by Angelica Steinker

Cue your dog to "weave" and click for weaving the 11th and
12th poles, reinforce after the last pole.  Ta da!  Your dog
just weaved the last two poles.  Now all you need to do is
keep backing your dog up two poles at a time.  Because
your dog always enters to the right of the first pole, moving
back two poles means she will enter correctly each time.
So when she is successful, for the next try, set her up next
to the 8th pole and then the 6th and so on.  Vary your click
point, but *at least 50% of the clicks should occur near the
10th pole*.  Depending on how long your dog has been
popping at the 10th pole you may be able to fix this in one
session, or it may take several weeks.

Always click when your dog's head is straight and in
alignment with the poles, and deliver your food or toy at
lightning speed before she turns her head.  You don't want
a head turn to become part of the behavior chain of
weaving.  As mentioned above, if you accidentally train a
head turn, you may be teaching your dog to pop out of the
poles.

*Weave Entries at Speed*
In order to make the weave entrance when your dog is
traveling at speed, she needs to take a collection stride
before the entrance.

Use differential reinforcement of excellent behavior (DRE)
to teach your dog that only accurate entrances pay.  To set
your dog up for success, begin with her close to the first

pole.  The closer your dog is to the first pole, the less speed she will have.  Build on success by gradually backing her up to increase speed.  When your dog is ready, add fast obstacles before the weaves such as a straight tunnel or even several straight tunnels.  This is like playing around the clock, except now you are adding more and more distance to increase your dog's speed.

**Tunnel!**
Most dogs seem to enjoy running through tunnels, which means that tunnel training usually provides immediate gratification.  To teach your dog the tunnel, take her up to it and allow her to investigate.  Click and reinforce her for approaching and investigating the tunnel.  After you click, consider reinforcing with a toy so that she is playing near the tunnel.  This can help create good attitude.

Photo by Suzanne Rider

Take a straight tunnel and push it together to make it as short as possible.  Have a helper hold your dog at one end of the tunnel, get down so your dog can see you on the opposite side and call her through.

Photo by Suzanne Rider

Click for stepping into the tunnel and reinforce when your dog exits.  This is the area of reinforcement.  If you don't have a helper, shape your dog to pass through the tunnel.  Do this by clicking and reinforcing for approaching the tunnel opening, touching the tunnel opening with one or two front feet, and finally passing through the tunnel.  Once your dog is passing through the tunnel start to click as she is coming out and, to encourage speed, toss your toy in the direction your dog is traveling.  Be careful.  If you click for entering the tunnel, she may pop back out and it may be harder to train her to pass all the way through.  Gradually pull the tunnel out to full length one to two-feet at a time.  Continue to click and reinforce your dog for committing to the tunnel (dog is almost at exit of tunnel) and toss your reinforcer to encourage speed.

The judge can create various tunnel shapes when designing a course, so introduce your dog to both U and S shaped tunnels.  Do this gradually by starting with very slight tunnel curves and build up to sharp tight curves.  At the upper levels of competition, judges sometimes stuff tunnels underneath the dog walk or the A-frame, be sure to practice both.

*Where's the Tunnel Entrance Game*
Play the around the clock game with the tunnel opening, so that your dog can confidently find the entrance to the tunnel regardless of her approach angle or speed.

Once she is performing the tunnel 90% of the time from all angles, begin playing send, lateral distance and recall games.  It will be very important that your dog perform tunnels independently of where you are or where you are moving.  A tunnel performed by your dog independently of you, allows you to move to a strategic position for the next part of the course.

*Tunnel Challenges*
Most dogs, whether agility trained or not, if left unsupervised on a field, choose to run through the tunnel because it is fun.  This means that running through the tunnel is self-reinforcing and this can be a potential problem.  Play some games that will shift your dog's reinforcement history away from the tunnel to other behaviors such as staying with you.  You want the performance of the tunnel to be under stimulus control.

This tunnel game teaches your dog stimulus control.  Begin by running side by side with your dog (introduced on p. 182).  Click and reinforce for staying with you and not taking any obstacles.  Gradually start running closer and closer to the tunnel and click for running past the opening.  If she takes the tunnel, don't reinforce, move further away from the entrance and try again.  Keep in mind you don't want more than two failures in a row.  By clicking and reinforcing for staying close, you are building a reinforcement history for being with you.

This game is particularly important for dogs that see tunnels from 60-feet away and are sucked into the opening as if it were a giant black hole.  Teaching your dog to go through the tunnel only on cue, teaches self-control.

**Chute!**
Since you have already taught the tunnel and it looks similar to the chute, teaching the chute will be easier.  Make the chute appear more tunnel-like by lifting its fabric

end so your dog can see the exit.  Enlist the help of another person and have that person hold your dog in front of the chute entrance while you lift the fabric.  Poke your head into the fabric opening and call your dog to you through the chute.

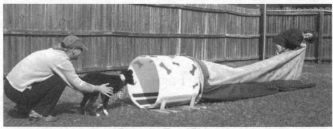

Photo by Tony Rider

Blink learning to run through the chute.

Click your dog once you are certain she will pass through the entire chute rather than popping back out.  Usually this means waiting until your dog is almost all the way through the fabric.  When you see your dog's nose emerging from the chute fabric, drop the fabric and take off running as hard as you can.  Since you have played the restrained recall game, your dog will take off at full speed to catch you.  Celebrate by playing a fun game when she reaches you.  As she gains confidence, shows no signs of hesitating and is actually straining to be released by the helper, lower the fabric a few inches.  Repeat the games described above.  Continue this process until the fabric is flat on the ground.  Click for pushing through the fabric and jackpot when she exits!

Photo by Suzanne Rider

Rev driving out of the chute and trying to catch up to his handler.

Henri is popping out of the chute; if he had raised his front end and head earlier while still in the fabric tube, he may have found himself tangled.

Photo by Pet Action Shots

Now that your dog is consistently passing through the chute without assistance, use DRE to get your dog to aim for the center of the fabric. Banking the inside of the fabric, or pushing through the fabric while traveling along a seam on the right or left side of the chute, or a dog throwing her head up can cause tangling. Only click and reinforce straight pushes through the chute fabric with your dog's head forward and lowered. To help set your dog up for success throw your toy straight ahead in the direction that your dog is traveling.

*Chute Safety*
If your dog gets tangled in the chute fabric, stay calm, quickly approach your dog and grab her while she is still covered in the fabric. This human contact will help your dog realize that you are there and will usually stop panicking. Quickly untangle her, and immediately ask her to perform the chute again; when she does, click and play her favorite game. Repeat this a few times to rebuild your dog's reinforcement history with the chute. If your dog refuses to go back in, no worries, just go back to holding the chute fabric open and retrain the behavior from there.

If you are unable to get straight travel through the chute fabric, place a toy or food tube target at the end of the chute for your dog to run to. This will likely prompt the desired behavior. If your dog has been banking or head popping the chute for years, the process of retraining will take time.

Agility trials are run in the rain.  Prepare for this by teaching your dog to push through a wet chute.  This is especially important for small dogs, because pushing through a wet chute can be hard work for a small dog.  Click for pushing through and give her a special reinforcer.

**Obstacle Challenges**
It is common for dogs to develop a quick affinity for some obstacles, and develop fear of others.  This section addresses both of these problems.

*The Black Hole*
The black hole is when your dog chooses to take a favorite obstacle off cue.  It's a stimulus control issue.  The black hole name is derived from dogs being sucked into, over or onto these obstacles even though the obstacle was hidden from view.  Your dog will somehow locate, as if via sixth sense, the favored obstacle and perform it.  That obstacle is often a tunnel.  However, this problem can occur with any obstacle with which your dog has developed a strong reinforcement history.  Trainers who consistently click and reinforce a dog for performing the 2O2ONT behavior can create a black-hole-contact-obstacle.

Generally, your dog develops the black hole challenge for four reasons:

The trainer has not gained stimulus control over the obstacle.  The solution is to proof your verbal and physical cues for this obstacle.  Click and reinforce your dog for doing this obstacle *only on cue* and click and reinforce your dog heavily for staying with you rather than taking obstacles when they aren't cued.  Create more reinforcement history for handler-focus rather than obstacle-focus.

The dog has been heavily reinforced for doing the black hole obstacle.  Agility training is about keeping your reinforcement history balanced, so it is roughly equal for all obstacles.  Keep in mind that some obstacles require more or less reinforcement according to how much your dog enjoys performing them.

Your dog finds the obstacle intrinsically reinforcing to do. In other words, she thinks that performing the obstacle is fun.  Again, the solution is simple; build up reinforcement history for staying with you and for doing other obstacles to re-establish the balance that you need.

Your handling is not clear, so your dog is making up her own course.  Your dog may be random sampling, trying to figure out what you want.  The next chapter will discuss handling in detail and will recommend that you develop your own consistent system of handling to avoid this situation.

When working through this challenge, watch your dog's head.  Click and reinforce as soon as her head turns towards you and away from the black hole obstacle.

*Fear*
Dogs don't refuse obstacles because they are dominant.  It is either a medical, training, handling or fear issue.  Fear is a tremendously powerful emotion.  It is a signal that death or injury may be eminent.  A fearful dog is learning impaired, as her brain is likely bathed in freeze, flight-or-fight chemicals.  If your dog is fearful of an obstacle, proceed very slowly.  Your dog sets the pace, not you.  It is important that your dog isn't forced to perform or even approach the feared obstacle.  All training should be done on a voluntary basis.  Using this method usually makes for slow progress, but it is the ideal training plan for the fearful dog.  Dogs don't refuse obstacles because they are dominant.  It is either a medical, training or fear issue.

When working with a dog near a feared obstacle your rate of reinforcement should be insanely high.  Click and treat with a rapid-fire progression and make just being near the "dreaded" obstacle a great thing.  Meals can be eaten, and games played next to the scary obstacle several times a day.  When near the feared obstacle, clicking and treating quickly and often can help build a reinforcement history for being close to the obstacle.  This is using classical conditioning alongside operant conditioning.  Classical conditioning will help change your dog's emotional state about the "dreaded" obstacle.

Only when your dog's fear dissipates will she be able to learn how to perform the obstacle.  Trying to train before is a waste of time, and may poison your cue and the obstacle because of the fear.  Cue poisoning occurs when fear, stress or worry become linked with the obstacle and cue.  If this has already occurred, you can heal the poisoned cue by retraining, using voluntary methods and adding a new cue.  The poisoned cue concept was developed by clicker training great Karen Pryor.  Poisoned cue research was performed by behavior analyst Jesus Rosales-Ruiz, Ph.D., and his students.

**Proofing the Obstacles**
For the rest of your dog's agility career continue asking your dog fun proofing questions.  Here are some ideas for maintenance proofing games.  See if your dog can do each obstacle while you:

- o  Wave your arms and scream as if you just won the lotto.
- o  Lie on the ground.
- o  Toss toys all around.
- o  Wear a weird wig and hat.
- o  Dress up in a costume.
- o  Accidentally bump into your dog or pretend to fall.
- o  Stand still.
- o  Stay 20-feet behind your dog walking slowly with a limp.
- o  Have a dog play, do agility, or be fed cookies near you.

## Sequencing

Now that your dog knows all the obstacles and you are ready to sequence, consider how many cues your dog will be performing in the ring before getting any reinforcement. Even if you are running a short novice course, your dog will need to perform a minimum of 20 behaviors to complete the course. To help her accomplish this, you will need to have the confidence and ability to perform at least 60 cues in practice without clicking or reinforcing.

Play the game of counting your cues, or have a training partner count your cues. Pick a number and do agility until you reach that number of cues, then click and reinforce the next excellent behavior you see. This way you are building up your dog's ability to play the agility game without being clicked and reinforced predictably.

If reinforcement always arrives after every three or so obstacles, your dog will become accustomed to this. The activity itself needs to become reinforcing. You won't have to do nearly as much maintenance training if each part of the agility obstacle sequencing reinforces your dog for the previous part. This means that the duration sit at the start is reinforced by the release "okay," which is reinforced by the jump cue, which is reinforced by the A-frame cue and so on.

The counting cues game gives your dog the opportunity to discover that responding to cues is reinforcing. It is also a mentally stimulating game as your dog is always guessing, "Am I going to get a click now? Maybe after this jump?" Above all, it is valuable for you to have the confidence that your dog can perform numerous behaviors and not require food or toys.

# Chapter 10    Click!  Handling

Clicker training is the language of training, handling is the
language of agility.  Handling communicates to your dog
which obstacle to take and which to avoid.  Handling
language is made up of body cues.  To be effective,
handlers need to know those body cues.  TAGTeaching is
a new concept of teaching yourself and others the
mechanical skills of handling.

Watching a tape of the agility world championships, you
see that there are many successful handling styles.  Some
handlers glide around the ring, barely making a sound.
Others seem frantic and scream their cues.  Whatever the
style, these handlers have reached the top of the game by
being consistent.

There it is!  That word consistent again!  Your handling can
only be effective if each movement is clear to your dog and
your dog knows what each movement means.  Handling is
the most complex aspect of agility.  It requires both the dog
and the handler to learn the proper handling movements.
The possibilities for either the dog or the handler to
become confused are great.  Avoid this pitfall by
developing a consistent handling language that is clear to
both you and your dog.

**What is TAGTeaching?**
Theresa McKeon, a top gymnastics coach, learned to
clicker train her horse.  She immediately saw its
applications in coaching her team of six to thirteen year old
gymnasts.  The results were remarkable.  The young
athletes took to the clarity and immediacy of hearing the
click when they performed a perfectly straight handstand or
other physical feat, increasing their learning speed and
motivation dramatically.  The gymnasts' body awareness
grew, and with it, their ability to perform precise behaviors.
Working with humans, Theresa called the method
TAGTeaching, or Teaching with Acoustical Guidance.

337

Along with scientist and clicker enthusiast Joan Orr and other partners, Theresa formed the company TAGTeach International, dedicated to bringing this information and technology to all sports training.

The TAGTeaching instructor makes use of a unique sound, a click, the word TAG or the ding of an electric bell, to mark the moment in which the desired behavior of the student occurs.

*How to Get TAGs*
In TAGging, one person learns while another person coaches.  The coach and the student agree on a TAG point, a specific, clearly described body position, which the coach marks with a signal (TAG) as it is accomplished. Examples of TAG points are the handler:

- o   Staying upright like a candle while turning his dog.
- o   Holding his arm six inches from his hip while his dog jumps a specific jump.
- o   Executing a handling move at a predetermined location.

Traditional coaching focuses on what is wrong. TAGTeaching focuses the student's mind on performing the TAG point, the correct behavior, not on avoiding a mistake.

The coach can TAG for an excellent training moment, outstanding handling move, or for catching the student doing anything in an ideal fashion.  If his dog is having trouble with weave entrances and he clicks and reinforces his dog for a weave entrance, the instructor may TAG the student.  If the student gets into an ideal position for a specific handling move, the instructor may TAG for that.

338

*Group Class Downtime*
Most group classes have down time, either before class or during class waiting for a turn.  Group class students can use this time to pair off and TAG each other.  Student pairs select a TAG point and alternate between student and coach roles.  The cool thing is that both parties are learning.

*Ideas for TAG Training*
Anything that is in need of training is a potential TAG point.  If your dog has a training issue, a TAG point can be created to address it.  If the handler has a handling issue, a TAG point can be set to work on the move.  The thing to remember is to set ONE TAG point at a time.  Require one behavior at a time just like you would when training your dog.

*Keeping Track of TAGs*
As an instructor, I am generous in the TAGs I give out, so my trainer friend Suzanne Rider had the brilliant idea of giving me a "TAG-O-Meter".  The TAG-O-Meter is a simple counter that you can purchase at an office supply store.

Students can use a string with beads on it to keep track of their tags.  For each TAG a bead is moved down the string.  Instructors can use office supply counters to keep track of how many tags they have given.

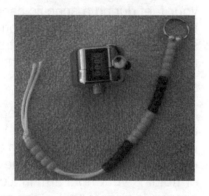

Photo by Suzanne Rider

The TAG-O-Meter is a valuable tool to help keep track of how many TAGs have been given to a student while he is running a course.  After the run, review with your student or training partner how many TAGs they received and why.

339

On occasion if the student does something wonderful, you can TAG jackpot — three TAGs at one time.

*TAGulator*
Students also need to keep track of their TAGs. You can use a string of beads to keep track of TAGs (see photo above). The string of beads is nicknamed a TAGulator.

*TAG Prize Ideas*
For many of my students the act of learning is self-reinforcing, but, hey, who doesn't enjoy a stuffed dog toy? What about a Frisbee or other fun dog gear? I place items that I think my students will enjoy into a box and when all students in the class reach 50 TAGs they each get to pick something out of the box.

*TAGTeaching Guidelines*
As in dog training, stop TAG sessions before the student becomes tired or bored. Switch to different behaviors frequently to keep the student's interest. End the session on success. TAGTeaching is intense. Most learners will suffer from focus fatigue if the sessions are too long. Use TAGTeaching for a specific skill set, such as where to put your feet during a specific handling move. During an hour-long group class there may only be one or two TAG sessions. During private instruction, it is possible to do more, but it is important to know your student's limits.

*TAGTeaching by Yourself*
Not all agility enthusiasts attend group classes or have access to a training partner. If you train alone, you can still use TAG teaching. Establish a TAG point, such as reaching a certain spot on the ground to do a front cross, or holding your right arm in a certain position. Find a person, any person (i.e. the neighbor's kid) to be your coach. Tell your coach what your TAG point is and to say TAG when they see you make the move, reach the spot or

whatever the TAG point is.  One of the advantages to this method is that anyone can coach as long as the person knows the TAG point.

The TAG method relies on the use of systematic and logical approximations.  This helps handlers gain clarity about what is required one body part at a time.  I recommend starting with TAGging the student for ideal arm and shoulder position, because arm position is a key TAG point.  If the arm and shoulder is correct, the rest of the handler's body (shoulders, hips and feet) usually falls into place.

## Handling Moves
This section introduces the basic handling moves and their TAG points.  They include start positions, pull turn, rear cross, front cross and false turn.  My handling philosophy is to keep it simple!

While it is fun to be creative and to develop your own system of handling, why reinvent the wheel?  If you base your handling on experienced world-class competitors, you can video those competitors and study their moves.  Then use the video tape to break the moves down into TAG points.

### Identifying TAG Points
To identify TAG points, videotape the entire handling move from beginning to end.  Start with what the handler's arms are doing, then identify TAG points for the feet and the rest of the body.  You want details.  Identify which foot is placed where and how much weight each foot is bearing.  If the handler is moving quickly, make note that this handling move will be executed on the balls of your feet.  Once you have completed the TAG points for the arms, move around the handler's body one section at a time: shoulders, head to feet, legs, hips and torso.

*Physical Challenges*
If you have a physical challenge (and in my experience almost all agility handlers do), find a handler who has the same physical abilities as you to imitate.  There are successful agility handlers in wheelchairs, with back problems and a wide variety of other physical challenges.  Once you find a successful handler that matches your physical abilities, use the TAGTeaching methods to establish TAG Points.

*Body Awareness*
The key to good handling is body awareness.  On the course, in order to have the mental room to tune into your body, make sure that you are absolutely clear what obstacles you will be performing and choose a handling strategy to get your dog from point A to point B.  It is impossible to be aware of what your body is doing if you are trying to remember where the next obstacle is or thinking about how you are going to get your dog turned toward the next series of obstacles.  TAGTeaching is an excellent way to develop body awareness.

To gain awareness of your feet, draw a straight line on the ground 20-feet long.  Use sidewalk chalk if you are indoors on matting or use powdered chalk outside on grass.  Place your left foot on the line, begin walking and have your coach "TAG" every time your left foot hits the line.  The first time keep your head down watching your feet, but the second time do it without looking.  The TAGging of the left foot will help you become aware of your left foot when you are traveling straight.  Repeat this game TAGging right foot contact with the line.  First walk, then jog and eventually run the line.

It is important for agility handlers to be able to travel in straight lines, or to move directly to a planned spot.  If you travel crookedly, you may accidentally signal your dog to take an incorrect obstacle.  Walking, jogging and eventually running straight lines helps you gain awareness of where you are placing your feet and what direction you are traveling.

An awareness of your shoulders is also critical to agility handling. "Why did the chicken cross the road?" "Because the handler's shoulders were pointing that way!" is an old agility joke. Your dog will travel in the direction your shoulders are facing. The motion of your arm is also important but shoulders determine where the arm will be.

To help gain shoulder awareness, have your coach TAG you for rotating your upper body and shoulders 90-degrees.

Photo by Suzanne Rider

Angelica before she has begun rotating. In TAGTeaching, this is called a start position. It is the position before you have attempted the behavior you are learning.

Begin in the position shown in the picture above, your start position. Your TAG point is to rotate your arms and shoulders 90-degrees to the left, without moving your feet.

Angelica after she has rotated her shoulders 90-degrees to her left. TAG!

Photo by Suzanne Rider

Now do this exercise in the other direction, rotating 90-degrees to the right. Once you are consistently successful, merge the straight line game with this shoulder rotating. Again, practice in both directions and then jog and eventually run.

Your arm is pivotal in agility handling. To help create an awareness of arms, assume a relaxed start position, arms at the sides, natural stance, weight evenly distributed on both feet. From this start position, try to "feel" the various arm position TAG points. Your coach may say, "The TAG point is to lift your arm six inches from your hip."

Here Angelica holds her hand six inches from her hip.

Photo by Suzanne Rider

The coach can then use this method to help the handler "feel" six, 12 and 18-inches.  Once the handler is successful with either arm while standing still, progress to arm movement while walking, then while jogging and finally while running.  This exercise is a great way to help handlers who swing their arms, accidentally signaling their dogs to take off courses.  The instructor calls out where the arm should be (six inches, 12-inches, etc.) to prompt the ideal arm position and then TAGs when it gets there.  The moment the instructor TAGs, the student can feel what that arm position feels like.

In addition to an awareness of what arms are doing, it is helpful to create a default of possible arm behaviors.

In the photo at left, Angelica demonstrates the bowl arm, which signals your dog to move ahead of you.  The photo to the right shows an arm that is horizontal with the ground, sigaling for the dog to move laterally away from the handler.  In both cases, elbows and wrists are straight.

Photos by Suzanne Rider

It is ideal for a handler to keep his elbow and wrist straight most of the time and to handle with the arm closest to his dog.  Which arm to use is a source of great debate among agility handlers.  In my mind using the arm closest to your dog makes sense, because that arm is most easily seen by her.

*The Magic Flashlight*
A great way of thinking about your arm signaling is to pretend that you are holding a "magic flashlight."

Wherever you shine the beam of the "magic flashlight" your dog will go.  Shine the magic flash light beam six-inches ahead of your dog's nose.  When using your "magic flashlight," keep your elbow straight and move your arm using your shoulder muscles.  Keeping your elbow straight most of the time will help avoid knocked bars and off courses, which occur more easily when your arm is bent.

A bent arm can allow lower-arm movement and cause wrong courses.  Jerky handler movements, arm or otherwise, can cause your dog to drop a bar.  In general, avoid jerky movements, especially when your dog is in the air over a jump.  This probably sounds challenging to do and it is, but we love this sport because of its challenges.

*Connection*
Connection is an agility term used to describe the line of communication between you and your dog.  Connection enables you to signal to your dog and your dog to respond. Either you or your dog can break connection.  Taking your eyes off your dog, even for a moment, can cause you to break connection.  To avoid this, make watching your dog a TAG point.  For a new handler watching their dog with their peripheral vision for one obstacle is an excellent TAG point.  As the skill of the handler improves, raise criteria to watching for two, three or more obstacles.  A handler could be TAGged for watching their dog while completing a very fast handling move.  The coach can infer if the dog is being watched, because of the timing of the handling moves, rather than actually being able to see the handler making direct eye contact.  If a handler stops watching their dog, the connection between dog and handler will be lost and this "disconnect" will be visible to an experienced coach.

Another way to lose connection is to handle too far ahead of or behind your dog.  Your arm signal consistently tells your dog where she is going, but there is a rubber band effect: if you handle too far ahead of your dog, the rubber band breaks and connection is lost.  If someone gives you directions and he is two streets ahead of your note taking, mental connection will be lost.  Signaling behind the location of your dog is also going to break connection and frustrate or slow the dog down.  A dog barking on course can be a sign of frustration because her handler isn't clearly telling her where to go.  If the person navigating a car trip keeps forgetting to tell you where to turn, you are going to get frustrated (I suggest biting his ankle).

*Consistent Handling Cues*
Consistency in handling is the only way your dog can know what a handling move means.  If one move looks just like another, your dog can't make sense of what you are signaling.  Just as verbal cues need to be different from each other in order to be clear to your dog, physical cues must be unique.  Each body cue you give your dog can only have one meaning.  Inconsistencies in body cues will cause your dog to become confused.

Many times handlers get exactly what they handle rather than what they meant.  The handler may have meant for his dog to go to the weaves, but because he never rotated his upper body and shoulders to show his dog the weave poles, the entrance is missed.  Because it is extremely challenging to achieve body awareness (what you actually did, not what you thought you did) it can be easy to blame your dog.  The truth is that it is always a training or handling issue.  Since we are the trainers and the handlers the dogs get off blame-free.

*Assessing Your Handling*
If you are already running agility, take a moment to find out how effective and consistent your handling is.  Get a sheet of paper and list your handling moves on the left side.  Then evaluate the effectiveness of each move.  Is the move consistently successful in practice?  What about competition? If the list shows that a certain move is not successful in competition but is during practice, you may want to have a friend video tape you in both training and

competition to see what is causing the move to be unsuccessful in competition.  Compare the move to other moves that you use.  Does it look similar to another move?  If so, pick one move and eliminate the other.

Some competitors hold their breath when they get nervous.  This can completely change the appearance of the handler's body, causing a limited range of motion and stiffness.  Tension can make a normally fluid well-rehearsed move look choppy.  Once your body tenses, your dog may not recognize your restricted handling cues or your timing may be off.  The change in appearance may cause your dog to slow down or misinterpret the move.

Another common problem is for a nervous competitor to lose confidence.  This manifests as tentative rather than confident signaling.  Increase your confidence in your handling by clearly defining each move and rehearsing it well.  Evaluation of your moves standardization and rehearsal will get you on track to make your competitive handling match your practice handling.

If you find a certain move isn't successful in training or competition, consider modifying it so it is clear to your dog.  Perhaps the move was never properly trained and your dog can't read it when you are stopped or are in a different position relative to your dog and the move is not generalized to that position.  You are the truth detective: investigate until your questions are answered.

If you find a move is successful at home, but not as successful in competition, here are some more ideas that may be helpful.

*If your dog is faster in competition than at home and you're not used to this speed, your timing may be off.*  Increase your dog's speed at home to duplicate the speed she is running at the trial.  Do this by playing motivational games and using DRE.  Run a friend's dog that is faster than your dog in practice, to help you learn faster timing. Alternatively, lower your dog's jump height by one or two increments so she will spend less time in the air and more time running, which will require you to speed up your handling.

*Instead of responding, your dog stares at you when you make the handling move.*  Establish specifically which move your dog is not responding to and in which context. Train this move while standing in one place, only moving the upper body, click and reinforce the response.  Be aware of the power of your eyes.  If your dog stalls when you are sending her, ask yourself what you are watching. If you are looking at your dog rather than at the obstacle you are sending your dog to, this may be the problem. When sending your dog ahead of you, look where you want her to go, using your peripheral vision to track her.

*Fast Feet*
In order to be the best handler you can be, you need to be quick on your feet.  This does not mean you have to be an Olympic sprinter — it means you must speed up and slow down according to what your dog needs.  If the best speed you have is a light jog, then that is your fast speed and walking is your decelerated speed.  If you can run, you will be alternating between running and jogging.  No matter what your physical ability, you will need two gears to communicate effectively with your dog.

*Speeding Up and Slowing Down*
Speeding up tells your dog to run hard and keep taking what is in front of her.  Slowing down tells your dog a change in direction is coming.

To learn to speed up while running, have another person TAG you for reaching forward with your leading leg, before your foot strikes the ground.  Most people drop their feet straight to the ground as they run.  This shortens stride and wastes energy.  Reaching forward as far as you can

349

increases the length of your stride and therefore your speed. Reaching your foot forward before it hits the ground becomes a TAG point.

Photos by Suzanne Rider

By focusing on reaching forward with your leading foot, you will cover more ground and increase your speed.

A second TAG point for increasing your sprinting speed is to focus on kicking your heel up high to your bottom after you push off from the ground. This TAG point increases the force with which you push off the ground, therefore increasing your speed. The increase in speed here isn't going to do much good because the lead leg reach is poor. Just like our dogs, the previous behavior of reaching forward was lost when the focus changed to the new behavior of heel up.

A second TAG point that will help increase your speed is kicking your foot up to your buttocks as your rear foot leaves the ground. Again, this does not take a whole lot of energy, but will help increase your speed by driving your body forward.

If you have a physical handicap, you can use a wheelchair to handle your dog and work with a physical therapist to establish TAG points that will help you improve your speed.  Agility handlers come from all walks of life and many have physical limitations.  Don't allow a physical challenge to keep you from pursuing a dream of running agility.  You can do it!

*Slow Down!*
Slowing down tells your dog that a change in direction is coming.  Whatever your initial speed, a sudden slowing down or stop, will cause most dogs to curl in toward you looking for their next cue.

Suddenly slowing down and speeding up requires some strength training.  Again, regardless of your physical condition, you can prepare your body for this and improve your speed with a little bit of training.  My students range from young kids to elderly people with various physical abilities.  All of them have learned to speed up and slow down to the best of their ability and are enjoying the game of agility with their dogs.

To get a feel for how your dog is affected by changes in your speed, run at full pace with your dog for a series of obstacles, then slow down.  Observe how slowing down affects your dog's behavior.  Observe what your dog does when you speed up.  World-class agility competitor Guy Blancke calls this "feeling the dog" and it is a very powerful exercise.  It allows you to "feel" how your movements affect your dog.  Use this information to plan your course strategy.

*How to Teach Speeding Up and Slowing Down*
Some dogs will take an obstacle without being directed to rather than check in with their handler if the handler stops or slows.  If your dog does this, it is easy to teach her that slowing down or stopping means, "check in with me."  Run your dog over a sequence and at a predetermined location

begin slowing down.  As you slow down, call your dog to you, click the response and reinforce when your dog is right next to you.  Your dog will learn that slowing down is followed by a recall and she will soon check in with you automatically.  You can then fade the recall and just click and reinforce her curling into you.

*Warming Up For Handling*
Whether you are a beginner or have been handling agility for years, proper warm up and stretching is important.  Every person is different, so check with a physical therapist for specific exercises.

When getting ready to work on your handling, begin with light stretches and jogging.  Once you are warmed up, do a few sprints at your top speed.  Frequently we handle at the speed that is comfortable to us rather than what is truly our top speed.  Develop the muscle memory of what your top speed feels like by making fast sprints part of your warm up routine.  Even if you have a physical disability, move as fast as you can so you have a feel for what your top speed is.  Establishing this baseline will help you decide what parts of the course you may want to speed up and slow down.

*Two Ways to Start*
There are two ways to get your dog started on your agility run.  You can lead-out ahead of your dog, while she waits, or you can do a running start together.  A running start is a fun way to start and it does not require your dog to hold any position prior to starting the run.

Photo by Angelica Steinker

Suzanne has lead-out ahead of Rev.  Her hand is pointing back at her dog for connection as she prepares to release him.

Photo by Suzanne Rider

Rev is ready to go and I am restraining him by placing my hand on his chest.

Photo by Suzanne Rider

The running start is complete.

To perform a running start, hold your dog back from doing the first obstacle by pushing on her chest. When ready, give your dog a gentle push backward away from the first obstacle and take off running. The slight push away from the first obstacle is intended to trigger your dog's opposition reflex, which will cause her to assertively drive forward toward the first jump.

The running start is popular among some handlers of small dogs. Dogs that are less motivated to do agility can also benefit from a running start. If you have a fast dog, a running start can present an entirely different set of handling challenges. This makes it a fun exercise for training. The challenge is that the handler will rapidly fall behind his dog. Many sequences are very different to handle when you are behind your dog, compared to if you are even with or ahead of her.

*Lead-outs*
A lead-out is when the handler leaves his dog in a sit or down at the start. He walks onto the course, strategically positioning himself to let his dog know the entire opening sequence rather than just the first jump. A lead-out is an advantage because it enables the handler to be ahead of his dog, which makes it easier for her to see handling signals. This is why it is important to train and proof your duration behaviors such as sit. You must be able to lead-out with confidence and know your dog will release only when you are ready.

The handler pictured has led out to the third jump.  Since both the dog and the handler's path are straight ahead this is a straight lead-out.  Note that the handler's left arm magic flashlight beam should be reaching back pointing six inches in front of the dog's nose indicating the path the handler wants the dog to take (the software design program doesn't allow handler arm adjustment).

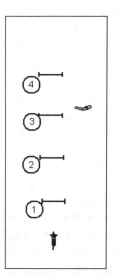

When leading out, use your shoulders and arms to show your dog where she is going.  Using your hand to shine the magic flashlight beam at the path you want your dog to take.

Begin practicing lead-outs on the flat without obstacles.  Once your dog has a 90% success rate, begin practicing with one jump.  Gradually build on success, until finally you can practice a long lead-out over a sequence of four or more obstacles.

*TAG Points for Straight Lead-out*
Feet and Legs:  Handler on the balls of his feet.  Knees bent and soft (unlocked) facing in the direction the dog will be traveling.
Upper body:  Leaning forward slightly.
Shoulders and arms: Shoulders facing in the direction you want your dog to go off the start line, arm closest to your dog pointing at her. The moment you release begin to shine the magic flashlight beam six inches ahead of your dog, arm furthest from your dog naturally at your side.
Head and eyes: Toggling between dog and first obstacle.

355

*TAG Points for Running Start*
Feet and Legs:  Parallel to dog's.
Upper body:  leaning forward slightly.
Shoulders and arms: shoulders facing in the direction you
want your dog to go, arm closest to your dog on your dog's
chest ready to give her a gentle push backwards, arm
furthest from your dog at side in a natural position.
Head and eyes: toggling between dog and first obstacle.

*Less Can Be More*
Being ahead of your dog is a good thing, but being too far
ahead can add challenges.  The greater the distance of the
lead-out, the more risk that you may lose connection with
your dog.  Long lead-outs can also encourage more
speed, which flattens the stride of most dogs.  This may
cause knocked bars.  It can also be difficult on your timing.
Your dog may misread which obstacle you are indicating
when she is far behind you.  It is your call if a long lead-out
is worth the risk.  However, in the agility ring, we are all
gamblers and taking chances is part of the fun.

**Handling Moves That Turn the Dog**
The pull turn, rear cross, front cross and false turn are the
most common handling moves used today.  (They have
different names in different countries and even in different
regions.)  These handling moves will help you complete
upper-level agility courses.

*Blind Crosses*
I don't recommend blind crosses.  It seems to me that it is
hard for a dog to distinguish between the handling move of
a blind cross, and a pull turn, described below.  Dogs can
also get confused as to which side of your body they
should race to if you use both front crosses, described
below, and blind crosses.  Rather than risk confusing a dog
by adding the blind cross move, it seems more ideal to be
able to continue using pull turns and front crosses.  Having
said this there are many handlers phenomenally
successful using blind crosses.  I coach what I believe to

be consistent and know to be successful based on my own experiences.

*Pull Turn*
Also called the pole turn (not to be confused with pole dancing), is among the simplest of handling moves.  The pull turn asks your dog to wrap around your body as you both turn in the same direction.  While this turn is physically the least demanding for the handler it does hold some challenges.

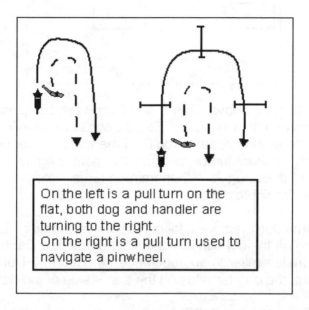

On the left is a pull turn on the flat, both dog and handler are turning to the right.
On the right is a pull turn used to navigate a pinwheel.

The diagram above pictures the path of the handler and the tightest possible path for his dog over the jumps.  Your dog's actual path will depend on her speed, size and training.  When practicing pull turns, tweak your handling style until you can consistently get your dog to perform the three jumps as tightly as possible.  The tightest path brings your dog close to the inside standard of all three jumps of a pinwheel.

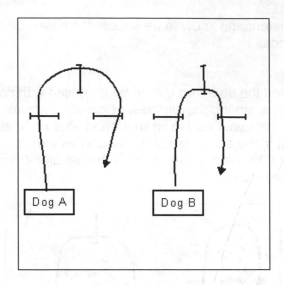

In the diagram above, Dog A and Dog B are completing a pull turn with their handler.  If these dogs are traveling at the same ground speed, Dog B's time will be faster going through the three jumps because her path is tighter (shorter) than Dog A.  When training turns, help your dog choose the tightest path.

Pull turns don't require a lot of movement: rotating and pushing off the outside leg or inside leg the handler turns. This turn is similar to an obedience "about turn".  During a pull turn, the dog remains on the same side of the handler.

*TAG Points for the Pull Turn*
The TAG points below assume that the dog is on the handler's left side.  Dog and handler are both traveling to the right.

Photo by Suzanne Rider

Brenna has decelerated as she moves towards the second jump of the pinwheel to begin the pull turn.

Photo by Suzanne Rider

She has rotated off her outside leg and is now running out of the pull turn.

The dog may be turning right just a little or a lot (270- to 360-degrees).  The pull turn can be used if the handler is slightly ahead of the dog, with the dog, or behind the dog.  If you are significantly ahead of your dog, another handling move, front cross or false turn, is usually a better option.

Begin with the TAG points for the lower body, starting with the positioning of the feet, then legs and hips, until the entire behavior is completed.

Lower Body
TAG POINT:  Handler softens knees and slows down using balls of feet, signaling to the dog that a turn is coming.
TAG POINT:  Handler rotates off the left (outside) foot shifting weight over to the ball of the right foot – turning his

upper and lower body as much as needed; you will not know which foot you will be caught on when it is necessary to complete the move.  Practice pushing and rotating off both your outside foot and inside foot.

TAG POINT: Handler speeds up out of the turn to reach next strategic handling position.

Upper Body

TAG POINT:  While slowing down, handler uses left arm to continue to signal his dog's path six inches ahead of the dog's nose.

TAG POINT:  Shoulders and hips are centered above each other.  If the handler bumps his hip outwards, it can cause wide turns or even send his dog off course.

TAG POINT:  While left foot is pushing off the ground during the actual turn, the handler uses his left arm to bring his dog around turn by placing the beam of the "magic flash light" six inches in front of his dog's nose.

TAG POINT:  Handler uses peripheral vision to watch dog.

TAG POINT:  While speeding up, handler uses his left arm to continue to signal the "magic flash light" beam six inches in front of the dog.

The game below is a great way to help your dog learn how to successfully execute pull turns.  When clicking your dog for turning with you, reinforce with either tug or food to help keep your dog close and focused on you.  If your dog swings wide or is not focused on you, pull turn execution is usually compromised.

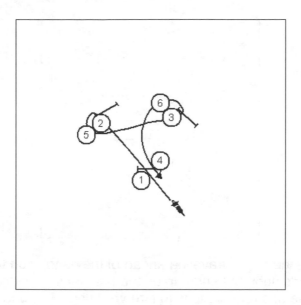

The diagram above shows the pattern of this exercise, start by only doing four obstacles and build up to #5 and #6. Play this game at your own risk because it can make you dizzy!

The pull turn game helped me tighten Nicki's wide floating pull turns. When I started playing this game with her, the jumps were 20-feet apart giving her plenty of room to turn. As she improved, I decreased the spacing until her path was only nine-feet from one jump to another.

*Rear Cross*
Also called cross behind or back cross, this move involves crossing behind your dog, so she is now on the opposite handling side.

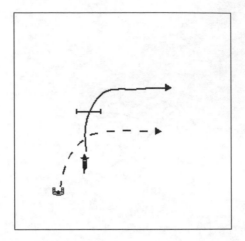

Above, the dog is traveling ahead of the handler on the handler's right, but ends up on the handler's left side. The purpose of a rear cross is to turn your dog. The dog turns when the handler performs the cross. Rear crosses are a fun way to communicate to your dog which obstacle you want her to take if she is facing options, as shown below.

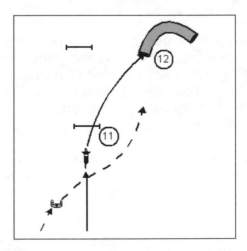

The diagram above shows the effective use of a rear cross. Without the rear cross, the dog would probably continue to the off course jump straight ahead, because the handler was heading that way. By using a rear cross, the handler clearly communicated that the next obstacle was the tunnel.

When rear crossing, keep your eyes on your dog.  Moving into the path your dog just traveled on will signal to her that a rear cross is coming.

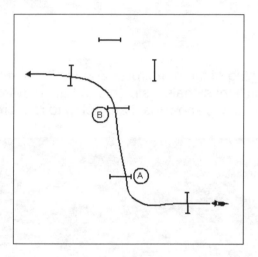

Assuming the dog is one obstacle ahead, as the handler reaches the upright marked A, he begins his rear cross moving toward the upright marked B.  The moment the handler begins to step into his dog's path after A, an experienced dog understands that a rear cross is coming, allowing her to adjust her stride, change leads and perform the next obstacle.

Photos by Suzanne Rider

The beginning of the rear cross, Zoomie is on my left, my magic flash light signals his path and I am moving into his space, letting him know that I am going to rear cross.

Zoomie has landed on his left lead and turned, I am preparing to cross behind him as my magic flashlight continues to signal his path.

Zoomie has committed to the last jump. I am following through and continuing to move toward the jump he is ready to take.

364

The rear cross is complete and I am preparing to reinforce
Zoomie with his toy.

*TAG Points for Rear Cross*
The TAG points below assume the dog is on the handler's
left, at the beginning of the move, but ends with the dog on
the handler's right.  In order to perform a rear cross, the
handler needs to be behind the dog.  If the handler is even
with or ahead of the dog, the handler will be unable to
perform a rear cross unless he slows down or stops.  In
those cases, the dog will continue to move because the
handler will signal the dog's path with the magic flashlight.

Lower Body
TAG POINT:  Handler slows down — signaling to the dog
that a change in direction is about to occur, knees are
slightly bent, weight is on the balls of the feet.
TAG POINT:  Handler steps into the path the dog has just
traveled on.
TAG POINT:  After the cross handler speeds up.

Upper Body
TAG POINT:  Handler's left hand is low magic flashlight
beam signaling six inches ahead of the dog's nose.
TAG POINT:  As the handler crosses behind the dog, the
handler's right hand follows through and continues to
signal the magic flashlight beam in the direction of the next
obstacle, shoulders support the arm movements and
consistently indicate the path the dog is about to take.

TAG POINT: Eyes on dog, peripheral vision on obstacles and dog's path.

*Rear Cross Game*
There are several games that teach dogs the rear cross. Before playing the rear cross game your dog must fluently perform the "go" cue, introduced in the Ground Games Chapter. Generally, in order for you to rear cross you will need your dog to be ahead of you, "go" helps you achieve that.

Performing lefts and rights on the flat as described in the Ground Games Chapter also prepares your dog for rear crosses. Finally, you can play two more games. The first introduces your dog to the hand signal that precedes you stepping into the path she has just traveled on and the second helps your dog learn your follow through on the landing side of the jump.

Pictured below are the two rear cross games.

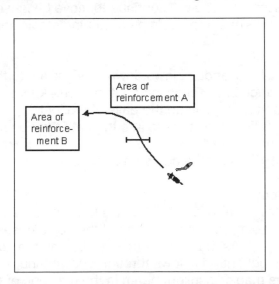

The game begins with the dog on the handler's left, the handler signals the jump with his left hand aiming the magic flashlight beam ahead of his dog at the jump, while saying "go". The handler clicks as his dog commits to the jump and then tosses a toy or food tube forward to the area of reinforcement labeled A. Three repetitions help ensure that your dog will travel ahead of the handler to the jump, eventually allowing the handler to cross behind. This game should also help prompt your dog to accelerate and perform an obstacle that you are signaling as you are pairing the hand signal for the jump with the toy toss.

Providing you have had success with the first game, now you can raise criteria by adding the rear cross. As before signal the jump and cue your dog to go, but this time tuck in behind your dog indicating the rear cross. As your dog commits to the jump, change hands beginning to signal the magic flashlight beam with the right hand. The left hand holds the reinforcer which is seamlessly tossed to the area labeled B. If your dog spins, don't toss your reinforcement, go back to playing the rear cross on the flat game. Be sure that your dog is set at an angle asking her to slice the jump as this sets your dog up to land on the left lead. Again, you are pairing your hand signal, now with the right hand, with the toy toss.

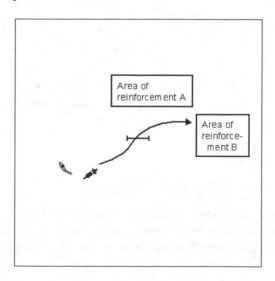

Above is the mirror image of the rear cross game.  As always play all games off both sides of your body.

*Front Cross*
The front cross is also used to turn a dog.  An advantage of a front cross is that it enables the handler to be ahead of his dog, or to get ahead of his dog, making it easy for his dog to understand where she is going because both the next obstacle and the handler are ahead of her.  For less motivated dogs, trying to catch the handler can be a fun game.  If you are less physically fit, or have a physical challenge, don't worry, you can still do front crosses.  By teaching your dog to send ahead of you and work away from you at lateral distance, you will be able to front cross even if you can't run.

When ahead of the dog's path, the handler steps into and across the dog's path, rotating in front of the dog.

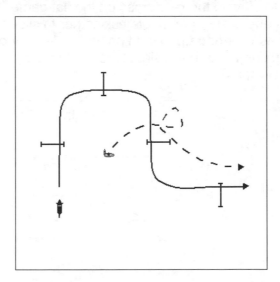

The path above is not exactly drawn as the handler will execute it: the loop is actually a tiny pivot.  The cross point of the loop indicates the *location* of the front cross.  The footwork of the front cross creates a line that points in the direction the dog is to travel.

It is possible to front cross when you are even with or behind your dog if the course requires your dog to turn 180-degrees, as shown in the diagram below.

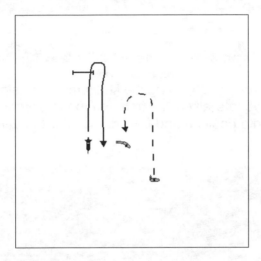

The above type of front cross is easy for beginners to practice on the flat.  Even though it looks very different it is a front cross.  The handler started with the dog on his left and ends with the dog on his right.  The handler caused the turn by moving into and in front of the dog's path.

The pictures below show Zoomie and I performing a front cross.  The front cross starts with Zoomie on my left and ends with him on my right.

Photos by Suzanne Rider

Zoomie is on my left taking the first jump, I am signaling for him to move laterally away from me to the second jump so I can get into position and front cross after the third jump.

As Zoomie commits to the second jump, I move to get into position to front cross.

As Zoomie commits to the third jump, I step into his path to start my rotation.  My left arm continues to signal his path.

As Zoomie jumps the third jump, I am shifting weight from my left leg to my right, preparing to move my left leg out of Zoomie's path, otherwise you may lose a knee cap.

I have rotated 180-degrees while reaching back with my left leg to move off of Zoomie's path.  I am following through with my right hand signaling Zoomie's path.

The front cross is complete, I am getting ready to reinforce Zoomie with his toy.

The actual footwork of the front cross, pictured above, is as follows: slow down on the left leg with knees bent and weight on the balls of the feet.  Next, rotate on the left foot, stepping into the dog's path with the right foot.  Finally, rotate on the right foot, stepping with the left foot in the direction the dog will be traveling.  The right foot then follows through and also steps in the direction the dog will be traveling.  Be sure to practice front crosses in both directions.  Most people have better timing in one direction. Practice your "weaker" side twice as much as your "stronger" side.

*Handler TAG Points for Front Cross*
The TAG points below assume the dog is on the handler's left, at the beginning of the move, but after the handler completes his front cross rotation, the dog will be on his right.

Lower Body
TAG POINT:  Handler decelerates to let the dog know a change in direction is coming, knees are soft and handler is on the balls of his feet.
TAG POINT:  Handler's right foot steps into what will be the dog's path.
TAG POINT: Handler's left foot rotates counter clockwise moving in the direction the dog will be traveling.

372

TAG POINT:  Handler's right foot follows through, signaling the next obstacle and direction the dog will be traveling.

Upper Body
TAG POINT:  While handler is decelerating, left hand is "magic flashlight" signaling the dog's path.
TAG POINT:  While handler is stepping into the dog with right foot, handler prepares to change "magic flashlight" from left to right hand.
TAG POINT: While handler is executing a reverse pivot counter clockwise, handler changes hands and starts signaling the "magic flashlight" with his right hand.
TAG POINT: As the handler's right foot follows through signaling the next obstacle, the handler's right hand "magic flashlight" also signals the next obstacle.
TAG POINT: Eyes on dog at all times, using peripheral vision to scan obstacles and dog's path.

The footwork of the front cross, if executed properly, should create a straight line.  You can determine the line the front cross will be on by using a simple formula developed by Elicia Calhoun.  While you perform the front cross, you will usually be moving between two obstacles. The upright of the first obstacle that is closest to you before you front cross, is point A.  The upright of the obstacle that is closest to you when you end the front cross, is point B. The trick of a good front cross is to stay as close as you can to the B point and to perform your front cross on the line formed between point A and B.

Photo by Suzanne Rider

Rubber spot markers indicate the A and B points, marker chalk, available at hardware supply stores can indicate the line the handler will be making the front cross on.  The photo assumes the same path for the dog as the diagram and pictures above.

Point A is the first upright the handler will get to before he makes his front cross and point B is the first upright he will get to after he makes his front cross.  The line is drawn from point A to B.  Use this line to play a fun TAG point game.  Have your coach give you a TAG for each front cross footfall that hits the line.

*The Front Cross Game*
To teach your dog the front cross, begin by playing the running side by side game on the flat with no obstacles. While connected to your dog, do the front cross motion and call your dog's name, asking your dog to turn 180-degrees while rotating into you.  Click your dog for turning into you. Then toss your toy as hard as you can to the area of reinforcement.

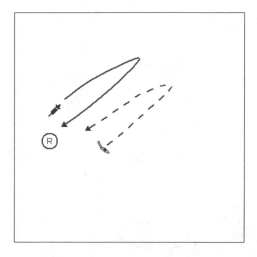

In the diagram above, the R in the circle represents the area of reinforcement.

This game teaches your dog that the step into her path signals a change in direction.  Your dog will learn to dig in and cut in ahead of your path so that she can hurry up and get to her area of reinforcement.  Click the turn and then toss your toy to the area of reinforcement so that your dog learns to accelerate out of the turn!

As you and your dog improve at front crosses, adding lateral distance will become extremely important.  It is possible to send your dog over several obstacles laterally away from you while you cut the corner and perform a front cross.  So, the "out" game will be of high importance in mastering front crosses.

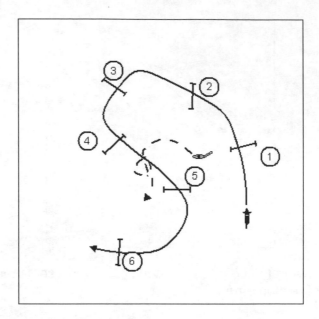

Above the handler, without covering a lot of ground, has used lateral distance to send his dog out to #2 and #3, enabling a front cross between #4 and #5.

*False Turn*
This move is one-half of a front cross; it is as if the handler were going to do a front cross, but then changed his mind. It enables the handler to place a kink in the dog's path.  If a dog has to hit a tricky weave pole entrance, the handler can use a false turn to adjust the dog's path, helping the dog find the entrance to the poles.

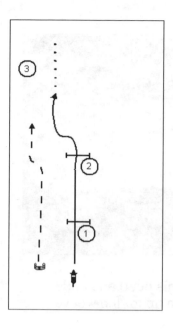

By performing a false turn after #2 and before #3, the handler avoids a missed entry into the poles and a refusal fault. The dog now has a straight entry into the poles. The dog's path is kinked after #2 by the handler briefly rotating into the dog, when the dog has turned sufficiently to be aligned with the weave poles the handler rotates back, signaling the poles.

*TAG Points for False Turn*
The TAG points below assume the dog is on the handler's left. There is no change of side during this move.

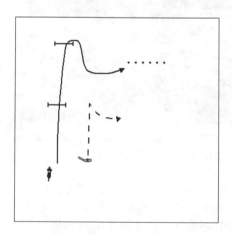

The handler appears to be engaging in a front cross but after pulling the dog and adjusting her path the dog is turned back to the original direction.

The handler can be parallel, slightly behind, or ahead of his dog to execute this move.

377

I have rotated into Zoomie to pull his head and body toward me.  This helps me line him up for the weave poles.

Photos by Suzanne Rider

Having sufficiently kinked Zoomie's path I rotate back to the original direction and send him to the poles.

When using a false turn, decelerate and then hold your rotation depending on how tight a turn you need.  For a tighter turn hold the position longer, for a tiny kink rotate for just a split second.

Lower Body
TAG POINT:  The handler decelerates to let the dog know a change in direction is coming, knees are soft and he is on the balls of his feet.
TAG POINT:  The handler's right foot steps into dog's path.
TAG POINT:  The handler holds the previous TAG point for a split second waiting for the dog to respond.
TAG POINT: The handler's left foot steps forward pointing at next obstacle and handler begins to accelerate.

Upper Body
TAG POINT:  As the handler slows down, his left arm continues to signal the dog's path with the "magic flashlight beam."
TAG POINT:  The handler's left arm is lowered and held tight to the body (using triceps muscle) to avoid accidentally pushing the dog away from the handler.
TAG POINT:  As the handler's right foot steps toward the dog, he switches the magic flash light from left hand to right hand and continues to use its beam to indicate the new path.
TAG POINT:  As the handler's left foot is signaling the next obstacle, the left arm's magic flash light also points at this obstacle.
TAG POINT: Eyes on dog at all times, using peripheral vision to keep track of obstacles and dog's path.

*False Turn Game*
To maintain false turns, play plenty of front cross games. For dogs that enjoy performing the obstacles, playing the front cross game is critical in maintaining a good false turn. Dogs that like doing the obstacles will learn you are "crying wolf," if you do too many false turns without enough front crosses.  The result is a handler who performs a false turn and a dog who ignores the move and continues driving to the next obstacle.  Consistently playing the front cross game will get the dog thinking, "turn" and the redirect of the false turn will be easy.  Be sure to always click the turn and reinforce in the area of reinforcement.

For clingy dogs that don't want to come off the handler, play the false turn game on the flat without any obstacles running side by side, begin rotating into your dog as if performing a front cross, then change your mind and after kinking your dog's path, turn back to the original direction. Click your dog for kinking and turning with you, then toss your toy to the area of reinforcement pictured below.

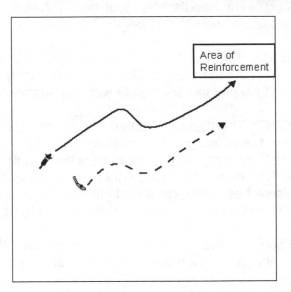

The opposite of clingy dogs that don't want to turn away from the handler are dogs like my Nicki. These dogs figure it is even faster if you avoid kinking your path in the first place, so when you false turn they tend to ignore the handlers attempt to kink the path and keep running full speed. These dogs are more reinforced by running fast and doing obstacles, then by turning or focusing on the handler.

Nicki is a very obstacle-focused dog and rather than playing the false turn game, I play lots of front cross games with her. When training, I frequently perform a front cross where I will be performing a false turn just to help keep her focused on me. I click and reinforce for turning with me, so I can build up a larger handler-focus bank account to balance the obstacle focus she naturally brings to agility. After front crossing, reinforce these dogs with tug or by tossing the toy behind you from in between your legs to encourage handler-focus.

**The Dog's Path**
A great way to practice handler-focus is to play the 'alphabet soup handling' game. This game teaches you to focus on handling your dog's *path* rather than the obstacles. This is easy because the game does not include obstacles. When handling a dog around a course, your focus *ought* to be on the path you intend your dog to take, rather than on the obstacles. Use powdered chalk to spell letters on the field, such as O, L, V, M, U, N, W, Z, C, L and M.

Photo by Suzanne Rider

Using marker chalk you can spell giant letters in the grass.

The goal is for the handler to indicate to his dog the path determined by the powdered chalk letter marked in the grass. Experiment to learn which handling moves direct your dog to travel on the chalk line path.

Alternately, you can play this game without marking the grass. The handler picks a letter, handles it path with the dog and the other students guess what the letter is.

Each completed stride of your dog while traveling on the chalk line can be a TAG. This game will teach you how to visualize and handle your dog's path. If you click and reinforce your dog for turning with you, you are using the game to create wonderful handler-focus.

**Proofing the Handling Moves**
Proof your handling moves with the proofing games you've already read about and others you developed.  The only difference is that you are asking your training partner to create distractions while you are performing the handling moves and your dog is responding to your handling.  As with all other training, your handling moves are not fully trained until your dog can respond to them, even while you are playing proofing games.

**Potential TAG Point Challenges**
While TAGTeaching is a great way to help students learn, you can encounter challenges.

What happens if the handler never does the movement the coach is waiting to TAG?  A TAG point should be easily attainable in two to three tries.  If the handler can't perform the TAG point, lower criteria by taking one step back in the process of shaping the behavior.

What if you want to TAG for more than one handling behavior at a time?  Build a behavior chain with one TAG point at a time.  If you are working on a rear cross, start with setting TAG points for the handler's feet.  Once the lower body behavior is established, focus on the behaviors of the upper body, one at a time.  When you have the entire rear cross behavior the coach can set a new TAG point that addresses the timing of the rear cross.  The key TAG point in handling moves will always be the positioning of the handler's arm, as that will enable ideal connection and help the handler with the timing of the move.

What if your training partner or student doesn't like the idea of being coached via TAGTeaching?  You have several options.  Experiment with different types of reinforcement.  Have a bystander drop chocolates in a box for every TAG, or use something else that the learner wants.  Have your partner observe TAGing in action and see the results.  The results are generally impressive.  Even if the learner doesn't like the process, he will like the result. Ask the learner to become the coach and TAG you. If you experiment with all this and your partner still does not like TAGging, accept your training partner's choice. Clicker training and TAG teaching are about reinforcing voluntary behaviors. No force, just fun!

**Peripheral Vision**
Peripheral vision is key to handling. Improve your peripheral vision skills while driving a car. Too often, when we are behind the wheel, we watch the road paying little attention to what we see in our peripheral vision. We can drive more defensively and improve our agility handling by engaging our peripheral vision, using it to gather information about the other cars and the environment around us. Using this skill will help you handle more effectively and maintain connection with your dog.

Other ideas to improve your peripheral vision:

- o Maintaining a soft focus — the more you hone in on an agility obstacle or any other detail, the less you will see your dog in your peripheral vision.
- o Scanning — or keeping your line of sight moving across the area in front of you. If you allow your eyes to settle on one spot, you are likely to lose your peripheral vision. Practice scanning while watching sports on TV. Keep your eye on the ball without moving your head.
- o Looking straight ahead and using your left and right hand to determine the boundaries of your side vision — is a great way to establish a baseline for your peripheral vision. You can then use this exercise to stretch that boundary by moving your hands back in small increments.

Standing in this position, raising and lowering the arms while wiggling your fingers, you can improve your peripheral vision. Use this training to help you keep track of your dog in the agility ring.

Photo by Angelica Steinker

**Does Your Dog Know This Move?**
If your dog is already agility trained, consider the following. Many handling moves can be intuitive to your dog. If you raise your arm, most dogs will move away from you and if you lower your arm, most dogs will move toward you. If you use a new handling move and your dog responds to it as you intended, you might assume your dog has learned the new move. For example a handler may rear cross and the dog may guess that this move means to change leads and turn the other way. If the handler does not repeatedly click and reinforce the turn and change of leads, however, the dog may not actually *learn* that she should turn because of the rear cross. Soon this dog is spinning on every rear cross and the handler is frustrated, because he thought the dog "knew" this move.

If you accidentally skipped the steps of teaching your dog your handling moves, it is likely that your dog may not be able to respond to them in a trial situation. To prevent the problem of your dog "guessing" what a handling move may mean, play the handling games, click and reinforce your dog for responding.

Another potential problem is that your dog may know the move but the information has not been generalized to other contexts — other agility equipment, other places and so on.  Playing proofing games while performing handling moves should help resolve this issue.

A great way to find out whether your dog understands a handling move is to use obstacle discriminations, situations when your dog has a choice of taking one of two or more obstacles.  Faced with the option of two obstacles, your dog must rely on your body movements to communicate which of the two to take.  Experiment and find out what responses your handling moves get from your dog, then adjust your training accordingly.

Try running silently.  Release your dog with "okay" and run a sequence without any verbal cues.  This will show you if your dog is "listening" to your handling moves.  If you are turned one way and your dog went another you know you need to work on handler-focus.

Another way to proof handling moves is to leave toys lying all over the training area.  These toys, people standing around, noises and so on will help you verify that your dog understands your body and verbal handling cues and will pay attention in many different circumstances.

Now strip out your body cues.  Stand still and experiment to see if your dog understands her verbal cues of left and right.  Ideally, she will be able to perform the left and right cues without any body cues from you.  When proofing my Border Collie Nicki on left and right I noticed that she was turning according to my head tilts.  After I faded that, she was cueing off my eyes.  If I looked left she turned left, if I looked right she turned right.  I decided not to fade that and so make sure I look in the direction that I want her to go!

**New Handling Move Game**
Whether you are learning your first handling move or adding a new one, train yourself and your dog.  First, create a plan.  Then, practice it without your dog.  Once

you are comfortable doing the move dog-less, to both the left and the right, invite your dog to join in the fun.

Suggested training plan for a new handling move:

1. Create a list of TAG points for the move.
2. Have your coach TAGTeach you the move without a dog; do it at a walk, then a jog and then a run.
3. Do the new move with agility equipment around you.
4. Perform the move with your dog on the flat with no agility equipment.
5. Do the move with your dog using only one jump.
6. Put it all together; the new move, your dog and an agility sequence with equipment.

The goal is to help you commit the move to your muscle memory, performing the move without thinking, before ever adding the equipment or your dog into the equation. By training new handling moves using approximations, you can be sure that both of you understand the handling move.

**Verbal Cues**
Verbal cues are used for the start line sit or down, release, directionals and obstacle performance. The cue "sit" places your dog in the duration sit position; the cue "okay" releases her. The cues "left" and "right" cue your dog to turn to her left and right, enabling her to see the next obstacle. The "look" cue is a directional indicating your dog should look behind her and "go" to run straight and take what she sees. The remaining verbal cues are for obstacle performance.

**Body Overshadows Verbal**
As descendants of predators, dogs are genetically wired to smell and see. This means that for most dogs your body cue will overshadow your verbal cue. I suggest not spending a whole lot of time on training body independent

verbal cues, other than left, right, go and look.  This way if you accidentally run to an incorrect position on course, you can use a well-timed verbal cue to repair your mistake.

Ideally, verbal cues are given as your dog commits to the previous obstacle.  If your dog is performing a sequence of jump, tire, jump, tunnel, the verbal cues would be "jump", then as your dog commits to that jump, "tire", then as your dog commits to the tire, "jump" and when your dog commits to the third jump the cue "tunnel".  Depending on the complexity of the course, it may be necessary to give cues even earlier and to stack them.

TAG training can help handlers with the timing of cues. Rather than using the TAG for a TAG point, the coach can say "now" to prompt the handler to give the verbal cue. Only an experienced agility handler will be able to accurately time this prompt.  Unlike dogs, handlers don't become prompt dependent, because the achievement of ideal timing is self-reinforcing.  Timely cues will cause the dog to run smoothly without slowing, spinning, or having to check in with you because she does not know where to go. Most handlers are reinforced by this.

Your dog's name can also be a handling cue, for both an emergency recall, or to create a head check.  A head check is when your dog maintains her path of travel but turns her head toward you.  Head checks are a great way of handling obstacle discriminations.  If you cue your dog to momentarily turn her head toward you while she continues to move, she never sees the obstacle that you don't want her to take.  Use part of your dog's name to get a head check and your dog's entire name to get a recall. For my dog Turbo, my head check signal is "Tur" and my recall is "Turbo."

To train a head check, give the cue while running side by side with your dog.  Having played the name game, this will prompt your dog to look at you.  Click the head check and reinforce with food or tug.  This method first prompts and then captures the head check.

### Head Check Addiction
Warning!  Once you have trained the head check, it can become addictive.  When running a fast dog, it can be tempting to give the head check cue frequently, to slow your dog down and allow you time to think.  Abandon this strategy, because running as fast as possible is part of your dog's fun.  Train both yourself and your dog to compete well at speed.  Only use the head check to prevent off courses or to let your dog know a change in direction is coming.

### Name Recall
A fun way to reinforce recalls is to cue your dog to "back" and, once your dog is 15 to 20-feet away, call her name and click for running towards you and then reinforce with food or tug when she gets to you.  You can even reinforce behind you to create speed for moving toward you.

You can also use your dog's name as an emergency recall.  If a dog gets loose and runs onto the field while you are running, or if you have accidentally sent your dog to the incorrect obstacle, you can use your dog's name to recall your dog to you.

### Timing Game
Chris Parker recommends handlers play this game to improve their timing.  Build a jump chute with eight-foot spacing between jumps.  If you are less experienced at this game or at timing your cues ideally, you may want to start with 12-foot spacing.  The larger the spacing the more "time" you have and the easier it is to succeed.  With tighter spacing, your cues need to be much faster.  Perform the sequence, (shown below), using front crosses.  The goal is to keep your dog turning tight and to prevent wrong courses.

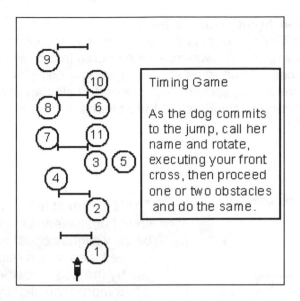

Timing Game

As the dog commits to the jump, call her name and rotate, executing your front cross, then proceed one or two obstacles and do the same.

As dog commits to jump, slow down, call name and execute front cross.  Travel one or two obstacles in the opposite direction before again calling, front crossing and turning your dog back again.  Because of the design of this exercise all front crosses will be pulling the dog around the respective uprights and then sending her in the opposite direction.

In order to ideally time your front crosses, slow down and then call your dog's name the moment your dog commits to the obstacle, (two front feet in the air), before the turn. Your coach can prompt you by saying "now".  Timing is a physical skill so you can practice your timing by playing video games.

As well as practicing your timing to improve your handling, start noticing the common obstacle patterns in the competition ring.  Use these patterns to train and prepare your handling for competition.

## Common Agility Course Patterns

Rhonda Carter explains that a simple way to look at course design is to chunk sections of the course into familiar sequences. All courses are made using a combination of lines, pinwheels, serpentines, boxes and zig zag patterns. Some courses include all of the patterns, others only a few.

*Lines*

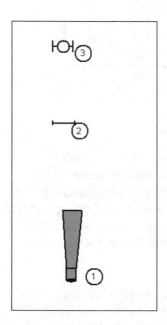

The diagram at left shows a line of obstacles. Lines can be very slightly offset and still be taken as a straight line by the dog. Obstacles offset more than slightly will require handling moves to ensure that the dog will take the obstacle. This is especially true if the dog is young and inexperienced.

Evaluate how many obstacles you can take in a straight line if you start alongside your dog. At what point will your dog get too far ahead and start curling back toward you? Use this data to establish handling strategies. If I know that my dog will curl after three obstacles and we are facing a line of five, I know I will need to use a handling move, such as a rear cross, to tell my dog to keep traveling straight for the last two obstacles. Without that handling move, I can predict that your dog will curl away from an obstacle back toward you and incur a refusal fault.

*Pinwheels*

The diagram at right shows a pinwheel.  Even if the obstacles, angles or spacing vary, the pinwheel concept is the same.  Use different obstacles, angles and spacing in training to create pinwheels, so your dog learns to recognize this pattern.

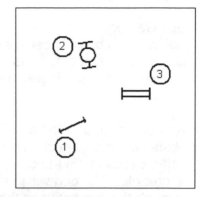

Establish where your feet need to be and what pinwheel handling strategy works best for you and your dog.  Know the spot you need to run to and turn if you are using a pull turn.  Which handling move gets you the best results?  Practice pin wheels with pull turns, rear crosses, front crosses and false turns so you know how each option works for you and your dog.

*Serpentines*

In the diagram at right, the three obstacles create a serpentine.  Even though both dog and handler may be used to seeing the traditional three jump serpentines, it is important to recognize this type of sequence and to implement a handling plan accordingly.

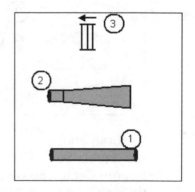

Which serpentine handling strategy works best for you and your dog? Experiment, evaluate and choose.  Be sure to gather data on how you handle serpentines when you are ahead of, alongside, or behind your dog and off either side of your body.

*Box Games*
Setting up a box of obstacles creates an array of challenges.  Not only does it present options, but also 90-degree turns, 180-degree turns, 270-degree turns and threadles.

A threadle, also called a pull through, refers to two obstacles next to each other that are performed in the same direction.  In the diagram below, jump #6 and #7 are a threadle.  The dog will jump #6 and then be pulled back through the gap between the two jumps to jump #7.

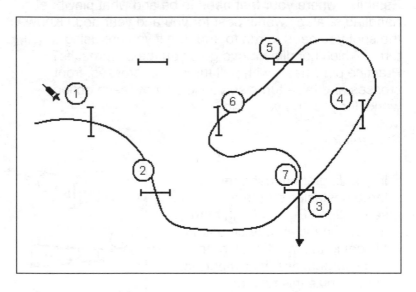

Pictured above is Greg Derrett's training exercise called the double box.  This set up allows you to practice, 90-degree turns, 180-degree turns, 270-degree turns and threadles.  #1-2 is a 90-degree turn.  #2-3 is a 180-degree turn.  #4-5 is a 270-degree turn and #6-7 is a threadle.

*Zig Zags*

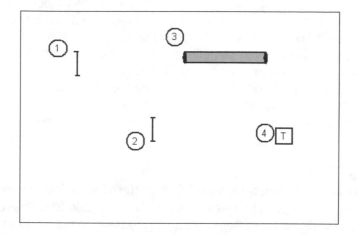

The diagram above depicts a zig zag pattern. This pattern is easily completed with rear crosses or, if the handler is fast, front crosses.

These five sequence patterns are predictable in the sense they will be part of the courses you run in competition. If you develop a handling plan off each side of your body, for each of the patterns and for when you are ahead, even with, or behind your dog then you will have designed your own successful method of handling. Congrats! Your dog will be able to anticipate what is to come because your handling system clearly tells her.

**Handle at Your Dog's Speed**
When learning how to handle, the main problem is that it all happens so fast! Just as it can be tempting to use your head checking cue more than you need to, you may also unconsciously delay your cues in an attempt to slow your dog down. Resist the temptation! Instead, over-prepare by pretending that you are running a dog that is even faster than your dog. When you can call your cues and signal your handling moves at the speed of the pretend dog, you know you are ready to go into the ring.

**Course Analysis**

At an agility competition, competitors are given a copy of the courses they will be running that day. Analyzing this course map to plan your handling strategy is a key to success. Begin with penciling in the path you want your dog to take. Then, using your dog's path as your reference, begin penciling in your own path. You can collect course copies by requesting them from your instructor or agility friends. Most competitors collect course maps.

*AKC*

The AKC (American Kennel Club) offers two titling classes for agility dogs. Titling means your dog is able to achieve titles (certificates entitling your dog to have initials added before or after her registered name). The Standard class includes the contact obstacles and a table, while the Jumpers with Weaves class includes only jumps, tunnels and weave poles. AKC offers three levels of agility Novice (for beginners), Open and Excellent. For more information visit the AKC website at www.AKC.org.

*NADAC*

NADAC stands for the North American Dog Agility Council. NADAC emphasizes safety and flow in their courses. There are no tables in NADAC classes. NADAC offers three levels of agility: Novice, Open and Elite. Trials usually offer a Standard and Gamblers combined course. Jumpers, Tunnelers, Weavers and Touch and Go may also be offered. Jumpers is a course of all jumps with an occasional tunnel. Tunnelers is a course of tunnels and Weavers is mostly weave poles, and some tunnels. Touch and Go is tunnels and contact obstacles. For some of the NADAC games all competitors run the same course, but the time allowed to run the course is shortened with each progressive level.

NADAC is tremendously popular in some parts of the country and not available in other parts. For additional information on NADAC, go to www.NADAC.com.

*USDAA*
The United States Dog Agility Association (USDAA) is one of the oldest American agility organizations. USDAA also offers three levels of agility: Starters/Novice, Advanced and Masters. USDAA classes are Standard, Jumpers, Gamblers, Snooker and Pairs relay. Jumpers is a course of mostly or all jumps. The Gamblers class contains an element of handling your dog at a distance. Snooker is a strategy game that emphasizes the handler's control of his dog. Pairs relay is a fun class that involves two dogs and two handlers, one running the first part of the course and the second dog and handler team running the second half. The website for USDAA is www.usdaa.com.

*Other Agility Organizations*
In addition to these three major organizations, other organizations offer agility competitions. Canine Performance Events (CPE) is a new agility organization that seems to be gaining rapid popularity. The United Kennel Club (UKC) offers agility with some different obstacles and a strong emphasis on control. Just for Fun is an agility organization started by Bud Houston that emphasizes fun. Bud is also involved in Tea Cup Agility, which is for small dogs only. For more information on any of these organizations, check the Appendix.

*Course Walk Through*
At competitions the judge allows time for handlers to walk the course and plan their strategy. You will need to memorize the course, focusing on segments by lumping obstacles into the constellations discussed in this book helps. Determine the ideal path for your dog to take. Get down to her level of sight. Evaluate what your dog will see and use that information to plan your dog's path.

Your dog's path will determine where she needs to turn. For each turn in your dog's path, ask yourself which handling move (pull turn, rear cross, front cross, or false turn) you will use.  The game is on: do your best to execute your handling plan while smiling!

**Handling Seminars**
Handling is about consistent communication with your dog. There are many handling styles out there.  Serious damage can be done to your dog's ability to understand your handling language if you train with people that teach different styles.  Find a handling style that makes sense to you and is compatible with what your dog knows and stick with it.

**Flow**
The concept of flow, or zoning, in sport psychology is used to describe a mental state of intense focus.  Activities done when in the "zone" are self-reinforcing.  Flow is fun!  Dogs also experience a similar state when engaged in an activity that they are accomplishing with great fluency.  This flow is self-reinforcing to a dog as it is to a handler.  For dogs that are highly reinforced by doing agility, well-timed cues by the handler can maintain behavior chains with high fluency.  The release and the first obstacle cue becomes the reinforcement for the duration sit at the start line, the release off the contact becomes the reinforcement for going into the 2O2ONT position and so on.

Even if your dog is not crazed by doing agility, but was clicker trained, properly timed cues will be reinforcing. Because of classical conditioning, your cues have become associated with good stuff — they have become positively reinforcing.

In *Don't Shoot the Dog*, Karen Pryor uses the example of how kids love to hear a recess bell ring because it signals that fun is about to begin.  With proper training, any cue you give your dog will have the same effect, providing you don't poison your cue by using negative reinforcement or punishment.  If you give your dog a cue, and then yell at your dog or give your dog leash corrections to comply, you have poisoned that cue.  Research in behavior analysis shows that cues taught to dogs using positive reinforcement prompt a happy attitude.  Cues taught with negative reinforcement prompt stress.  Interestingly when a cue that was taught using negative reinforcement is repeatedly given after a positively trained cue the stress responses begin to occur after the positively trained cue is given.  The previously happy cue predicts the "poisoned" cue.

Precise, accurate handling is both a science and an art, and there are many things that you can do to improve your handling.  Timing is a physical skill, so if it isn't as fast as you want it to be, keep practicing.  With practice your timing will improve.

Just in case I have not said it enough, the most important thing to focus on is giving clear and consistent body cues.  Only then, can your dog run both clean and fast.  Agility is a blast — enjoy the journey of learning to handle!

# Chapter 11   Click! The Adventure Begins

You are in the "clicker training agility know". You now face choices. How high should you jump your dog in training? How many trials a year to attend? What is best for your dog? What does your dog want? So much of agility is about achievement and us. I recently spoke to a top competitor in a different dog sport. Everything this person said was centered on himself; his dog was only mentioned in terms of how she would help him attain more fame. I challenge agility competitors world-wide to be different, to keep the focus on the dog and to make all decisions based on what is best for the dog not on what will help secure money or ego enhancement. Agility is a game we play with our dogs.

Dogs don't care about blue ribbons and they don't care about a run being qualifying or non-qualifying. Dogs truly just want to have fun, and some, like my Turbo, truly just want to be a couch potato. Consider what your dog wants. If your dog is not addicted to agility, consider another dog, or limiting competing to your dog's favorite environments. Dogs don't often have a vote in what we choose for them, but we can give them one. We can watch their body language, their expressions and we can listen to what they say. When you listen, you hear that they have something to say about everything.

Photos by Suzanne and Tony Rider and Spot Shots

What do these dogs have in common?
They are all smiling. That is what agility is
all about, making your dog smile.

## The Best Teachers

Many dogs enjoy agility but for various reasons they still present a wide array of training challenges.  These dogs are our best agility instructors.  Our training and trialing frustrations are actually gifts.  The challenges we face allow us the opportunity to learn, and only by learning can we become the best we can be.

My first agility dog, Moose, taught me more than all the seminars I have attended.  Moose taught me that force does not work with most terriers.  Moose taught me that if I were forceful, he too would resort to the use of force.  Moose taught me that it is truly possible, even for a terrier, to love his "work".  Moose shaped me to find another way, to find clicker training.  I listened to all he had to say, even when it was painful for me to hear.

One day after only a few years of competing Moose told me something was wrong.  He told me it was time to stop trialing and to just be a pet.  He told me by showing me that he was unable to differentiate one cue from another.  He showed me by staring aimlessly at nothing.  Odd obsessive behavior had always been normal for Moose, but this was different.  I knew something was wrong.  Years later I finally learned, he had canine cognitive dysfunction, doggie Alzheimer disease.  The years that came were hard; it was a long good bye.  I will eternally miss my Moosie-man, my best teacher.  His lessons made me a better trainer and person.

With every dog, I have learned valuable lessons.  When I added my first Border Collie, Nicki, I learned that breed differences really do exist.  I learned that I had to work anywhere from ten to one hundred times harder to get my Jack Russells to do the same behaviors as my Border Collie.  The Border Collie wanted to do agility; two of my Jacks wanted to do what they felt like, which usually had nothing to do with agility.  Ah, the joy of learning the lesson of loving what is.  Love them the way they are.  Avoid fighting with genetic and biochemical make up, this is always a losing battle.

**Responsibility is Power**
Nicki taught me about taking responsibility. She did not lecture me; she gently guided me to see the truth. When I first got Nicki, I lacked a handling system. She was my first Border Collie and fast. I had no access to consistent instruction, so I was free falling. Patiently Nicki taught me. All the times I was absolutely certain she had made a "mistake" she smiled and continued to play with me. Thanks to her patience, I became aware of the truth. It was always me. Whether it was a handling error, or a training error (I was both the handler and the trainer). If Nicki failed to respond to a cue, it was the result of my training. If Nicki did not respond to a handling cue as I had intended, it was the result of my inconsistent handling. With this realization came empowerment and freedom. If what Nicki did was truly the result of my training and handling, then it could all be modified.

I made a lot of mistakes training Nicki and I still do, but our journey has been fun! Many of the mistakes I made, like letting her watch other agility dogs run (which to this day haunts us when she sneaks a peak at the dog running in the other ring) are the result of my training. Of course, Nicki is genetically and biochemically wired to eye, stalk and obsess, but what she does when I run her is *still* the result of my training. Taking responsibility opens the door to learning.

Literally every dog I have ever met or seen, has taught me something. Sometimes I learn something about that dog's behavior motor pattern, sometimes it is something about the owner. It is amazing the stories a dog can tell if you learn to listen.

As you journey through the agility world, allow your dog to be your teacher. Allow your dog to tell you what will work, and what won't.  What brings her joy?  Stress?  How would she like to spend her life?  It is your choice to consider what your dog thinks and feels.  If you choose to listen, your reinforcement will be learning, respect and true love.

# Appendix 1 Glossary of Terms

While writing this book I found it difficult to find clear definitions of operant conditioning, classical conditioning and behavioral terms. As a result, I have compiled a glossary of the scientific and agility terms referred to in this book and some extras that should be helpful. I have been as accurate as I could, mistakes in any of these definitions are my own.

When I did not write a term's definition, the author's name is in parentheses. Scientific definitions are subject to disagreement; researchers often and vehemently argue how terms should be defined. I picked definitions that made sense in terms of dog training, but at times I listed two definitions to allow you to choose which you prefer.

If you long to be the best trainer you can be, learn to love the games of operant and classical conditioning. An understanding of the science of how animals, including humans, learn will enable you to think critically and logically. You are then free to choose what to include or exclude from your training program. Let the fact that positive reinforcement is the most powerful way to modify behavior guide you.

# A – B

**Acquisition**
The learning phase, or up curve phase, of either classical or operant conditioning (Jean Donaldson).

**AKC**
Abbreviation for the American Kennel Club, a national dog registration and dog show association. For further information see www.AKC.org.

**Antecedent stimulus**
A stimulus preceding, coming before, a behavior that controls performance of the behavior (also known as **cue,**

**signal, discriminative stimulus, SD**) (Pamela Reid). A prompt can also be an antecedent stimulus.

**Approximation**
Any portion of a defined behavior (Karen Pryor).

**Association**
This can also be called **pairing**. The process by which a stimulus becomes linked with another stimulus (Pamela Reid).

**Autoshaping**
An increase in genetically programmed or innate behavior in the presence of specific reinforcement of that behavior (Karen Pryor).

**Aversive** or **Aversive Stimulus**
Something an organism will work to avoid (Karen Pryor). Aversives by definition cause an organism stress, thus they should be avoided or at least minimized. Stress is incompatible with fun and win/win training.

**Backward Chaining** or **Backchaining**
In backward chaining, the end (terminal) behavior is established first because this response leads directly to reinforcement. Once this new behavior has been established, a cue is introduced for this behavior. Then the next-to-end behavior is trained, and reinforced with the cue for the final behavior (Karen Pryor).

Backchaining or Backward Chaining is the development of a chain of responses by training the last behavior in the chain first, then the next to last, and so on until the entire chain is performed as a single complex behavior (Pamela Reid).

**Baseline**
The rate of occurrence of a behavior before training is introduced (Karen Pryor).

## Backward Conditioning
Backward conditioning refers to the presentation of the unconditioned stimulus (UCS) before the conditioned stimulus (CS). Let's say you're trying to condition a dog to like the grooming table by pairing it with chicken. The order that would work is: 1) dog on grooming table 2) helping of chicken. Backwards conditioning would be: 1) helping of chicken 2) dog on grooming table. You won't get love of the table this way. You'll get, at best, nothing, and at worst — if the dog really hates the table, fear of chicken because it predicts the dreaded table (Jean Donaldson).

## Behavior Chain
Also known as **chaining**. Chaining is appropriate for teaching a complex sequence of responses (Pamela Reid).

## Behavior System
Konrad Lorenz coined the term behavior systems as a replacement for the term instinct. Behavior systems describes behaviors that are linked together and that appear to be innate. Also called **fixed action patterns** and, more currently, **modal action patterns**.

## Bite Inhibition
A process through which, as the result of puppy play, dogs learn to inhibit hard biting.

## Blocking
Failure of an animal to attend to a novel stimulus when it is presented in a compound with an already learned stimulus (Jean Donaldson). Pair a click with a treat until a dog drools at the sound of the click. Then present the click and a verbal "yes" at the same time and repeat for ten repetitions. Then test both the click and the verbal "yes" and find that "yes" fails to elicit drooling. The "yes" was blocked. Blocking is not the same as overshadowing.

**Bridge** or **Bridging**
A stimulus that bridges or spans the temporal (time) gap between the behavior and the reinforcer (Karen Pryor). The clicker is a bridge. Using a verbal "yes" marker, is also a bridge.

**Buja Board**
Generally a 2-foot by 2-foot piece of plywood with a tennis ball in a sock staple gunned on the bottom side. This enables dogs to get used to the wobbling motion that will ultimately become the teeter. Named after clicker trainer Brenda Buja.

# C – D

**Capturing**
Also called **catching** by some trainers. A procedure in which a naturally-occurring behavior increases in frequency through reinforcement (Pamela Reid).

**Classical Conditioning**
Learning that results when associations are formed between stimuli (also known as **respondent conditioning, Pavlovian conditioning, S-S learning**) (Pamela Reid).

Classical conditioning is the process by which one stimulus becomes linked with and predicts the arrival of another stimulus (Diana Bird). Pavlov rang the bell, presented food, and the dogs drooled when they heard the bell, because they had made the association that the bell signified that the food was coming.

**Classical Counterconditioning**
A procedure which overlays an existing emotional response by conditioning another conditioned emotional state that is counter to the original one (also known as **cross-motivational transfer**) (Pamela Reid). This is the procedure by which you change a dog's emotional response. Fear can become joy.

408

**Clickerwise**
This non-scientific term is dog trainer lingo used to describe a dog that is in the proper mental state to perform cues or learn via operant conditioning. Arousal or stress can interfere with a dog's ability to be "clickerwise" (Karen Pryor).

**Closed Economy**
A training procedure requiring the learner to work for all reinforcement. If you are using a closed economy, your dog never sees a food bowl. All of the dog's food is consumed during training sessions.

**Commitment Point**
Your best guess at what point your dog has made the decision to perform the specific behavior you are working on. When jumping, the commitment point is when the dog has her two front feet in the air.

**Compulsive Training** or **Compulsion Training**
Training that forces the dog to perform or withhold behaviors in order to escape or avoid unpleasant events. Compulsion training is win/lose or lose/lose and in direct contrast to clicker training.

**Conditioned Emotional Response**
An emotional response conditioned to an originally neutral stimulus (Pamela Reid). Emma Parson's game of "where's the monster?" (in Chapter 5) is an example of a conditioned emotional response. In agility, a common conditioned emotional response can be elicited from dogs by the term "ready," usually an excited emotional response.

**Conditioned Negative Punisher**
A stimulus that acquires punishing properties as a result of repeatedly being presented just prior to the absence or withdrawal of a reinforcing stimulus (also known as **no reward marker**, **non-reward marker**) (Pamela Reid).

When the dog performs an unwanted behavior the trainer says "too bad" and places the dog in time out. "Too bad" predicts time out for the dog.

## Conditioned Negative Reinforcer
A stimulus that acquires reinforcing properties as a result of repeatedly being presented just prior to the absence or withdrawal of an aversive stimulus (Pamela Reid). A leashed dog darts out ahead of the handler, the handler says "no" and then begins yanking on the leash repeatedly until the dog falls into heel position next to the handler. Not part of clicker training but, unfortunately for dogs, used by many trainers.

## Conditioned Punisher
A stimulus that acquires punishing properties as a result of repeatedly being presented just prior to the delivery of a primary punisher (Pamela Reid). Another win/lose that will likely become a lose/lose. You won't have a happy dog or speed if you train using conditioned punishers. For example, when the dog does an unwanted behavior the trainer screams "BAH" and throws a noisey object near the dog. "BAH" becomes a conditioned punisher and will elicit stress in the dog, and damage the dog/trainer bond.

## Conditioned Reinforcer
A stimulus that acquires reinforcing properties as a result of repeatedly being presented just prior to the delivery of a reinforcing stimulus (also known as **secondary reinforcer, marker**, **bridge**) (Pamela Reid). The sound of the clicker is a conditioned reinforcer.

## Conditioned Response
Abbreviated CR, a response elicited by the presence of a conditioned stimulus, often similar to the unconditioned response (Pamela Reid). Pavlov's dogs drooling after the bell rang was a conditioned response.

**Conditioned Stimulus**
Abbreviated CS, a stimulus that acquires significance as a result of repeatedly being presented just prior to the delivery of an unconditioned stimulus (Pamela Reid). When Pavlov first rang the bell nothing happened. Once classical conditioning had occurred, the dogs began to drool when hearing the bell. The bell had become a conditioned stimulus.

**Consequence**
A stimulus that either reinforces or punishes an animal's behavior (Pamela Reid). Operant conditioning follows an ABC formula. Antecedent → Behavior → Consequence. (Cue → behavior → consequence).

**Contingent Observation**
A procedure that contains elements of time out in which observation of pleasurable activities is possible but participation is not (Pamela Reid). If you put one of your dogs in a crate, and in view of the crated dog, you play with the second dog, the crated dog is experiencing contingent observation. (Behavior analysts typically call this an inclusionary time out.)

**Continuous Schedule**
Abbreviated CRF – a schedule in which each occurrence of a response is reinforced (Pamela Reid). When a behavior is in acquisition, you should reinforce every occurrence. When the behavior is in maintenance, you differentially reinforce only the excellent responses.

**Countercondition** or **Counterconditioning**
There are two forms of counterconditioning, classical and operant. Classical counterconditioning is a procedure which overlays an emotional response by conditioning a new emotional state that is counter to the original one (also known as **cross motivational transfer**) (Pamela Reid).

Operant counterconditioning is a procedure in which the animal is conditioned to perform a behavior that is physically incompatible with the target behavior, in response to antecedent stimuli that originally signaled the target behavior (Pamela Reid).

**Criteria**
A clearly articulated standard of performance that the dog must achieve in order to be reinforced — this may be a single behavior or a chain of behaviors (Jean Donaldson).

**Decision Point** or **Commitment Point**
A term that refers to something about the dog's behavior suggesting the dog has made a commitment. In agility, it is generally common to say that the dog has committed to an obstacle when the dog has two feet over or on the obstacle.

**Default Behavior**
The behavior that has the highest likelihood of occurring; a preferred behavior. It could be the first behavior trained, or a behavior that is assumed to be enjoyable to the dog.

**Deprivation**
Withholding of a reinforcer or necessity (food, water, attention, freedom) for a period of time, with the intent of increasing motivation (Karen Pryor).

**Desensitization**
Presentation of a stimulus at a level of intensity that elicits little or no response from the dog, then gradually increasing the intensity of the stimulus (Karen Pryor). This is the process by which a fearful dog will get used to the bang of the teeter, and the movement of the teeter, but only if the approximations are tiny and the training very gradual.

**Differential Reinforcement of Excellent Behavior (DRE)**
A schedule of reinforcement that is selectively reinforcing more accurate, more intense or faster performances (Karen Pryor).

**Differential Reinforcement Schedules**
Differential Reinforcement — reinforcement of some behaviors but not others, depending on some specified properties of the behavior.
There are three types of differential reinforcement schedules that are most commonly used by dog trainers:
1. **Differential Reinforcement of Excellent Behavior** (DRE). A schedule that trainers can use to selectively reinforce more accurate, more intense or faster performances of a behavior or behavior chain.
2. **Differential Reinforcement of Other Behavior** (DRO). A schedule that a trainer can use to selectively decrease a behavior that is unwanted by differentially reinforcing *all* other behavior.
3. **Differential Reinforcement of Incompatible Behavior** (DRI). A schedule that a trainer can use to selectively decrease an unwanted behavior by differentially reinforcing any behavior that is physically incompatible with the unwanted behavior (Pamela Reid).

**Discrimination**
The process of learning to respond to certain stimuli and not others (Pamela Reid).

**Discriminative Stimulus**
Abbreviated Sd — a stimulus in the presence of which a behavior is likely to be reinforced (Pamela Reid). Cues are discriminative stimuli.

**Displacement Behaviors**
Arise when an animal is in conflict or frustrated and are almost always related to feeding or grooming behaviors.

Displacement behaviors are not unique behaviors genetically selected for, but are species wide. Examples are sniffing and scratching (Karen Pryor). Many signs of stress are displacement behaviors.

## DRE
### Differential Reinforcement of Excellent Behavior
(**DRE**). A schedule that trainers use to selectively reinforce more accurate, more intense or faster performances. Very similar to shaping by successive approximation (Pamela Reid).

## Drive
A hypothetical source of energy for behavior to explain why animals are internally motivated to engage in different behaviors at various times (Pamela Reid). Not a scientific term, but dog trainer lingo.

## Duration Behavior
A behavior that must endure for a period of time (Pamela Reid).

# E – F
## Extinction or Extinguishing
A procedure in which the reinforcement of previously reinforced behavior is discontinued (Pamela Reid). Note you can't extinguish a self-reinforcing behavior. Many dog behaviors are self-reinforcing, such as barking, digging and so on.

## Extinction Burst
A temporary increase in the frequency of a behavior that accompanies the early phases of an extinction program (Karen Pryor).

## Fading
The gradual removal of antecedent stimuli, such as a prompt or cue (Karen Pryor).

**Fake Front**
Also called **false turn** and **reverse flow pivot**, this agility handling move is one half of the front cross. The move is used to pull the dog's path toward the handler to give the dog a better approach angle or a strategic advantage for the next obstacle.

**Fault**
In agility, when an error has occurred and the judge deducts points.

**Fixed Action Pattern**
An innate pattern of behaviors that may interfere with the training process. Once the fixed action pattern is triggered the animal will continue with the series of behaviors even if the environmental trigger for it has been removed. Border Collies can get what agility trainers call sticky, stopping or moving very slowly, when their predatory fixed action pattern is activated.

**Fixed Interval Schedule**
A schedule of reinforcement that dictates that the first correct response after a set amount of time has passed is reinforced (i.e., a consequence is delivered). The time period required is always the same, therefore predictable to the animal.

**Fluency**
The fast and rapid response to cues with minimum latency. Latency is the interval between the presentation of an antecedent (cue) stimulus and performance of the behavior (Pamela Reid).

**Forward Chaining**
Development of a chain of responses by training the initial behavior in the chain first, then the second, the third, and so on until the entire chain is performed as a single complex behavior (Pamela Reid). Forward chaining is scientifically proven to be less effective than backward

chaining, but is rampant in dance, music and martial arts classes!

**Free Shaping or Free Behavior Shaping**
Shaping refers to the procedure in which a new behavior is developed by the systematic reinforcement of behaviors or behavioral elements, each of which more and more closely resembles the goal behavior. The word free refers to the lack of prompting used in this process (Pamela Reid). Free shaping requires a high level of skill from the trainer to avoid unnecessary frustration in the learner. Free shaping a behavior that you ultimately want to be very precise, may not be a good idea — precise behaviors usually require some prompting.

**Front Cross**
An agility handling move during which the handler crosses in front of the dog's path to signal a change in direction.

# G – H –I – J – K
**Gamblers**
A game played in competitive agility that consists of two phases. The first phase is a point accumulation phase, and the second a gamble phase. The gamble is designed to test the handler's ability to direct his dog from a distance. Depending on the level of the gamble, the handler will be required to handle his dog anywhere from 15- to 30-feet away.

**Generalizing** or **Proofing**
Generalization is when a cued behavior becomes more probable in the presence of one stimulus or situation as a result of having been reinforced in the presence of another stimulus or situation (Pamela Reid).

**Habituate** or **Habituation**
The ability to stop reacting to a meaningless stimulus is called habituation (Pamela Reid). When you put your dog on the **Buja Board** and within a few minutes the dog stops

showing any concern about the movement under her feet, she has habituated to the **Buja Board** movement.

**Involuntary Behavior**
Responses that are not under the animal's control and are unlikely to be controlled by consequences (Pamela Reid). It is probably impossible to put a dog's eye blink on cue because the eye blink is involuntary.

**Jackpot**
A larger or higher-value reinforcer than the norm (Pamela Reid).

**Jump Start**
Also called reinforcer sampling. You allow the dog to see the reinforcer you plan to use, as a way to increase motivation (Pamela Reid). Flashing food or a toy as a way to help get the dog motivated are examples of jump starting. The problem is that the motivation is dependent on the flashing of food or toy and you won't have either in the agility competition ring.

**Kong Toy**
A special dog toy made of nearly indestructible rubber, which can be stuffed with food and left with the dog as a chew toy. For more information visit www.KongCompany.com.

# L – M
**Latency**
The interval between the presentation of an antecedent stimulus and performance of the behavior (Pamela Reid).

**Latent Learning**
Learning that occurs but is not demonstrated or realized until there is motivation to show the accompanying changes in behavior (Pamela Reid).

## Lead Out

An agility handling move used at the start line. The dog is asked to stay and the handler moves out onto the course. This enables the handler to recall the dog over the first set of obstacles, and is used to achieve a strategic advantage.

## Learned Helplessness

A condition a dog may experience when she feels that unpleasant events are not controllable. In experiments in which dogs are shocked, if they can escape the shock, they experience frustration and anxiety. But if the dog cannot control or predict the shocks, after initial experimentation the dog will collapse and fail to respond to the shocks at all. It is as if the dog gives up because she knows she can't do a thing about it; she cannot adapt. It is not clear to her what behavior will cause her to receive a shock, so she does not determine any connection between consequences and her behavior. Consequences, whether reinforcing or punitive, don't affect these dogs and they appear depressed and despondent. It can be very difficult to rehabilitate such dogs. Rehabilitation revolves around convincing the dog that she can, in fact, control and predict events (gain some stability); in other words, building confidence (Steven Lindsay).

## Learned Irrelevance

Also called the **pre-exposure effect**, the dog learns that a signal is not predictive and, therefore, irrelevant. Subsequent conditioning of the signal is retarded (Pamela Reid).

## Learned Laziness

The most problematic contingency is when a dog is exposed to a situation in which reinforcement is equally likely to occur whether or not the specified response occurs — that is, the reinforcer and response occur independently of each other. In training, the non-contingent presentation of food may result in various interference effects collectively referred to as Learned Laziness (Steven Lindsay).

**Learning**
The process whereby an animal experiences certain relations between events (Pamela Reid). Our dogs are always learning. What is your dog learning right now?

Changes in behavior resulting from experience (Jean Donaldson).

**Learning Set**
The phenomenon of an animal becoming progressively more proficient at solving new problems as a result of extensive experience solving similar problems (Pamela Reid). This is why clicker training is such a great gift to dog trainers: it helps dogs learn to learn, increasing their abilities to problem solve.

**Limited Hold** or **Limited Hold Schedule**
A restriction placed on a schedule requiring that the behavior be performed within a time limit in order for reinforcement to be delivered (Pamela Reid).

**Loading**
As in "loading the clicker" — the process of repeatedly presenting the clicker sound just prior to the delivery of a reinforcing stimulus so that it comes to acquire reinforcing properties (also known as **magazine training**) (Pamela Reid).

**Lumping** and **Splitting**
These terms were coined by clicker training greats, Marian and Keller Breland, and Bob Bailey. Lumping is a common training error of attempting to combine steps of training with the intent of speeding up learning. In reality, it accomplishes the opposite. Splitting is the proper way of training, always breaking down the behaviors to the

419

smallest possible components.  This is the fastest and most ideal way of training new behaviors (Pamela Reid).

**Luring** or **Prompting**
Using some stimulus to elicit the behavior you wish to reinforce.  For example, using the reinforcer to draw the dog's attention and luring the dog into doing what you want, or you can use physical props to guide a dog into doing what you want.  Physically touching your dog with varying amounts of pressure to get the dog to do what you want is also a form of prompting (Pamela Reid).

**Maintenance**
The persistence phase of training in which associations learned during acquisition are repeatedly confirmed (Pamela Reid).

**Management**
Controlling the dog's environment so that you encourage desirable behavior, and discourage/prevent undesirable behavior (Pamela Reid).

**Marker**
A stimulus that signals to the animal the precise behavior that caused her to earn reinforcement (Pamela Reid).

**Masters** or **Master's Level**
The highest level of difficulty in the United States Dog Agility Association's (USDAA) agility tests.

**Motivation**
Psychological energy that arouses a dog to engage in particular behavior (Pamela Reid).

# N – O
**Negative Contrast**
Depressed responding that follows delivery of reinforcement that is of lower value than the norm (also known as disappointment effect) (Pamela Reid).  Negative

420

contrast is something to avoid in your training. Make sure that all your reinforcers are of high value to your dog or start lower and move upwards.

## Negative Punishment
A procedure that involves the removal of a reinforcing stimulus as a consequence for a behavior and results in the decrease in the probability of that behavior (Pamela Reid). An example is timing your dog out in her crate for a short period of time.

## Negative Reinforcement
A procedure that involves the removal of aversive stimulus as a consequence for a behavior and results in an increase in the probability of that behavior (Pamela Reid). Repeatedly yanking on your dog's leash to force her into heel position is an example of negative reinforcement.

## Non-Contingent Reinforcement
Delivery of reinforcement irrespective of the dog's behavior (Pamela Reid). Feeding treats to your dog even though she is not engaging in a behavior is an example of non-contingent reinforcement.

## Non-Qualifying
In agility, a run that incurred errors will usually be non-qualifying. Non-qualifying runs don't earn points toward coveted agility dog titles.

## Novel Stimuli
A new stimulus (event) not previously experienced (Pamela Reid).

## Off Course
In agility when a dog takes an incorrect obstacle it is called off course and is faulted by the judge.

**One Trial Learning**
A single presentation of behavior consequence resulting in changes in behavior.

**Operant Conditioning**
Learning that results from contingent relationships between behavior and its consequences (also known as **instrumental conditioning**, **Skinnerian conditioning**, **S-R learning**) (Pamela Reid).

Operant conditioning works in four ways: Positive Reinforcement, Positive Punishment, Negative Reinforcement and Negative Punishment.

**Positive Reinforcement**
A procedure that involves the application of a reinforcing stimulus as a consequence for a behavior and results in an increase in the probability of that behavior (Pamela Reid).

**Positive Punishment**
A procedure that involves the application of an aversive stimulus as a consequence for a behavior and results in a decrease in the probability of that behavior (Pamela Reid).

**Negative Reinforcement**
A procedure that involves the removal of an aversive stimulus as a consequence for a behavior and results in an increase in the probability of that behavior (Pamela Reid).

**Negative Punishment**
A procedure that involves the removal of a reinforcing stimulus as a consequence for a behavior and results in the decrease in the probability of that behavior (Pamela Reid).

**Opposition Reflex**
Sometimes called the **balancing reflex**. The opposition reflex is when an animal leans into pressure rather than yielding to it (scientifically known as **positive thigmotaxis**) or the tendency for a dog to resist pressure.

**Overshadowing**
If two stimuli are presented together, one will dominate the other even though both would be effective if presented separately (Pamela Reid). Present a verbal "yes", click at the same time, and then feed to create a conditioning effect. After conditioning takes place, dog is drooling. Test both separately and find that only the click elicits the conditioned response. The more salient, more noticeable, click conditioned and the verbal "yes" was overshadowed.

# P — Q — R

**Pack Theory**
According to Dr. Ray Coppinger, Ph.D., author of the book *"Dogs: A Startling New Understanding Regarding their Evolution and Origin,"* dogs are not pack animals like their ancestor the wolf. Coppinger explains that it used to be thought that people domesticated wolves but the current scientific theories indicate that it is much more likely that wolves evolved into dogs as the result of scavenging human garbage. Another interesting book is *Dominance Theory in Dogs* by James O'Heare. This book extensively discusses how the theory of dominance is not useful when applied to dogs, because it does not accurately predict behavior.

**Pair** or **Pairing**
The process by which two stimuli become linked (Pamela Reid).

**Pattern Training**
Also called **patterning** or **overlearning**. Once behavior is trained to your chosen criteria, doing an enormous number of repetitions beyond that which would be normally required (Pamela Reid).

**Ping-Ponging**
This term was first referenced in print by Morgan Spector in "Clicker Training for Obedience." Ping-ponging refers to bouncing your criteria gently back and forth while still

overall increasing it. Pam Reid says, "criteria refers to a behavior or a behavior chain that the dog must emit in order to receive reinforcement." If you were taking a test and each question you responded to, was progressively harder than the previous one, you would soon feel drained and mentally exhausted. If, however, the teacher was smart and ping-ponged the questions, easy then hard then easy again, you would likely do much better on the test. That is how dogs also prefer to have their knowledge tested. If you are working the weave poles, alternate between easy and more challenging while overall raising criteria.

### Play Behavior Systems
Konrad Lorenz coined the term behavior systems as a replacement for the term **instinct**. Behavior systems describes behaviors that are linked together and that appear to be innate.

### Postreinforcement Pause
A pause in responding following reinforcement; associated with fixed interval or fixed ratio schedules of reinforcement (Paul Chance). If your pattern of reinforcing becomes predictable to the dog, you may get a postreinforcement pause, the dog temporarily shows a decrease in motivation until she anticipates the time of potential reinforcement is closer.

### Proofing
A program of discrimination and generalization training (Pamela Reid).

### Pull Turn
An agility handling move in which the handler rotates the dog around his body, turning the dog in the same direction as he is turning. Also called **pole turn**.

## Popping
In agility, an incorrect performance of the downside of a contact obstacle. The dog leaps down the ramp so that her front end bears most of her weight and the hind end lifts temporarily off the contact obstacle. Popping is also used for a dog that fails to complete the weaves, "popping" out of the poles.

## Positive Contrast
Enhanced responding that follows delivery of reinforcement that is of higher value than the norm (also known as the **elation effect**) (Pamela Reid). Using positive contrast is fun and win/win dog training.

## Positive Punishment
A procedure that involves the application of an aversive stimulus as a consequence for a behavior and results in a decrease in the probability of that behavior (Pamela Reid). An example is a person hitting a barking dog with a rolled up newspaper. The hitting of the dog decreases probability of barking.

## Positive Reinforcement
A procedure that involves the application of a reinforcing stimulus as a consequence for a behavior and results in an increase in the probability of that behavior (Pamela Reid). In this book when the term reinforcement is used, positive reinforcement is meant.

## Premack Principle
Access to preferred activities function as reinforcement for the performance of less preferred behaviors (also known as **Grandma's Law**) (Pamela Reid). Nicki prefers playing Frisbee over heeling, so I heel Nicki before we play Frisbee. As a result heeling predicts play with the Frisbee and heeling has become more fun to Nicki. A win/win.

## Prompting

The presentation of a stimulus in order to elicit a given behavior (Pamela Reid). You can use food or a toy to draw the dog's attention and lure her into doing what you want, or you can use physical props, i.e. your hands, targets or barriers, to guide a dog into doing what you want.

## Proofing

A program of discrimination and generalization training (Pamela Reid).

## Punishment

A procedure that when applied to the dog, results in a decrease of the probability of that behavior (Pamela Reid). The application of punishment will cause the animal stress. That is why excellent dog training minimizes its use. Incidentally it is impossible to train without any punishment because simply withholding your click and reinforcement, which is necessary for learning, is **Negative Punishment**.

## Random Sampling

A term used to describe what the dog does during training sessions in which she is encouraged to offer behaviors from her repertoire. (Trainer is not cueing any specific behavior.) Random sampling can interfere with duration behaviors, so put it on a verbal or contextual cue.

## Rapid Fire Clicking and Reinforcing

The act of repeatedly clicking and reinforcing in order to communicate to your dog that she is to hold the current position. This is how the dog is taught to hold the 2O2ONT position in agility. It is also how you can teach a dog to hold a sit, down or stand position. (Usually, I prefer the "asking questions" — proofing method — to increase duration.)

**Rate of Reinforcement**
Frequency with which reinforcement is delivered (Pamela Reid).

**Ratio Strain**
If the requirement of a ratio schedule is too high, the animal will slow down, take breaks or stop working altogether. This implies that the animal is not prepared to put in that much effort for the amount of reinforcement received (Pamela Reid).

Disruption of the pattern of responding due to stretching the ratio of the reinforcement too abruptly too far (Paul Chance). Actually, I think this term should be renamed "Arnie Strain" because my mom's Jack Russell, Arnie, is the king of ratio strain, post-reinforcement pause and anything else that will give a trainer gray hair.

**Rear Cross**
In agility, a handling move used to turn the dog that requires the handler to cross behind the dog's path.

**Reinforcement**
For the purposes of this book when reinforcement is mentioned, positive reinforcement is meant. Reinforcer refers to a positive reinforcer.

**Reinforcement History**
Refers to the series of responses corresponding to a particular contingency of reinforcement for a particular operant response (James O'Heare). Reinforcement history exists because of classical conditioning. Classical conditioning causes your dog to associate good and bad events with you or other things in her environment. Things that your dog likes that are linked with you increase your dog's reinforcement history with you. Alternately, things that your dog dislikes that are linked with you decrease your reinforcement history with your dog. Reinforcement

history is similar to a bond your dog establishes with you, people, agility obstacles, cues, handling moves and so on.

## Reinforcement Schedules
The rules governing which responses earn reinforcement (Pamela Reid).

## Reinforcer Sampling
A antecedent procedure that places the animal in contact with a reinforcer prior to responding in order to stimulate performance, also called **jump start** (Pamela Reid).

# S – T
## Salience
How noticeable something is (Pamela Reid). For example, when teaching your dog to take a jump rather than the A-frame, consider that the A-frame is far more salient to the dog than the jump because it is wider, higher and more solid. Set the dog up for success by placing the jump in her path and the A-frame out of her path. This will increase the jump's salience.

## Satiation
Occurs after a large amount of one type of reinforcement has been experienced (Pamela Reid). You are reinforcing with food and the dog becomes full.

## Scalloping
A result of using a fixed interval schedule of reinforcement. It becomes predictable to the dog when the next reinforcement will be delivered so the trainer observes a dramatic drop off in responding immediately after reinforcement. As the dog approaches the time of reinforcement the vigor with which the behavior is performed or the number of responses will increase (Jean Donaldson).

### Scribe
A volunteer at an agility trial that assists the judge and notes the faults that the judge is signaling.

### Self-Reinforcing
Any behavior that does not require external reinforcement in order to be maintained.  The behavior itself is intrinsically reinforcing to the animal.  Most dogs enjoy barking so, if ignored, barking will not decrease.

### Sensitizing
Instead of habituating to a repeated stimulus, sometimes the dog's reaction to it will become even stronger. Thunderstorm phobia is an example of sensitizing. Sensitization is not stimulus specific and as the result of sensitization any novel stimulus can trigger a heightened response (Pamela Reid).

### Serpentine
A pattern of agility obstacles that requires the dog to travel in one direction followed by a 180-degree turn in the opposite direction.

### Shaping
Shaping, actually shaping by successive approximation, is the process by which the trainer differentially reinforces approximations of the desired behavior.  The trainer begins by reinforcing the behavior already in the dog's repertoire that vaguely most resembles the desired behavior.  Next, the trainer adjusts the criteria for reinforcement so that the form of the behavior gradually shifts to the desired behavior (Pamela Reid).

### Signal
A stimulus or event that conveys information about the occurrence or non-occurrence of an event that is significant to the dog (also known as **cue, antecedent stimulus, discriminative stimulus, SD**) (Pamela Reid).

**Single Event Learning**
The process by which a dog habituates or sensitizes to a stimulus that is repeatedly presented.

**Splitting** and **Lumping**
These terms were coined by clicker training greats, Marian and Keller Breland, and Bob Bailey. Splitting is the proper way of training. Always breaking down the behaviors to the smallest possible components. This is the fastest and most ideal way of training new behaviors. Lumping is a common training error of attempting to combine steps of training with the intent of speeding up learning. In reality it accomplishes the opposite.

**State Dependent Learning**
The mental state of the dog is linked to what she learns. If the dog learns to sit when calm, she will more likely remember this cue when calm, and less likely to remember what "sit" means when in an aroused state.

**Stimulus**
Anything the dog can perceive is a stimulus (Pamela Reid).

**Stimulus Control**
Also called **signal control** or **cue control**, said to have occurred when a stimulus (also known as **signal** or **cue**) systematically affects the performance of a behavior (Pamela Reid).

**Success Point**
The specific criteria that your dog is able to perform successfully. Find your dog's success point and build on it, rather than focusing on what is going wrong.

**Success Rate**
Frequency of correct responses (Pamela Reid).

## Superstitious Behavior
The modification or maintenance of a behavior by accidentally or unintentionally reinforcing it (James O'Heare).

## Suppress
The animal ceases to perform a behavior (Pamela Reid). Punishment suppresses behavior, however the punishment is also associated with the punisher via classical conditioning. Your cues can also be associated with punishment, thus poisoning them. Suppressing your dog's behavior is a lose/lose. Teach your dog other behaviors. A win/win.

## Targeting or Target Training
Training that involves teaching the animal to make contact with a target and then using movement/placement of the target to prompt behaviors (Pamela Reid).

## Two On and Two Off Nose Touch Position (2O2ONT)
In agility, a method used to train contact obstacle performance that requires the dog to go into a position where two hind feet are on the contact obstacle and two front feet are on the ground with the dog touching her nose to the ground. This method was developed by Stacy Peardot and Susan Garrett.

## Threadle or Pull Through
A pattern of agility obstacles numbered by the judge in a way to require the dog be brought back between two obstacles. Called threadling, because it is similar to pulling a thread through the eye of a needle.

## Time-Out
A procedure designed to reduce the probability of a target behavior in which access to reinforcement is removed for a particular time period contingent upon the performance of an undesired behavior. Either the animal is removed from

the reinforcing environment or the environment is removed from the animal.

There are three types of time-out:

1.  Dog is removed — you gently take dog and place her in her crate.
2.  Owner/reinforcement is removed — you leave.
3.  Contingent observation — dog gets to watch while other dog gets her reinforcement. Possibly useful to build motivation, possibly less useful to eliminate behavior.

All three types of time-outs are effective. Depending on the dog, a certain type may be more effective than others. (Pamela Reid) The use of negative punishment can be indication of poor training. Ideal agility training minimizes the use of negative punishment.

**Timer**

A volunteer that times a dog's agility run by starting the clock as the dog's nose crosses the start line and ending it the moment the dog's nose crosses the finish line.

**Trajectory**

In agility, the path that the dog takes while jumping is called the trajectory. The desired trajectory is usually a perfect half circle arc.

**Trial**

A single presentation of stimulus-stimulus or behavior-consequence or stimulus-behavior-consequence (Pamela Reid). Just to be confusing, the term trial is also a term for an agility competition.

# U – V – W – X – Y – Z
**Unconditioned Response**

Abbreviated UCR — a response elicited by the presence of an unconditioned stimulus, in the absence of any prior learning (Pamela Reid). Your dog's eye blinking (UCR) as the result of you blowing a puff of air into it (UCS), is an example of an unconditioned response.

**Unconditioned Stimulus**
Abbreviated UCS – a stimulus of significance to the animal in the absence of any prior learning (also known as primary reinforcement, unconditioned reinforcement, unconditioned punishment) (Pamela Reid). A puff of air (UCS) that you blow into your dog's eye and causes the dog to blink is an example of an unconditioned stimulus.

**USDAA**
Abbreviation for the United States Dog Agility Association. For more information visit www.USDAA.com.

**Variable Schedule of Reinforcement**
Schedules of reinforcement that are made contingent upon the performance of a variable number of responses before one is reinforced (Pamela Reid). Humans are generally not good at being variable and even if they are, it is better to use differential reinforcement of excellent behavior.

**Voluntary Behavior**
Responses that are under the animal's control and are likely to be controlled by consequences (Pamela Reid). Clicker training is based on clicking and reinforcing behaviors that are voluntarily offered by the dog, not forced, or coerced.

**Wrong Course**
In agility when a dog takes an incorrect obstacle, it is faulted as a wrong course.

**Yellow Contact Zone**
An area located at the bottom of the contact obstacles that is painted yellow. In order to prevent incurring faults while running an agility course, dogs are required to touch this yellow area in a clear fashion that is visible to the judge.

434

# Appendix 2 Recommended Resources

All the books listed below are available at
www.Dogwise.com, www.CleanRun.com,
www.CourteousCanine.com or at
www.ClickerTraining.com.

## Agility
*The Agility Record Book* by Marie Logue available at
   www.recordbooks.net
*Agility Success* by Angelica Steinker available at
   www.CleanRun.com
*Agility Tricks* by Donna Duford available at
   www.CleanRun.com
*The Book of Games* by Bud Houston available at
   www.CleanRun.com
*The Clean Run Source Book* by Clean Run Productions
   available at www.CleanRun.com
*Clicker Agility for Fun and Fitness* by Diana Bird
*Competing in Agility* by Cindy Buckholt available at
   www.CleanRun.com
*Course Design* by Stuart Mah available at
   www.CleanRun.com
*Jumping from A to Z* by Chris Zink and Julie Daniels
*The Jumping Issue* by Clean Run Magazine.
*Jumping seminars* by Susan Salo available nationwide for
   more information contact Susan at: jumpdogs@aol.com
*Peak Performance* by Chris Zink

## Aggression
*Aggressive Behavior in Dogs* by James O'Heare
*Bringing Light to Shadow* by Pamela Dennison
*The Canine Aggression Workbook* by James O'Heare
*Changing People Changing Dogs* by Dee Ganley
*Click to Calm* by Emma Parsons
*Dogs Bite but Balloons and Slippers are More Dangerous*
   by Janis Bradley
*Fatal Dog Attacks* by Karen Delise
*Fight!* by Jean Donaldson

*Mine!* by Jean Donaldson

## Clicker Training
*The Book of Challenges* by Kay Laurence
*Click N Sniff: clicker training for scent discrimination* by
    Deb Jones
*Clicker Training Foundation* by Kay Laurence
*Clicker Training Intermediate* by Kay Laurence
*Clicker Training Novice* by Kay Laurence
*Clicker Training for Obedience* by Morgan Spector
*Clicker World Obedience* by Kay Laurence
*Click for Joy!* by Melissa Alexander
*Dances with Dogs* by Kay Laurence
*Don't Shoot the Dog* by Karen Pryor
*Karen Pryor on Behavior* by Karen Pryor
*Lads Before the Wind* by Karen Pryor
*Quick Clicks, 40 Fast and Fun Behaviors to Train with a
    Clicker* by Mandy Book and Cheryl S. Smith
*Special Weave Pole Training Issue* by Clean Run
    Magazine
*Teaching People Teaching Dogs* magazine by Kay
    Laurence
*Walk with Me* by Kay Laurence

## Dog Behavior
*Canine Neuropsychology* by James O'Heare
*The Canine Separation Anxiety Workbook* by James
    O'Heare
*The Culture Clash* by Jean Donaldson
*Dogs: Startling New Understanding of Canine Origin,
    Behavior and Evolution* by Ray Coppinger and Lorna
    Coppinger
*Dominance Theory and Dogs* by James O'Heare
*Excel-Erated Learning* by Pam Reid, Ph.D.
*Front and Finish Articles* by Chris Bach
*The Third Way Instructor's Manual* by Chris Bach

## Advanced Texts
*Aggressive Behavior in Dogs* by James O'Heare

*Applied Dog Behavior and Training* vol. I and vol. II, by
   Steven Lindsay
*Coercion and Its Fallout* by Murray Sidman
*The Domestic Dog* by James Serpell
*Genetics and the Social Behavior of the Dog* by Scott and
   Fuller

## Positive Training
*Fun and Games with Dogs* by Roy Hunter
*Fun Nosework for Dogs* 2$^{nd}$ Edition by Roy Hunter
*More Fun and Games with Dogs* by Roy Hunter
*The Other End of the Leash* by Patricia McConnell
*The Power of Positive Dog Training* by Pat Miller
*So Your Dog is Not Lassie* by Fisher and Delzio
*Whale Done!* by Kenneth Blanchard, Thad Lacinak, Chuck
   Tompkins and Jim Ballard

## Online Learning
For trainers interested in furthering their education
   www.CynologyCollege.com provides online courses and
   diploma programs in dog behavior, training, learning
   theory and professional behavior consulting.

## Recommended Videotapes/DVDs
Canine Cineradiography: A study of bone and joint motion
   as seen through moving x-rays by Rachel Page Elliott
Chris Bach the Third Way Foundation Video Series
Clean Run Productions Agility World Championship Videos
Clicker Fun – three tape series by Deborah Jones, Ph.D.
Dogs Need Massage Too!  Canine Massage Video by
   Angela Wills
Foundation Training Video tape 1 and 2 by Greg Derrett
Julie Daniels Agility DVD
The Language of Dogs, 3-DVD set by Sarah Kalnajs
Pets Incredible DVD www.Petsincredible.com
Sue Sternberg Videos www.SueSternberg.com

## Recommended Magazines
Agility Action, available at www.agilityaction.com

Agility in Motion the first DVD bimonthly agility videozine.
www.agilityinmotion.com
Clean Run Magazine. The magazine for all agility
enthusiasts. Available at www.cleanrun.com
The Clicker Journal available at
http://www.clickertrain.com/journal.html
Dog Trainer's Journal a new publication dedicated to the
art and science of dog training.
www.DogTrainersJournal.com
Teaching Dogs Magazine. The best clicker magazine.
www.Learningaboutdogs.com
The Whole Dog Journal Magazine available at www.whole-
dog-journal.com

## Referenced Studies

Allen, C., & Bekoff, M. (1996). Intentionality, social play,
and definition. Readings in Animal Cognition ed. Bekoff
and Jamieson.
Baleviciute, G. (1999). Effect of a human contact and
object-oriented play exercises on the development of
behavior features favourable for search training of the
domestic dog. Acta Zoologica Lituanica. 9, 27-34.
Bekoff, M. (1997). Deep Ethology. Retrieved on August
23, 2005 at http://cogprints.org/161/00/199710001.html
Bekoff, M. (1972). The development of social interaction,
play and metacommunication in mammals: An
ethological perspective. *Quarterly Review Biology, 47,*
412-434.
Bekoff, M. (1974). Introductory Remarks - Symposium on
Play. American Zoologist, 14, 266.
Bekoff, M. (1977). Social communication in canids:
Evidence for the evolution of a stereotyped mammalian
display. *Science, 197,* 1097-1099.
Bekoff, M. (1995). Play signals as punctuation: the
structure of social play in canids. *Behaviour, 132,* 419-
429.
Bekoff, M., & Allen, C. (1998). Intentional communication
and social play: how and why animals negotiate and
agree to play in *Animal Play Evolutionary, Comparative*

*and Ecological Perspectives ed. Bekoff and Byers,
Cambridge Press.*

Bekoff, M., & Allen, C. (2002). The evolution of social play: interdisciplinary analyses of cognitive processes *in The Cognitive Animal. Bekoff, M., Allen, C. and Burghardt, G.M. (ed)*, 429-435.

Blackshaw, J. (2000). Chronic stress in housed dogs. Retrieved on August 23, 2005 from http://vein.library.usyd.edu.au/links/Essays/2000blacksha w.html

Brown, S. (1998). Play as an organizing principle: clinical evidence and personal observations. *Animal Play Evolutionary, Comparative, and Ecological Perspectives, Cambridge Press.*

Byers, J. (1998). Biological effects of locomotor play: getting into shape or something more? *In Animal Play Evolutionary, Comparative, and Ecological Perspectives, Cambridge Press.*

Curl, P. (2004). An evaluation of dog-training techniques: an assessment of efficacy and welfare. Retrieved on August 23, 2005 from http://vein.library.usyd.edu.au/links/Essays/2004/curl.htm l.

Eisenberger, R. (1989). Can response force be shaped by reinforcement? Perceptual and Motor Skills, 68, 725-726.

Estes, W. (1944). An experimental study of punishment. Psychological monographs. 263, no. 3.

Fagan, R. (1981). *Animal Play Behavior:* Oxford University Press.

Garnier, F., Benoit, E., Virat, M., Ochoa, R., Delatour, P. (1990) Adrenal cortical response in clinically normal dogs before and after adaptation to housing environment. Laboratory Animals, 24, 40-43.

Gibbs, N. (1980). New brain research suggests that emotions, not IQ, may be the true measure of human intelligence. Time Magazine 146, 14.

Girard, I., McAleer, M.W., Rhodes, J.S., Garland, Jr., T.

(2001). Selection for high voluntary wheel-running increases speed and intermittency in house mice. The Journal of Experimental Biology, 204, 4311-4320.

Henry, J. D., & Herrero, S. M. (1974). Social play in the American black bear: its similarity to canid social play and an examination of it's identifying characteristics. *American Zoologist, 14,* 371-389.

Hill, H. L., & Bekoff, M. (1977). The variability of some motor components of social play and agonistic behavior in infant eastern coyotes, Canis latrans var. *Animal Behaviour, 25,* 907-909.

Holford, P., (2003). Depression: the nutrition connection. Primary Care Mental Health, 1, 9-16.

Iwaniuk, A. N., Nelson, J. E., & Pellis, S. M. (2001). Do big-brained animals play more? Comparative analyses of play and relative brain size in mammals. Journal of Comparative Psychology, 115(1), 29-41.

Kabaila, A. (2004). The effects of current training techniques and environmental factors on dog behavior. Retrieved on August 23, 2005 at http://vein.library.usyd.edu.au/links/Essays/2004/kabila.html

Koteja, P., Garland, Jr. T., Sax, J.K., Swalow, J.G., Carter, P.A. (1999). Behavior of house mice artificially selected for high levels of voluntary wheel running. Animal Behavior, 58, 1307-1318.

Minueur, Y., Prasol, D., Belzung, C., Crusio, W. (2003). Agonistic behavior and unpredictable chronic mild stress in mice. Behavior Genetics, 33, 513-519.

Panksepp, J. (1998). Rough and tumble play: the brain sources of joy. Affective Neuroscience. Human and animal emotions. Oxford University Press: New York

Pellis, S. H. (2002). Keeping in touch: play fighting and social knowledge. in The Cognitive Animal. Bekoff, A., Allen, C., and Burghardt, G.M. (ed), 421-427.

Pellis, S. M., & Pellis, V. C. (1998). The structure-function interface in the analysis of play fighting. Animal Play Evolutionary, Comparative, and Ecological Perspectives ed. Bekoff and Byer, Cambridge Press.

Prato-Previde, E., Custance, D., Spiezio, C., Sabatini, F.

(2003). Is the dog-human relationship an attachment bond? An observational study using Ainsworth's strange situation. Behaviour, 140, 225-254.

Robbins, T.W., Everitt, B.J. (1996). Neurobehavioral mechanisms of reward and motivation. Current Opinion in Neurobiology, 6, 228-236.

Rooney, N. Bradshaw, J. (2002). An experimental study of the effects of play upon the dog-human relationship. Applied Animal Behavior Science, 75, 161-176.

Rooney, N. J., Bradshaw, J. W. S., & Robinson, I. H. (2000). A comparison of dog-dog and dog-human play behaviour. Applied Animal Behaviour Sciences, 66, 235-248.

Rooney, N. J., Bradshaw, J. W. S., & Robinson, I. H. (2001). Do dogs respond to play signals given by humans? Animal Behavior, 61, 715-722.

Rooney, N. J., and Bradshaw, J.W.S. (2003). Links between play and dominance and attachment dimensions of dog-human relationships. Journal of Applied Animal Welfare Science, 6(2), 67-94.

Rooney, N. J., and Bradshaw, J.W.S. The effects of games on the dog-owner relationship. Retrieved February 3, 2005, from http://www.bsas.org.uk/meetings/annlproc/Pdf2003/015.pdf

Siviy, S. M. (1998). Neurobiological substrates of play behavior: glimpses into the structure and function of mammalian playfulness. Animal Play Evolutionary, Comparative, and ecological Perspectives, Cambridge Press.

Smuts, B., & E., B. (2002). Ethogram for Dog Play Self-Handicapping Study Revision Jan 2002.

Spinka, M., Newberry, Ruth C., and Bekoff, Marc. (2001). Mammalian play: training for the unexpected. The Quarterly Review of Biology, 76(2), 141 - 168.

Tipton, C., Carey, R., Eastin, W., Erickson, H. (1974). A submaximal test for dogs: evaluation of effects of training, detraining, and cage confinement. Journal of Applied Physiology, 37, 271-257.

Thompson, K. V. (1998). Self assessment in juvenile play.

Animal Play Evolutionary, Comparative, and ecological
Perspectives, Cambridge Press.
Voith, V.L., Wright, J.C., Danneman, P.J. (1992). Is there
a relationship between canine behavior problems and
spoiling activities, anthropomorphism, and obedience
training? Applied Animal Behavior Science, 34, 263-272.
Weyand, P.G., Sternlight, D.B., Bellizzi, M.J., Wright, S.
(2000). Faster top running speeds are achieved with
greater ground forces not more rapid leg movements.
Journal of Applied Physiology, 89, 1991-1999.
Wilson, S. C., & Kleiman, D. G. (1974). Eliciting play: a
comparative study. American Zoologist, 14, 341-370.

## Recommended Websites
You can find a list of these links on
www.ClickandPlayAgility.com that will enable you to
browse directly on the internet, rather than type in the links.

The Applied Companion Animal Network  www.acabn.com
a resource for dog owners on pet behavior, training and
problem solving.
International Institute for Applied Companion Animal
Behavior. www.iiacab.com. Resources for professional
trainers and behavior consultants.

## Canine Health Websites
http://www.itsfortheanimals.com/HEMOPET.HTM
www.caninerehabilitation.com
www.CanineIcer.com
This website sells dog ice packs and wonderful carpal
supports. These supports, similar to ones used on
horses, protect the dog's front leg wrists from potential
damage created by the pounding first stride on the A-
frame and landing on the front end after jumping.
www.OFFA.org
This is the official site of the Orthopedic Foundation for
Animals, a non-profit organization that tracks hip
dysplasia, and elbow dysplasia. The site also contains
info on CERF, which is an ophthalmologic exam passing

or failing the dog for genetic eye defects which may cause a dog to go blind.  On this website you can actually enter kennel names, registration numbers, or OFA numbers to search for health screened animals. OFA also contains information on other genetic problems.

www.optigen.com/
This website provides DNA screening for common and serious dog illnesses.

www.PennHip.org
The website for a hip dysplasia screen, commonly used by the clicker trained service dog community and others interested in rigorous and accurate screening.  PennHip is considered superior to OFA screening by many, including myself.

http://w3.vet.upenn.edu/research/centers/penngen/
The Section of Medical Genetics is dedicated to pursuing clinical and basic research on inheritable diseases of companion animals to better understand the disease processes and to develop novel therapeutic approaches.

http://www.vetgen.com/
Using VetGen's services, combined with our valuable DNA Profiling and DNA Storage, for the first time in history, animal breeders and owners have the opportunity to eliminate targeted inherited diseases in a growing number of breeds.

## Animal Emotions
http://www.nwf.org/internationalwildlife/2001/emotionso01.html
A link to an article "Natural Passions" discussing displays of affection, happiness, sadness and other emotions in animals.

## Agility Websites
www.AgilityNerd.com
This is a training blog that is organized for agility enthusiasts.

www.agilityrecord.com

This site can help you track your competition agility titles and legs.

www.cleanrun.com

This is the site of Clean Run Agility Magazine, the best agility magazine available, and one of the best dog magazine's in the world.

www.DogwoodAgility.com

This is the official site of agility great Bud Houston and contains info on his electronic agility magazine, his camps, and much more.

## Various Info and Clicker Training Sites

www.4m.com

Another great dog bookstore.

www.AgilityAbility.com

A very informative and useful dog agility website.

www.AKC.org

If you are interested in competing in the AKC flavor of agility this is the site for information and forms.

www.apdt.com

The Association of Pet Dog Trainer's website.

www.clickersolutions.com

A superb clicker training website.

www.clickertraining.com

Karen Pryor's wonderful website which features news, info and retail sales of the best clicker gear available.

www.courteouscanine.com

The author's website.

www.CynologyCollege.com

A website for professional dog trainer education.

www.dogagility.org

This is the website for Tea Cup Agility. This association sanctions competitions that are for small dogs running 16 inches in jump height and lower.

www.docna.com

This is the website for Dogs on Course of North America a new agility venue that is quickly gaining popularity.

www.dogpatch.org

A fun website for anything dog.

www.dogwise.com
   The website for the greatest doggie bookstore on the
   web.
www.genuinedoggear.com
   Retail and wholesale sales of dog toys, leashes and dog
   gear.
http://www.k9cpe.com/
   This website is for Canine Performance Events an
   association offering agility titles with various levels and
   games.
www.LearningAboutDogs.com
   This is the website of master clicker trainer Kay
   Laurence.
www.Nosetouch.com
   The site for the electronic training products "Touch It"
   and
   "Hit It" used to train nose touches and running contacts
   for agility.
www.sitstay.com
   One of the best websites for anything dog!
www.SueSternberg.com
   If you have an aggressive dog Sue Sternberg's website
   sells excellent videos and books.  Sue Sternberg can
   read dogs like most people read a book.
www.thekongcompany.com
   The Kong Toy is an excellent chew toy that you can stuff
   to keep your dog busy when you are not home.
www.trainthethirdway.com
   Chris Bach's website.  Information on her THIRD WAY
   training philosophy and training techniques.
www.USDAA.com
   The website of the United States Dog Agility Association,
   provides info and forms.

## Recommended Software
Clean Run Course Designer Software, available at
   www.cleanrun.com
This software will help you design your own courses.

Sniffy the Virtual Rat software, available at
http://www.wadsworth.com/psychology_d/special_feature
s/ext/sniffy/index.htm
This software is a blast for the operant and classical
conditioning buff.

## Recommended Agility and Clicker Training Emailing Lists

http://groups.yahoo.com/group/agility-equipment/
A list for people interested in making their own agility
equipment.
http://groups.yahoo.com/group/CleanRun/
An Agility list for readers and fans of the Clean Run Dog
Agility Magazine.
http://groups.yahoo.com/group/clickerdogs/
A list for clicker trainers.
http://groups.yahoo.com/group/ClickHerd/
A list for herding enthusiasts teaching herding behaviors
with a clicker.
http://groups.yahoo.com/group/ClickSport/
A list for dog sport enthusiasts who train with the clicker.

## Agility Equipment Manufacturers

A1 Agility Equipment Phone: 585-396-3009
http://www.a1agilitydog.com/
Action Agility Equipment Phone: 909- 679-3699
http://www.actionk9.com/
Agility by Carlson Phone: 717-597-5076
Agility Dog Nova Star Equipment
http://www.agilitydog-novastarr.com/
Agility Equipment
http://www.agility-equipment.com/
Agility for Less
http://www.agilityforless.com/
Camelot Agility Equipment
http://www.camelotaussies.com/AgilityEq4Sale.htm
Dog Tube
http://www.dogtube.com/
J and J's Dog Supply Phone: 1-800-642-2050

446

http://www.jjdog.com/
Max200/Pipe Dreams Agility Equipment
www.Max200.com
Mick Tini's Agility Equipment Phone: 519-632-9444
http://www.k9sports.ca/
NTI Global Tunnels
http://www.ntiglobal.com/DogAgility/Index.htm
Over Rover! Agility Equipment Phone: 866-837-7683
http://www.overrover.com/
Paw-Z-Tracks Agility Equipment Phone: 403-248-8744
http://www.paw-z-tracks.com/
Paul's Dog Agility Works Phone: 780-995-1376
http://www.paulsdogagilityworks.com/
Rocket Dog Agility Equipment Phone : 1-888-699-6116
http://www.rocket-dog.com/
Train Agility Equipment
http://www.trainagility.com
WeavePoles.Com
http://www.weave-poles.com/

# Appendix 3    Training Plan Ideas

A good training plan is flexible, because every dog is different. The training plan charts in this appendix allow adjustments for each dog and handler team. The charts create a framework for the approximations described in this book. The completion of the training process will likely take six months to two years if you practice on a daily basis. When in doubt take more time rather than less.

When following any training plan, only advance to the next approximation if you are able to play the games at a success rate of 90 percent. Use the charts below to ensure that your dog has been trained and prepared for fun matches and trials. Consider first trialing in NADAC tunnelers and jumpers or USDAA jumpers, usually these classes are more flowing and less demanding for a dog new to agility. You can build up to AKC jumpers with weaves and eventually enter the standard classes when your dog demonstrates consistent confidence.

If you are a group instructor consider giving your students one TAG for each check mark. The charts below offer a starting point, ideally customize charts for each dog and handler team. Award TAGs for exercises that are skipped because the dog does not require the approximations. For example, a tiny 8-inch jumper will not need to train the 2O2ONT behaviors. Be generous when reinforcing.

*Individual Dog and Handler Team Agility Training Charts*
Place a check mark and date as each item is completed. Games listed below are from Chapters 1-4. The Nightmare on Elm Street game is completed when you have designed the nightmare and completed the nightmare proof you described. Ideally, games, restrained recalls and the food dish game are integrated into your daily interactions with your dog. For easy reference, next to each behavior you will find the page number where the game is described.

449

The length of this list may seem overwhelming, however many check marks can be achieved in only a few minutes of training. I feel grief when I near completing a check list for one of my own dogs, because teaching a dog to play agility is heaven on earth to me.

| Foundation | Explained by Instructor | Completed | Proofed |
|---|---|---|---|
| Attention game p.37 | | | |
| Passive attention game p.42 | | | |
| On/off switch game p.49 | | | |
| Food dish game p.65 | | | |
| Timing game p.70 | | | |
| Reinforcer toss on spot game p.73 | | | |
| Nightmare on Elm Street game (design your nightmare) p.79 | | | |
| Your dog's signs of stress (create list) p.113 | | | |
| Restrained recall game p.121 | | | |
| Game inventory : Food games (create list) Chap. 5 | | | |
| Games inventory : Toy games (create list) Chap. 5 | | | |
| Games inventory : no food no toys (create list) Chap. 5 | | | |
| Other : | | | |

The games listed below are from Chapter 5. All games listed should be put on cue, trained to duration, body independent and proofed. If body independence does not apply NA was placed into the chart.

| Ground games | On cue | Duration | Body Independent | Proofed |
|---|---|---|---|---|
| Sit p.155 | | | | |
| Down p.157 | | | | |

| Ground games | On cue | Duration | Body Independent | Proofed |
|---|---|---|---|---|
| Stand p.166 | | | | |
| Okay p.156, 162 | | | | |
| Hand targeting p.167 | | | NA | |
| Target stick game p.165 | | | NA | |
| Left p.173 | | | | |
| Right p.173 | | | | |
| Running side by side game – dog on right p.169 | | | NA | |
| Running side by side game – dog on left p.169 | | | NA | |
| Front crosses – both sides p.368 | | | NA | |
| Set up game (front or heel position) p.161 | | | NA | |
| Lead out game p.163 and Chap. 10 | | | NA | |
| Magic flashlight game p.171 | | | NA | |
| Name game p.172 | | | | |
| Jump in chair game p.172 | | | NA | |
| Fork lift game p.172 | | | NA | |
| Out game p.174 | | | NA | |
| Go game p.177 | | | | |
| Back game p.182 | | | | |
| Turn on forehand game p.185 | | | NA | |
| Look game p.186 | | | | |
| Leave it p.187 | | | | |
| Get it p.187 | | | | |
| Other : | | | | |

The chart below lists games from the contact training chapter taking you through the entire process. If a certain skill set did not apply to a game an NA was placed into the chart.

| Contact games | 90% Success | In Front Position | Off Handler's Left | Off Handler's Right | Behind Dog | Proofed |
|---|---|---|---|---|---|---|
| Flat boards p.207 | | NA | | | NA | |
| Buja board game p.233 | | | | | | |
| Bang noise game p.234 | | | | | | |
| Cavaletti games p.208 | | | | | | |
| Nose touch games p.210 | | | | | | |
| Position game p.213 | | | | | | |
| Hold game p.217 | | | | | | |
| Okay game p.217 | | | | | | |
| Slide game p.219 | | | | | | |
| Slat games under first slat p.225 | | | | | | |
| Slat games one slat p. 225 | | | | | | |
| Slat games two slats p.225 | | | | | | |
| Slat games three slats p.225 | | | | | | |
| Target faded p.226 | | | | | | |
| Slat games four slats p.225 | | | | | | |

| Contact games | 90% Success | In Front Position | Off Handler's Left | Off Handler's Right | Behind Dog | Proofed |
|---|---|---|---|---|---|---|
| Slat games five slats p.225 | | | | | | |
| Other : | | | | | | |

The chart below takes you through the games listed in the jumping chapter. For some of the games the columns send and recall didn't apply and in those cases NA was placed in the chart.

| Jumping games | Off Handler's Left | Off Handler's Right | Send | Recall | Lateral Distance | Run with Dog | Proofed |
|---|---|---|---|---|---|---|---|
| Cavaletti games : straight line p.264 | | | | | | | |
| Cavaletti games : various angles p.268 | | | | | | | |
| Cavaletti games : various spacing p.269 | | | | | | | |
| Cavaletti games : curved p.270 | | | | | | | |
| Jump chute games : straight p.271 | | | | | | | |
| Jump chute games : off set angles p.272 | | | | | | | |
| Jump chute games : off set spacing p.272 | | | | | | | |

| Jumping games | Off Handler's Left | Off Handler's Right | Send | Recall | Lateral Distance | Run with Dog | Proofed |
|---|---|---|---|---|---|---|---|
| Oval p.277 | | | NA | NA | | | |
| Pinwheel p.278 | | | NA | NA | | | |
| 270-degree p.279 | | | NA | NA | | | |
| 180-degree p.280 | | | NA | NA | | | |
| Three sided box p.282 | | | NA | NA | | | |
| Four sided box p.281 | | | NA | NA | | | |
| Double box p.281 | | | NA | NA | | | |
| Five sided box p.282 | | | NA | NA | | | |
| Eight sided box : serpentine p.283 | | | NA | NA | | | |
| Eight sided box : threadle p.283 | | | NA | NA | | | |
| Eight sided box : keep out p.283 | | | NA | NA | | | |
| The S exercise p.284 | | | NA | NA | | | |
| Other : | | | | | | | |

The chart below covers games from the contact and obstacle chapters.

| Obstacles | Around the Clock | Wrap p. 88 | Send 5 feet | Send 10 feet | Send 15 feet | Send 20 feet | Recall 5 feet | Recall 10 feet | Recall 15 feet | Recall 20 feet | Lateral 5 feet | Lateral 10 feet | Lateral 15 feet | Lateral 20 feet | Proofed – including rear cross and front |
|---|---|---|---|---|---|---|---|---|---|---|---|---|---|---|---|
| Single bar jump p. 247 | | | | | | | | | | | | | | | |
| One bar jump p. 248 | | | | | | | | | | | | | | | |

454

| Obstacles | Around the Clock | Wrap p. 88 | Send 5 feet | Send 10 feet | Send 15 feet | Send 20 feet | Recall 5 feet | Recall 10 feet | Recall 15 feet | Recall 20 feet | Lateral 5 feet | Lateral 10 feet | Lateral 15 feet | Lateral 20 feet | Proofed – including rear cross and front cross |
|---|---|---|---|---|---|---|---|---|---|---|---|---|---|---|---|
| Panel jump p.296 | | | | | | | | | | | | | | | |
| Double jump p.292 | | | | | | | | | | | | | | | |
| Triple jump p.293 | | | | | | | | | | | | | | | |
| Tire jump p.297 | | | | | | | | | | | | | | | |
| Broad jump p.293 | | | | | | | | | | | | | | | |
| Winged jumps p.249 | | | | | | | | | | | | | | | |
| Tunnel p.327 | | | | | | | | | | | | | | | |
| Chute p.329 | | | | | | | | | | | | | | | |
| Table : hop on p.298 | | | | | | | | | | | | | | | |
| Table : speed to p.298 | | | | | | | | | | | | | | | |
| Table : torque p.298 | | | | | | | | | | | | | | | |
| Table : sit p.298 | | | | | | | | | | | | | | | |
| Table : down p.298 | | | | | | | | | | | | | | | |
| Table : hold p.298 | | | | | | | | | | | | | | | |
| Table : okay p.298 | | | | | | | | | | | | | | | |
| A-frame Chap.7 | | | | | | | | | | | | | | | |
| Dog walk Chap. 7 | | | | | | | | | | | | | | | |
| Teeter Chap. 7 | | | | | | | | | | | | | | | |
| Three poles p.309 | | | | | | | | | | | | | | | |
| Channel width of dog p.314 | | | | | | | | | | | | | | | |
| Channel ¾ width of dog p.314 | | | | | | | | | | | | | | | |
| Channel ½ width of dog p.314 | | | | | | | | | | | | | | | |
| Channel ¼ width of dog p.314 | | | | | | | | | | | | | | | |
| 6 poles closed p.314 | | | | | | | | | | | | | | | |
| 12 poles closed p.314 | | | | | | | | | | | | | | | |

Below are the games from the handling chapter, including games that teach the dog the handling moves. Standing in place did not apply to several games and NA was placed in the chart when that was the case. Games can be played on the flat with and without a dog. When playing the games over obstacles, walking and jogging can be done without the dog if the handler needs to increase the speed of his handling or improve his timing to match his dog's working speed. It may not be possible to play all of the games listed with all dogs, ideally customize this and all the charts to each dog and handler team.

| Handling | In Place | Walking | Jogging | Running | One Jump | Sequence |
|---|---|---|---|---|---|---|
| Arm 0-inches from hip p.343 | | | | | | |
| Arm 6-inches from hip p.344 | | | | | | |
| Arm 12-inches from hip (no photo) | | | | | | |
| Arm parallel to ground p.345 | | | | | | |
| Bowl arm p.345 | | | | | | |
| Rotate arm and shoulder 90-degree in front of body p.344 | | | | | | |
| Magic flashlight p.345 | | | | | | |
| Connection game : 2 obstacles p.346 | | | | | | |
| Connection game : 4 obstacles p.346 | | | | | | |
| Connection game : 6 obstacles p.346 | | | | | | |
| Connection game : 8 obstacles p.346 | | | | | | |
| Connection game : 12 obstacles p.346 | | | | | | |
| Connection game : 16 obstacles p.346 | | | | | | |
| Connection game : 20 obstacles p.346 | | | | | | |
| Connection game : 24 obstacles p.346 | | | | | | |
| Line speeding up and slowing down game p.349 | | | | | | |
| Pull turn p.357 | NA | | | | | |

456

| Handling | In Place | Walking | Jogging | Running | One Jump | Sequence |
|---|---|---|---|---|---|---|
| Pull turn game for dog p.361 | NA | | | | | |
| Rear cross p.361 | NA | | | | | |
| Rear cross game for dog p.366 | NA | | | | | |
| Front cross p.368 | NA | | | | | |
| Front cross game for dog p.374 | NA | | | | | |
| False turn p.376 | NA | | | | | |
| False turn game for dog p.379 | NA | | | | | |
| Line p.390 | NA | | | | | |
| Pinwheel p.391 | NA | | | | | |
| Serpentine p.391 | NA | | | | | |
| Box p.392 | NA | | | | | |
| Zig Zag p.393 | NA | | | | | |
| Other : | | | | | | |

# Appendix 4 Explanation of Titles and Tracking of Legs

In agility competition, a run that is good enough to go toward earning a title is called a qualifying run. A qualifying run means a "leg" toward a title was earned. Most titles require three legs.

Since there are so many venues of agility competition, I am going to present a very basic overview of the rules for what can earn a leg and titles in only AKC and USDAA agility.

At this writing, the following agility venues are available:
American Kennel Club www.AKC.org
Canine Performance Events www.k9CPE.com
North American Dog Agility Council www.NADAC.com
Tea Cup Dog Agility www.dogagility.org
United States Dog Agility Association www.USDAA.com
New venues sporadically pop up and certain flavors are more popular in certain geographical locations.

Rulebooks are available on each organization's website. It is time well spent if you read the rules before you enter and compete.

*Explanation of Faults*
There are basically five types of faults: refusals, wrong courses, table, time and elimination.

- o  Refusals are when the dog approaches the correct obstacle, but then turns back on her path and away from the obstacle. Avoid refusals by clearly signaling the obstacle and not leaving any questions in your dog's mind about where she is going next.

- o  Wrong courses occur when the dog either on her own, or because the handler signaled it, begins to take or completes an incorrect obstacle or even several obstacles.  Just like with refusals, if you clearly signal your dog's path you can avoid wrong courses.

o  Table faults are assessed if your dog releases herself or is released by you before the 5-second count is complete.  Generally the table count is, "five, and four, and three, and two, and one, and go."  It is important to wait until the count is over including the "o" of the judges "go" before releasing the dog.

o  Before dogs and competitors run the course the judge uses a wheel to measure the length of the course in yards.  The judge uses this measurement to come up with the standard course time.  This time varies depending on the height of the dog.  Small dogs are given more time to complete the course and large dogs are given less time, since they are faster.  If a dog and handler team don't complete the course in the allotted time, time faults are assessed.  Usually the number of time faults is one to three points per second over standard course time.

o  Knocked bars and missed contacts are considered a failure to perform the obstacle.  Assessment of a failure to perform any obstacle means the team can't qualify.  A contact is considered to be missed if no part of the dog touches the yellow of the contact zone.  If the judge sees even one toe nail in the yellow there is no fault.  In AKC all yellow contact zones are judged except for the up contact of the A-frame.

o  Certain rule violations are taken more seriously and, as a result, a dog and handler team can be asked to leave the ring.  If your dog relieves herself in the ring this will cause her to be eliminated and the judge will ask you both to leave the ring. The handler cussing, the unsafe performance of an obstacle, most touching of the dog or touching an obstacle will also cause an elimination. Even if you accidentally touch an obstacle, you will be eliminated. The rules state that if the handler accidentally touching the dog aids the performance of the dog, then the team is eliminated. So even accidental contact can cause you to be eliminated if the judge determines that it helped the dog perform the course.

## AKC Qualification Chart

| Type of Fault | Novice A & B (score required 85) | Open (score required 85) | Excellent A (score required 85) | Excellent B (score required 100) |
|---|---|---|---|---|
| Refusal – 5 faults | 2 permitted | 1 permitted | 0 permitted | 0 permitted |
| Wrong Course – 5 faults | 2 permitted | 1 permitted | 0 permitted | 0 permitted |
| Table Fault – 5 faults | 2 permitted | 1 permitted | 0 permitted | 0 permitted |
| Time Faults (dog's course time over what judge allowed) | Up to 15 faults or 15 seconds over course time permitted | Up to 15 faults or 7 seconds over course time permitted | Up to 15 faults or 5 seconds over course time permitted | 0 permitted |
| Failure to Perform (dropped bars/ missed contacts) | 0 permitted | 0 permitted | 0 permitted | 0 permitted |
| Elimination Faults | 0 permitted | 0 permitted | 0 permitted | 0 permitted |

The chart above is intended for use as a guideline. Ideally train your dog to where she can at least run an open course cleanly and then begin competing in Novice.

Novice A classes are for people new to the sport. Novice B classes are for experienced competitors with a young dog.

## USDAA Qualification Chart

| Type of Fault | Starters and Novice (no faults to qualify) | Advanced (no faults to qualify) | Masters (no faults to qualify) |
|---|---|---|---|
| Refusal | Up to three permitted (just wasting time) | 0 permitted | 0 permitted |
| Wrong Course | 0 permitted | 0 permitted | 0 permitted |
| Missed Contact | 0 permitted | 0 permitted | 0 permitted |
| Table | 0 permitted | 0 permitted | 0 permitted |
| Dropped Bar | 0 permitted | 0 permitted | 0 permitted |
| Elimination | 0 permitted | 0 permitted | 0 permitted |

Just like AKC Novice B, Novice is for young dogs with experienced handlers. Starters is for inexperienced dogs and handlers. USDAA rules differ slightly from AKC rules. While AKC does not judge refusals at the weave poles in Novice, USDAA does not judge refusals at all in the Novice or Starters classes, however, to qualify, no faults at all are allowed.

## AKC Title and Leg Tracker

| Title | Leg Date, Location & Judge | Leg Date, Location & Judge | Leg Date, Location & Judge |
|---|---|---|---|
| Novice Standard (NA) | | | |
| Novice Jumpers (NAJ) | | | |
| Open Standard (OA) | | | |

| Title | Leg Date, Location & Judge | | | | Leg Date, Location & Judge | | | | Leg Date, Location & Judge | | |
|---|---|---|---|---|---|---|---|---|---|---|---|
| Open Jumpers (OAJ) | | | | | | | | | | | |
| Excellent Standard (AX) | | | | | | | | | | | |
| Excellent Jumpers (AXJ) | | | | | | | | | | | |
| Masters Standard (MX) | 1 | 2 | 3 | 4 | 5 | 6 | 7 | 8 | 9 | 10 | Comments |
| Masters Jumpers (MXJ) | 1 | 2 | 3 | 4 | 5 | 6 | 7 | 8 | 9 | 10 | Comments |

463

| Master Agility Champion (MACH) | Speed Points 750 | Double Qs 20 | Comments |
|---|---|---|---|
|  |  |  |  |

Use the chart above to keep track of your AKC qualifying runs. Every time you have a qualifying run enter the date, score and name of judge. Dogs entered in Novice earn legs toward their Novice titles (NA and NAJ). Once you have earned a title you can move up to the Open level in that class. In Open you can earn the OA and OAJ and once you have completed either of those titles you can move into Excellent A in the corresponding class. In Excellent A you earn legs toward your AX and AXJ. Either title gets you into Excellent B in that class. Once you have earned both the AX and the AXJ, you have only three titles remaining MX, MXJ and the MACH. All three of these titles require more legs than the previous titles. MX and MXJ both require ten legs each. The MACH requires both 750 speed points and 20 double Q's. Speed points are earned by being under course time. Each second under course time is a speed point. First or second placements can increase the number of speed points.  A double Q is earned when a dog qualifies in standard and jumpers with weaves on the same day.  For dogs that continue to compete beyond the MACH they can add a number after the MACH for each additional time they have reached the MACH criteria.  You can find some dogs with MACH9 before their names, this means they have reached the MACH criteria 9 times!

AKC also offers a program called Preferred which allows dogs to compete at one jump height lower then they measured.

AKC Jump Heights
Height is measured at the withers, where the dog's neck attaches to the body.

11-inches and under jump 8-inches.
14-inches and under jump 12-inches.
18-inches and under jump 16-inches.
22-inches and under jump 20-inches.
Over 22 inches jump 24-inch jumps.

Many competitors choose to compete with a young dog in the preferred program, because if the dog measures over 22-inches the dog can jump the lower 20-inches instead of 24-inches.  Preferred is also a great program for older dogs that are no longer able to jump their full jump height. The Preferred program also offers titles.

# USDAA Championship Program Title and Leg Tracker

| Title | Standard 1 | Standard 2 | Standard 3 | Gamblers 1 | Jumpers 1 | Pairs Relay 1 | Snooker 1 |
|---|---|---|---|---|---|---|---|
| Agility Dog (AD) | | | | | | | |
| Advanced Agility Dog (AAD) | | | | | | | |
| Masters Agility Dog (MAD) | | | | | | | |

**Agility Dog Champion (ADCH) – Masters titles in each game and 5 Tournament legs**

| | Leg 1 | Leg 2 | Leg 3 | Leg 4 | Leg 5 |
|---|---|---|---|---|---|
| **Gamblers Master (GM)** | | | | | |
| **Jumpers Master (JM)** | | | | | |

| | Leg 1 | Leg 2 | Leg 3 | Leg 4 | Leg 5 |
|---|---|---|---|---|---|
| Relay Master (RM) | | | | | |
| Snooker Master (SM) | Super Q 1 (Top 15% of class) | Super Q 2 | Super Q 3 | Leg 4 | Leg 5 |
| Tournament Classes Required for Championship: Steeplechase, Grand Prix and DAM Tournaments | Leg 1 | Leg 2 | Leg 3 | Leg 4 | Leg 5 |

USDAA offers a program that demands versatility of a dog and handler team. However, it also offers flexibility. This chart is not complete there are additional titles available from USDAA but I have charted the most common titles. Like, AKC, USDAA offers titles in two programs Championship and Performance. Championship is for handlers whose dogs jump full height and Performance is one jump height lower then full height.

467

USDAA Jump Heights
Dogs height is measured at the withers.

12-inches and under jump 12-inches.
16-inches and under jump 16-inches.
21-inches and under jump 22-inches.
Over 21-inches jump 26-inches.

USDAA includes four games called jumpers, snooker, relay and gamblers. Jumpers is a course of mostly jumps, tunnels and may include weave poles. Snooker is a strategy game similar to the snooker billiard game. It emphasizes control and speed. Relay requires two dog and handler teams. One team runs the first part of the course and the second team runs the last part. Gamblers offers both strategy and a distance handling challenge. The judge draws a line that only the dog but not the handler may cross. The challenge is for the handler to direct the dog over the "gamble" without stepping on or over the line.

As you can see the first title in USDAA requires qualifying runs in standard in addition to the games classes, pushing dog and handler teams to show versatility. At the Master's level in snooker, handlers are challenged to earn super Q's meaning that not only do they qualify but that they qualify in the top 15% of their class.

To earn the coveted ADCH dogs must show tremendous versatility, accuracy and speed in addition to five legs in Tournament classes. Tournament classes are Grand Prix, Steeplechase and DAM. Grand Prix is a special competition that focuses on qualification for the USDAA World Championship. Steeplechase is a tournament that offers a jumpers course with an A-frame and weave poles emphasizing speed. DAM, which stands for Dog Agility Masters, tournaments are team events. Three dogs and handlers create a team that competes in five different classes. Regular competitions can include one of the three tournaments, check your agility trial premiums and the USDAA website (www.USDAA.com) for more information.